7/02

HAMLET
NEW CRITICAL ESSAYS

Erratum for *Hamlet: New Critical Essays*
edited by Arthur F. Kinney

On page i, the volume number for this
series, Shakespeare Criticism, is listed
incorrectly as 23. This title is actually
Volume 27 in the series.

SHAKESPEARE CRITICISM

PHILIP C. KOLIN, *General Editor*

HAMLET
New Critical Essays

Edited by
Arthur F. Kinney

Routledge
New York & London

Published in 2002 by
Routledge
29 West 35th Street
New York, NY 10001

Published in Great Britain by
Routledge
11 New Fetter Lane
London EC4P 4EE

Routledge is an imprint of the Taylor & Francis Group.
Copyright © 2002 by Arthur F. Kinney

Printed in the United States of America on acid-free paper.

Cover illustration: *Henry Irving as Hamlet*, by permission of the Folger Library.

10 9 8 7 6 5 4 3 2 1

Library of Congress Cataloging-in-Publication Data
Hamlet : new critical essays / edited by Arthur F. Kinney.
    p. cm. — (Shakespeare criticism ; v. 27)
    Includes bibliographical references and index
    ISBN 0-8153-3876-7 (acid-free paper)
    1. Shakespeare, William, 1564–1616. Hamlet. I. Kinney, Arthur F.,
1933– II. Series.
  PR2807.H2657 2001
  822.3'3—dc21   2001019247

Contents

Illustrations

General Editor's Introduction

PHILIP C. KOLIN

The continuing goal of the Shakespeare Criticism Series is to provide the most significant and original contemporary interpretations of Shakespeare's works. Each volume in the series is devoted to a Shakespearean play or poem (e.g., the sonnets, *Venus and Adonis, Othello*) and contains 18–25 new essays exploring the text from a variety of critical perspectives.

A major feature of each volume in the series is the editor's introduction. Each volume editor provides a substantial essay identifying the main critical issues and problems the play (or poem) has raised, charting the critical trends in looking at the work over the centuries, and assessing the critical discourse that has linked the play or poem to various ideological concerns. In addition to examining the critical commentary in light of important historical and theatrical events, each introduction functions as a discursive bibliographic essay citing and evaluating significant critical works—books, journal articles, theater documents, reviews, and interviews—giving readers a guide to the vast amount of research on a particular play or poem.

Each volume showcases the work of leading Shakespeare scholars who participate in and extend the critical discourse on the text. Reflecting the most recent approaches in Shakespeare studies, these essays approach the play from a host of critical positions, including but not limited to feminist, Marxist, new historical, semiotic, mythic, performance/staging, cultural, and/or a combination of these and other methodologies. Some volumes in the series include bibliographic analyses of a Shakespearean text to shed light on its critical history and interpretation. Interviews with directors and/or actors are also part of some volumes in the series.

At least one, sometimes as many as two or three, of the essays in each volume is devoted to the play in performance, beginning with the earliest and most significant productions and proceeding to the most recent. These essays, which ultimately provide a theater history of the play, should not be regarded as different from or rigidly isolated from the critical work on the script. Shakespeare criticism has often been informed by or has significantly influenced productions. Over the last thirty years or so Shakespeare criticism has understandably been labeled the "Age of Performance." Readers will find information in these essays on non–English speaking productions of Shakespeare's plays as well as landmark performances in English. Editors and contributors also include photographs from productions around the world to help readers see and further appreciate the ways a Shakespearean play has taken shape in the theater.

Ultimately, each volume in the Shakespeare Criticism Series strives to give readers a balanced, representative collection of the most engaging and thoroughly researched criticism on the given Shakespeare text. In essence, each volume provides a careful survey of essential materials in the history of the criticism of a Shakespearean play or poem as well as cutting-edge essays that extend and enliven our understanding of the work in its critical context. In offering readers innovatively and fulfilling new essays, volume editors have made invaluable contributions to the literary and theatrical criticism of Shakespeare's greatest legacy, his work.

Philip C. Kolin
University of Southern Mississippi

Introduction

ARTHUR F. KINNEY

When you consider a major achievement of writing such as a play by Shakespeare, you are continually reinterpreting it. This object is there and it's like a sputnik, it turns round, and over the years different portions of it are nearer to you, different bits are further away. It's rushing past and you are peeling off those meanings. In that way a text is dynamic. The whole question of what Shakespeare intended doesn't arise, because what he has written not only carries more meanings than he consciously intended, but those meanings are altered in a mysterious way as the text moves through the centuries. If you dig into it you find some new aspect, and yet you never seize the thing itself.

Peter Hall[1]

Let me entreat, and beseech, and adjure, and implore you not to write an essay on Hamlet. In the catalogue of a library that is very dear to me, there are about four hundred titles of separate editions, essays, commentaries, lectures, and criticisms on this sole tragedy, and I know that this is only the vanguard of the coming years. To modify the words, on another subject, of my ever dear and revered Master, the late Professor Child, I am convinced that were I told that my closest friend was lying at the point of death, and that his life could be saved by permitting him to divulge his theory of Hamlet, I would instantly say, "Let him die! Let him die! Let him die!"

H. H. Furness[2]

PROLOGUE

The meanings of Shakespeare's *Hamlet* are infinite; its significance, inexhaustible. Kenneth Branagh—who has acted Hamlet on the stage, has made a production of *Hamlet* the subject of the play-within-the-play for his own film, *In the Bleak Midwinter*, and has adapted the play and directed it as a four-hour epic—notes that Shakespeare's best-known work "has consumed me, to varying degrees, for the last twenty years."

I first encountered *Hamlet* when Richard Chamberlain, T.V.'s Doctor Kildare, played the title role on British television. I was eleven years old and from a background (Irish, Protestant, working-class) which had given me little preparation for watching Shakespeare. I was sufficiently distracted on that Sunday evening to leave my overdue homework uncompleted. I felt very uneasy when the Ghost of Hamlet's father appeared. There were no great special effects to heighten the audience's fear, but the atmosphere of the scene was unsettling. I was dragged away from the screen shortly afterwards to a tardy bedtime. It continued to affect me as I tried, unsuccessfully, to sleep. . . . Over the following few years, *Hamlet* took on different shapes. One was a picture of Laurence Olivier on the cover of an old L.P. record, lying (unused) in a corner of the English Department Stock Room. Later still, the record itself was played in class, the master's sepulchral reading of "To Be or Not to Be" set against Walton's eerie score. I knew nothing of "fardels" or "bodkins," but I knew that here was "something." (xi)

Still later, having seen Derek Jacobi in the television serialization of *I, Claudius*, he noticed in his hometown newspaper that Jacobi was opening in *Hamlet*—the first production of the Prospect Theater Company—at the New Theatre in Oxford, a half-hour away by train. Branagh still hadn't read the play; he had been to the theater only twice. But there in Oxford he found that "the story was gripping, and I wanted at every moment to know 'what happened next.' Much of the language I did not understand and yet the actors' commitment to each line convinced me that I knew what they were feeling."
Afterward,

as I traveled home that summer evening twenty years ago my overwhelming feeling was of having connected with an extraordinary energy. In the play itself and chiefly in the character of Hamlet, I experienced the insistent hum of life itself. He was passionate, humorous, cruel, intelligent, courageous and cowardly, but unmistakably and gloriously brimming over with life. In the production and in Jacobi's performance I had been taken on an emotional rollercoaster. It made me reflect on my relationships with my parents, the prospects of my adolescent love affair. It set my heart and my head racing. I felt I had encountered a genuine force of nature, and on that journey home and for sometime afterwards, its memory made me glad to be alive. But then I was fifteen.

What followed this revelation was a sequence of imaginings, possibilities, meditations, adaptations, and embodiments, leading to playing the title role for Adrian Noble in the 1992 production of the Royal Shakespeare Company and again in his own 1995 film for Castle Rock Entertainment. "I longed to allow audiences to join Fortinbras on the plain in Norway, to be transported, as Hamlet is in his mind's eye, back to Troy and see Priam and Hecuba" (xiv). Branagh's intentions were local, composite, overarching, the "inflexion of a subjective view of the play which has developed over the years. Its intention was to be both personal, with enormous attention paid to the intimate relations between the characters, and at the same time epic, with a sense of the country at large and of a dynasty in decay" (Branagh xiv–xv).

During the ambitious filming of Branagh's 1995 *Hamlet*, Russell Jackson, the critric and scholarly consultant, recorded the restless interpretations in a diary. On Wednesday, January 3, he notes that "Ophelia (Kate Winslet) and Hamlet have been having an affair (yes, they have been to bed together, because we want this relationship to be as serious as possible) since the death of Hamlet senior. (Effect of a surge of feeling in time of bereavement and crisis?)," adding, "Kate Winslet plays Ophelia vulnerable but not cowed, Dickie Briers is getting more than anger in Polonius—some loving apprehension." In an entry marked "Thursday 4–Monday 8 January," Jackson notes that "Ken steers Derek [Jacobi] towards seeming even more vulnerable as Claudius, 'quietly anxious' about Hamlet after the 'nunnery' scene, rarely openly angry, even when Rosencrantz and Guildenstern have screwed up. So, when he does flare up, becomes desperate, it will be more shocking." Finally, on Wednesday, January 24, "Last full day of rehearsals: work on the play scene and Hamlet's meeting with the Players, who begin to seem a sort of ideal, alternative family. (The only one we see that is not dysfunctional?)" (Jackson in Branagh 177–81). Further changes would occur during the filming in this ever-renewable play.

Indeed, there is no end to meanings in *Hamlet*, since in "holding the mirror up to nature" (3.2.20), to changing human nature, it is ever capable of transference and transformation. In one week of April 2000 in western Massachusetts, two strikingly dissimilar *Hamlet*s were produced: *Hamlet—Asalto a la Inocencia*, adapted and directed by Sheryl Stoodley and Jonathan Croy with additional text by Migdalia Cruz at Thornes Market in Northampton, at Forum Theater at Holyoke Community College, and at CityStage in Springfield; and Heiner Muller's *Hamletmachine* directed by Tanya Kane-Parry at the Curtain Theater of the University of Massachusetts at Amherst. In a joint review entitled "Assaults on *Hamlet*: Two 'responses' to tragedy smash conventional expectations," Chris Rohmann summarizes each of them:

> What if Gertrude, Hamlet's mom, were an ambitious Puerto Rican street kid, a Latina Cinderella who caught the eye of a Danish King Charming and grabbed the opportunity to improve her station in life? What if their bi-racial son were driven by a macho sense of honor to avenge his father's murder, but was left paralyzed by ambivalence, a child of two cultures and of neither? . . . *Hamletmachine* asks a different question: What if Hamlet's ambivalence were sexual as well as moral? What if the existential doubt that gnaws his spirit sprang from a soul-crushing ideology? And what if Hamlet's girlfriend, Ophelia, weren't a suicidal doormat but a feisty mirror image of Hamlet—the angry child of a murdered father, bent on revenge but ultimately powerless?

Rohmann notes, "Both productions take brash liberties with their textual sources. Serious Play has cut Shakespeare's text by half, then augmented it with modern interpolations. These include several monologues and dialogues written by playwright Migdalia Cruz, mostly for Hamlet and Gertrude, based on conversations with the young actors playing these roles, Arnoldo Rivera and Candy Santiago. The dialogue is punctuated with sudden outbursts of Spanish, especially at moments of high emotion." As for the "consciously postmodern staging" of *Hamletmachine*, the director "uses Muller's text as a grab-bag from which some passages are plucked, some repeated, and some ignored. One of the few direct quotes from Shakespeare is 'Denmark is a prison' —a prison of the spirit where noble impulses are twisted into cynical self-mutilation. In Kane-Perry's version, the phrase constantly recurs and finally mutates into 'I am my own prisoner.'"[3] (Rohman 2000)

Like staged productions, film too continually metamorphoses Shakespeare's play. Just a month later (in May 2000), Elvis Mitchell notes in *The New York Times* that the movie director Michael Almereyda, setting "his voluptuous and rewarding new adaptation of the play in today's Manhattan," catches the city's "contradictions of beauty and squalor . . . and New York becomes a complex character in this vital and sharply intelligent film." Inspired, perhaps, by the 1987 film *Hamlet Goes Business* by director Aki Kaurismaki, the corporate world of Almereyda's *Hamlet* is a colder vision of capitalism where Claudius has risen to head the Denmark Corporation after the death of Hamlet's father. "But where Mr. Kaurismaki presented his take as a slapstick tragedy that bordered on sadism, Mr. Almereyda layers his cool-to-the-touch version with a luxuriant paranoia compounded by the constant deployment of video cameras and listening devices." The idea is not as remote as it might seem at first: the consistent spying in the original *Hamlet* coincided with the extensive network of spies Francis Walsingham instituted during the reign of Elizabeth I at the initial writing of the play. For Mitchell, such a parallel can be alarmingly acute. "Mr. Almereyda has created a new standard for adaptations of Shakespeare, starting with an understanding of the emotional pull of the material that corresponds with its new period and setting. Hamlet's soliloquies are now interior monologues except for the 'To be or not to be' speech, which he delivers in a Blockbuster video store, using the blue in the company logo and the word 'Action' emblazoned on the shelves to fit in with the mood and color of the rest of the picture."[4]

At the dawn of the new century, adaptation extended to fiction, too, in the prequel novel by John Updike, *Gertrude and Claudius*. Drawing sequentially on the three versions of the story Elizabethans knew—those of Saxo Grammaticus, François de Belleforest, and Shakespeare—Updike envisions a far more complicated and considerably sadder Gertrude, married against her will to a man much older than she. As Geruthe describes Horvendile (the elder Hamlet) to Fengon (Claudius):

"He saw me first as desirable property, and of his property he is a considerate enough caretaker. But, yes, in that he has taken me from the days of my life, and encouraged in me a mummifying royal propriety, I do hate him. You, by daring me to love, have led me to see how badly tended I have been. But the world is such. He is my master. Outside of Elsinore, I am nothing—less than a female serf, who has at least her native sturdiness, her hungry sprats, her beanpatch, her straw bed." . . .

"Enamorata, it may be death to keep me," Fengon warned. "Amors, mors." He stroked her tingling hair and tugged a strand in illustration. "Fate cuts the sailor some slack, but then the line pulls taut." (Updike 132–33)

As a prequel, Updike's fiction wrestles under the shadow of the great play that will follow it. Gertrude is more sympathetic; she is also more complicated. Her desires, during her marriage to Hamlet, to wish him dead, to prefer Claudius, haunts her, arousing dread forebodings of guilt. She tells Claudius,

"Now little Hamlet has it, that same gift. Of making me feel dirty and ashamed and unworthy. I have a confession. No, it's too terrible to say." She waited to be coaxed, then went on, uncoaxed. "All right, I'll *tell* you: I'm glad the child isn't at Elsinore. He would sulk. He would try to make me feel shallow, and stupid, and wicked." (Updike 165)

Despite haunting premonitions, Gertrude longs to improve her lot. "Even with so muted a celebration in prospect, a marriage draped in mourning, Gertrude found these narrowing November days brightened. What we once did imperfectly, we yearn to perfect in the second doing" (Updike 169). Premonitions for Gertrude become (in Updike's prequel) sensible, almost visible.

King Hamlet in Gertrude's sense of him became almost palpable, quickening all of her senses save that of sight, her ears imagining a rustle, a footstep, a stifled groan, the nerves and fine hairs of her sixth sense tickled and brushed by some passing emanation, though the corridor was windless, and no newly snuffed candle or fresh-lit fire could account for the whiff of burning, of smoke, of char, of roasting. And upon this sense was visited an impression of pain; he seemed, this less than apparition but more than absence, to be calling her name, out of an agony—*Gerutha*, as she had been in the deeps of time. . . . What did dead Hamlet want of her? . . . The blessed dead do not haunt the living; only the damned do, tied to the living fallen, and her late husband had been a model of virtue and a very pattern of kingship. *He wants me still to be hi*s was her intuition; the King loved her, had always loved her, and her infidelity, that while living he had in his royal preoccupations overlooked, now tormented him so that she could smell his burning flesh and almost hear his strangled voice. (Updike 194–95)

The ghostly sense of King Hamlet lends pain to the world of Gertrude and Claudius, provides the edge of doom. The irony of readers' knowing what follows gives Updike's poised conclusion a poignancy as well as a sense of inevitability.

> The era of Claudius had dawned; it would shine in Denmark's annals. He might, with moderation of his carousals, last another decade on the throne. Hamlet would be the perfect age of forty when the crown descended. He and Ophelia would have the royal heirs lined up like ducklings. Gertrude would gently fade, his saintly gray widow, into the people's remembrance. In his jubilation at these presages, the King, standing to make his exit, announced boomingly that this gentle and unforced accord of Hamlet sat so smiling to his heart that, at every health he would drink today, the great cannons would tell the clouds. And his queen stood up beside him, all beaming in her rosy goodness, her face alight with pride at his performance. He took her yielding hand in his, his hard sceptre in the other. He had gotten away with it. All would be well. (Updike 210)

By thus humanizing the central characters of Shakespeare's play, Updike deepens both its irony and its tragedy, fashioned for another culture four centuries after its composition.

THE TEXT OF *HAMLET*

Shakespeare's play invites such responses because the past lives (and the future of Denmark) are felt absences whenever we see or read his play. We want, perhaps need, to know more; and that *more* is what prompts centuries of interpolations, amendments, conflations, and adaptations. But there is also a sense in which *Hamlet* requires our active complicity, for the text we have presents us with awkward inconsistencies, even lacunae. What, for instance, are we to make of the Horatio we do have in the play? In 1.1, the Danish Horatio is familiar with King Hamlet, Danish political affairs, and the rumors swirling around the ramparts of Elsinore, as a visitor from Wittenberg summoned home for the funeral of the King; yet in 1.4 he is innocent of the Danish habit of drinking and remarks of the King, "I saw him once" (1.2.185). Nor does he seem to know Fortinbras (unless Shakespeare changed his mind while writing the play). In 1.1, Horatio describes young Fortinbras as a soldier "Of unimprovèd mettle hot and full" who "Hath in the skirts of Norway here and there / Sharked up a list of landless resolutes" (1.1 95–97). This description is far removed from that of the disciplined soldier who seeks permission from Claudius to cross Denmark to invade Poland—

> Go, captain, from me greet the Danish king.
> Tell him that by his licence Fortinbras
> Claims the conveyance of a promised march
> Over his kingdom. You know the rendezvous.
> If that his majesty would aught with us,
> We shall express our duty in his eye,
> And let him know so (4.4.1–7)

—and the military leader whose election to the very throne of Denmark as young Hamlet's successor "has my dying voice" (5.2.298).

Hamlet, too, presents problems. For one thing, how old is he? In 5.1, the grave-digger (the First Clown) tells us he has "been sexton here, man and boy, thirty years" (149–50) and that he took up his job "that day that our last King Hamlet o'ercame Fortinbras" (132–33), "the very day that young Hamlet was born" (136). This is confirmed by his reference to Hamlet's childhood recollections of being carried about by Yorick, the king's jester, who "has lain in the earth three-and-twenty years" (160). Hamlet, then, is clearly thirty years of age. But as a student at Wittenberg he should be in his early twenties; his adolescent refusal to acknowledge his stepfather might make him seem even younger. On the other hand, his schoolmate Horatio, who recalls at first hand the death of old Fortinbras (1.1.82ff.) could be about forty. Secondly, when does Hamlet first think of *The Murder of Gonzago*, *The Mouse-trap*? Musing on the actor playing Priam, he thinks,

> I have heard that guilty creatures sitting at a play
> Have by the very cunning of the scene
> Been struck so to the soul that presently
> They have proclaimed their malefactions;
> For murder, though it have no tongue, will speak
> With most miraculous organ. I'll have these players
> Play something like the murder of my father
> Before mine uncle. . . .
> The play's the thing
> Wherein I'll catch the conscience of the King. (2.2.566–73; 581–82)

But he has already done just that very thing: asked if the players can do *The Murder of Gonzago*, he thought to write "a speech of some dozen or sixteen lines which I would set down and insert in't" (2.2.518–19), and sought their permission and approval. Or, again, how does Hamlet view life after death? He says to himself, shortly before he meets Ophelia, that death is

> The undiscovered country from whose bourn
> No traveller returns (3.1.81–82)

and that this "puzzles the will," but nearly all of 1.5 has confronted Hamlet with a dead traveler returned as a ghost and Hamlet's response, if still uncertain, has nevertheless not so puzzled him that he has not commanded the players to test the veracity of the Ghost. Even at the end of the play, he appears confused. He will trust God and His providence—he will "defy augury. There's a special providence in the fall of a sparrow" (5.2.157–58), yet he is hardly passive ("The readiness is all," 5.2.160) and, reinforced by the Ghost's command in his mother's closet and his determined murder of Rosencrantz and Guildenstern and his

sudden reappearance at Elsinore eagerly prepared to combat Laertes, he is neither uncertain nor passive.

Or what are we to make of Gertrude's second marriage? By the laws of the
Catholic and Established churches of Shakespeare's day, drawing on Leviticus
20:21, Gertrude's marriage to her brother-in-law was considered incestuous, a
deep moral offense. (Such marriages, in fact, did not become legal in England
until 1960.) Such a marriage deeply affects Hamlet, although he does not question its actual legality; such a marriage does not even bother any other member
of the Danish court, despite insistence elsewhere on moral conduct (1.3.10-44,
2.1.1–48, and 5.1.209–12, for example). In such a universe, at such a court, is the
Ghost purgatorial or demonic, and where would this put providence? At its very
center, then, as well as in its untrammeled consequences, the threads of the story
of *Hamlet* come unwound. As critics have noted through the centuries, much is
left unexplained in the play; much may forever be inexplicable. There is mystery
at the heart of the work. But when, as in *Hamlet*, epistemology consistently
elides with eschatology, interpretations become imperative and, in a play as rich
as *Hamlet*, always potentially various. Discrepant readings and discrepant productions have, since the sixteenth century, been the result.

THE EARLIEST RECORDS

Even the initial "facts" about *Hamlet* are disturbingly uncertain. James Roberts,
printer, entered into *The Stationers' Register* on July 26, 1602, "A booke called
the Revenge of Hamlett Prince [of] Denmark as yt was latelie Acted by the Lord
Chamberleyne his servantes," yet the first quarto was not actually printed until
the following year, and by a different printer, Valentine Simmes. Roberts printed
the second quarto, later in 1604. But by then, the play had already been staged,
although just when it was first staged is also unknown. In a listing of
Shakespeare's works that Francis Meres published in *Palladis Tamia* in 1598,
Hamlet is not mentioned; yet in his edition of Chaucer likewise published in
1598, Gabriel Harvey reports that "The younger sort takes much delight in
Shakespeare's *Venus and Adonis*, but his *Lucrece* and his *Tragedy of Hamlet,
Prince of Denmark* have it in them to please the wiser sort" (232). It is likely,
though, that Shakespeare's *Hamlet* was written about the time of *Julius Caesar*
(1599), since the references to Caesar in *Hamlet* then take on enhanced, even
parodic, meaning (1.1.106.5–15; 3.2.93–95). This evidence may thus establish
the date of composition and playing at around 1598.

But these are not the only references we have to *Hamlet*. Apparently contrary to Francis Meres, Philip Henslowe records in his *Diary* a performance of
Hamlet at the theater of Newington Butts in June of 1594 (21) and Thomas
Lodge, in 1596, alludes to the "ghost which cried so miserably at the Theatre
[another playhouse], like an oister-wife, Hamlet, revenge." Indeed, way back in
1589 Thomas Nashe descants on a play called *Hamlet*:

It is a common practice nowadays amongst a sort of shifting companions, that run through every art and thrive by none, to leave the trade of *Noverint*, whereto they were born and busy themselves with the endeavors of art, that could scarcely Latinize their neck-verse if they should have need. Yet English *Seneca* read by candlelight yields many good sentences, as *Blood is a beggar* and so forth; and if you entreat him fair in a frosty morning, he will afford you whole *Hamlets*—I should say handfuls of magical speeches. But . . . *Seneca*, let blood line by line and page by page, at length must needs die to our stage; which makes his famished followers to imitate the Kid in Aesop who, enamoured with the Fox's newfangles, forsook all hopes of life to leap into a new occupation, and these men, renouncing all possibilities of credit or estimation, to intermeddle with Italian translations. (Nashe, *Workes* ed. R.B. McKerrow III: 315–16)

Most scholars and historians conclude from these early references that there were at least two *Hamlets*, and that the earlier one mentioned by Henslowe, Lodge, and Nashe, the "*ur-Hamlet*," was written by someone else. Just what that play was like and who wrote it is still unknown, but if the mocking Nashe means to leave clues, then perhaps the author was Thomas Kyd (Kid) whose father had been a scrivener (*Noverint*). Kyd died in 1594, the known author of a single extant play, *The Spanish Tragedy* (printed in 1592), a work of considerable accomplishment both poetically and psychologically (although not as accomplished as Shakespeare's play). *The Spanish Tragedy* shares similarities with Shakespeare's *Hamlet*, and even verbal echoes, but these may have grown out of Kyd's interest in Senecan tragedy—revenge plays such as *Medea*, commonly studied in grammar schools and sometimes publicly performed, may have suggested an earlier, rougher work: the *ur-Hamlet* preceding *The Spanish Tragedy*. Geoffrey Bullough lists

Over a score of parallels in incidents and situations [that] exist between *Hamlet* and *The Spanish Tragedy*. These include: (1) A Ghost which repeatedly demands revenge; (2) A secret crime revealed but needing verification; (3) An oath taken on the cross of a sword-hilt; (4) The avenger falls into doubts which are removed; (5) The avenger assumes madness, and a woman really goes mad; (6) The revenge is delayed and the avenger reproaches himself; (7) A contrast is drawn between the tardy avenger and someone else whose father (*Hamlet*) or son (*The Spanish Tragedy*) has been murdered; (8) The avenger meditates on suicide; (9) He uses dissimulation, as do his enemies; (10) The woman loved by the son is warned by her father and brother; (11) The avenger discusses the art of the theatre; (12) A play-within-the-play is a decisive moment; (13) The catastrophe occurs during an alleged entertainment; (14) Both plays have a character ([named] Horatio) who is a faithful friend; (15) Hamlet knows in the closet-scene that his father's Ghost comes to chide him: (16) Hieronimo pretends a reconciliation with his enemy Lorenzo: Hamlet offers Laertes a sincere reconciliation; Laertes dissembles; (17) A spy is set to watch the lovers; (18) A brother hates his sister's lover and kills him treacherously; (19) A woman dies by suicide; (20) Conflicts between two kingdoms involve the coming and going of

ambassadors; moreover each play is set in a moral climate of intrigue, crime and
hypocrisy. The mind of each hero is almost unhinged by grief and frustration,
and there are violent Senecan speeches in each play. (Bullough 16–17)

While many of these similarities are common to revenge plays generally, the
shared characteristics are nevertheless telling. "At the heart of these plays," W.
Thomas MacCary writes, "is the obsession with honor. A man loses his honor if
he fails to uphold his obligations to friends and family; a woman loses her honor
if she is unchaste or allies herself with a man socially inferior to her" (MacCary
15). And with Kyd especially, Shakespeare's *Hamlet* shares formal orations,
rhetorical tropes, repeated speeches of self-interrogation, and metatheatricality.
Where Kyd's Hieronimo stages a masque to expose his son's murderers,
Shakespeare's play is full of scripts meant to test other characters: the Ghost's
instructions to Hamlet; Polonius's scripts to Reynaldo and to Ophelia; Claudius's
script to the court in 1.2 and to Laertes in 4.5.

Two other texts precede Shakespeare's *Hamlet*, and perhaps any and all
*Hamlet*s. The more important, and quite clearly the ultimate source for
Shakespeare, is the twelfth-century Latin *Historiae Danicae* by Saxo
Grammaticus, first printed in 1514; it was followed by several editions in Latin
and a translation into Danish in 1575 and may have taken on increased impor-
tance around 1590-1600 as James VI of Scotland and his wife, the Danish Queen
Anne, became strong contenders to succeed Elizabeth I on the throne of England.
As Saxo tells his story, Rorik, king of Denmark, marries his daughter Gerutha to
Horwendil, whose family has some claim to rule in Jutland. But Horwendil also
distinguishes himself by killing King Kroll of Norway. After their marriage,
Horwendil and Gerutha give birth to a son, Amleth. But Horwendil's brother
Feng, presumably younger, is jealous of Horwendil and ultimately kills him and
marries his sister-in-law, the widow Gerutha. Amleth is aware that his father was
murdered, and, in fear for his own life, feigns madness, concealing his own intelligence and integrity. Feng grows suspicious and tests Amleth—he asks some
young men at court to take Amleth to the forest where he meets a girl he has long
known. If he is stupid, Feng reasons, he will do nothing; but if he is sane, he will
"yield to wantonness." Amleth seduces the girl but swears her to secrecy.
Returning to court, he confesses his actions, but the girl denies them and again
he appears mad. Now he comes before Gerutha, unaware that a courtier has been
set to spy on him once again. But Amleth discovers the spy in the straw of the
bed, stabs him, dismembers him, and flushes the body parts down a sewer to be
eaten by swine. He then scolds his mother:

> Most infamous of women! dost thou seek, with such lying lamentations to hide
> thy most heavy guilt? Wantoning like a harlot, thou hast entered a wicked and
> abominable state of wedlock, embracing with incestuous bosom thy husband's
> slayer, and wheedling with filthy lures of blandishment him who had slain the
> father of thy son. (Bullough 66)

Here the stories depart. The Scottish Queen Hermutrude kills her suitors to seduce Amleth (a point impolitic in the last years of Elizabeth I) and accompanies him to Britain, where he already has a wife. In time, Amleth is killed by King Wiglek of Denmark, Rorik's successor; and Hermutrude, who protested she would not outlive her husband Amleth, immediately marries King Wiglek in actions transposed by Shakespeare into the dumb show preceding *The Murder of Gonzago*. Treachery is as central to Saxo as to Shakespeare:

> Thus all vows of women are loosed by change of fortune and melted by the shifting of time; the faith of their soul rests on a slippery foothold, and is weakened by casual chances; glib in promises, and as sluggish in performance, all manner of lustful promptings enslave it, and it bounds away with panting and precipitate desire, forgetful of old things, in the ever hot pursuit after something fresh. So ended Amleth. Had fortune been as kind to him as nature, he would have equalled the gods in glory, and surpassed the labours of Hercules by his deeds of prowess. A plain in Jutland is to be found, famous for his name and burial-place. (Bullough 79)

The possible second source is François de Belleforest's lugubrious retelling of Saxo in "The Tragical Historie of Hamlet, Prince of Denmark," in his collection *Histoires Tragiques*, published in French in seven editions between 1564 and 1582 but not translated into English until 1608.

In addition, Bullough reprints probable or possible sources from Titus Livius's *Romane Historie*, translated into English by Philemon Holland (1600); *Agamemnon* translated by John Studley (1566) and *Troas* translated by Jasper Heywood (1581 ed.); in Thomas Newton's *Seneca, His Tenne Tragedies* (1581); Paolo Giovio's *Eulogies of Men Famous for Warlike Virtue* (1575); *The Tragedie of Dido Queene of Carthage* by Christopher Marlowe and Thomas Nashe (1594); and the anonymous *Warning for Faire Women* (1599), as well as analogues in the anonymous *Hystorie of Hamblet* (1608); I. G.'s (John Gordon's) *Henrici Scotorum Regis Manes* (1587); the St. Alban's *Chronicle*; the anonymous *Tarltons Newes out of Purgatorie* (c. 1590); Nathaniel Woods's *Conflict of Conscience* (1581); and Pyrocles's story in Sir Philip Sidney's *Arcadia*, I.8. (Bullough 80-81). Each possibility throws its own slanted perspective on *Hamlet* when held up to the mirror of its own nature. None of them wholly evolves into *Hamlet*, but all of them are refracted in Shakespeare's play, reflecting the play's unsettledness, its susceptibility to variants.

QUARTO AND FOLIO *HAMLET*

Such myriad contemporary works might turn Shakespeare's *Hamlet* like a kaleidoscope were it not that the play, coming down to us in three performance texts in Shakespeare's lifetime, is itself myriad and kaleidoscopic. The first quarto, (Q1, 1603) which, claims its title-page, "hath been diverse times acted by his

Highnesse servants in the City of London: as also in the two Universities of Cambridge and Oxford, and elsewhere" is the shortest (2,154 lines). It is unique in putting the "to be or not to be" soliloquy and the "nunnery scene" at the start of six scenes leading up to Hamlet's advice to the players rather than at its close, allowing Hamlet's plan to use the play to catch the King's conscience to come just before the performance of *The Murder of Gonzago*. In Q1 Laertes seeks personal revenge for his father's death, but he does not lead a rebellion, and Gertrude, hearing from Hamlet of his father's murder and from Horatio of the plot to kill her son in England, explicitly changes her allegiance from king to prince: "conceal, consent, and doe my best, / What stratagem soe'er thou shalt devise." In the "to be or not to be" soliloquy, Hamlet's hope of a happy life after death prevents him from suicide.

The second Quarto (Q2, 1604) adds a number of speeches, including the soliloquy beginning "How all occasions do inform against me" and the confirmation of Osric's embassage through Gertrude and her desire that Hamlet "use some gentle entertainment to Laertes, before you fall to play" (which, in the Folio, is Hamlet's own idea). The First Folio (F, 1623), at 3,535 lines, includes more banter with Rosencrantz and Guildenstern (while omitting their knowledgeable involvement of killing Hamlet in England) and the satire on boy actors (in 2.2).

But the dates and sequence of publication do not necessarily indicate a preferential ordering of texts—or that Q1, apparently nearest in time to the play's composition, is necessarily closest to Shakespeare's initial intention. Indeed, the printing of Q1 is so garbled that it seems unlikely that Shakespeare had a hand in it or that printers were working directly from any fair (good) copy of Shakespeare's "foul papers," his own manuscript. The investigation and study of Harold Jenkins for Arden 2 (soon to be replaced by the Arden 3 text, edited by Ann Thompson and Neil Taylor), concludes that

> Of [the] three texts, each of the last two [Q2 and F], though largely substantive, owes something to its predecessor, while the first [Q1], the only wholly independent text, has all the unreliability of a memorial reconstruction [that is, pieced together for the printer by one or more actors or members of the audience from one or more performances, probably by notation and dictation]. Q2, the one which stands closest to the author, [therefore] leaves obscure a number of passages which are not represented in the other two at all. . . . On the other hand, F contains passages not in Q2 which are certainly authentic as well as incidental addition almost as certainly spurious. In the matter of variant readings, since F as well as Q1 reflects playhouse deviation from the Shakespearean original, agreement between these two does not authenticate a reading against Q2, and in view of Q2's partial dependence on Q1, agreement between those two, especially in the first act, does not authenticate a reading against F. Moreover, with F also dependent on Q2, agreement even between the two good

texts affords no guarantee, and it is obviously possible for all three to be wrong together. (Jenkins 74)

Alternatively, changes between Q2 and F may result either from Shakespeare's revisions (on second thought and/or because of performance) or from subsequent performances: when his two fellow shareholders in the playing company known as the King's Men, Heminge and Condell, called in the company's properties to memorialize Shakespeare after his death in the great First Folio of 1623, they probably chose what was on hand, and arguably the most playable at the time. (Indeed, MacCary thinks, with others, that "much of what Q2 contains and F lacks as exposition and expansion [is] of an allusive, scholarly nature—what Shakespeare might have originally written . . . but later deleted because they did not 'play well.'") (MacCary 4)

CULTURAL CONTEXTS

Whichever text or texts we choose, however, *Hamlet* in turn refracts cultural conditions and beliefs of Shakespeare's time. Tudor medicine would describe Hamlet as melancholic (suffering from what Freud called dementia praecox, we call depression) caused by a superabundance of black bile in his body chemistry that throws health out of balance. "Touching that which comes by Melancholy, sundry things are to be considered," the revered theologian William Perkins writes in *The Whole Treatise of the Cases of Conscience* (1608):

> 1. And first of all, if it be asked what Melancholy is? I answer, it is a kind of earthy and black blood, specially in the spleen, corrupted and distempered. . . .
> 2. The second is, what are the effects and operations of Melancholy? Ans. . . . There is no humor, yea nothing in man's body, that hath so strange effects, as this humor hath being once distempered. . . . Now the effects thereof in particular, are of two sorts. The first, is in the brain and head. For this humor being corrupted, it sends up noisome fumes as clouds or mists which do corrupteth the imagination, and makes the instrument of reason unfit for understanding and sense. Hence follows the first effect, strange imaginations, conceits and opinions framed in the mind. . . . [And] because it corrupteth the instrument [the mind], and the instrument being corrupted, the faculty cannot bring forth good but corrupt actions. (Perkins XII:2, 193, XII:2, 191–92; sigs. M8–M8v)

Perkins's source, in part, is *A Treatise of Melancholy* by Timothy Bright (1586) which Hamlet's behavior faithfully limns.

> There are sorts of unnatural melancholia. . . . They rise of [from] the natural humors, or their excrements by excessive distemper of heat, burned as it were into ashes in comparison of humor, by which the humor of like nature being mixed, turneth into a sharp lye. . . . This sort raiseth the greatest tempest of perturbations and most of all destroyeth the brain with all his faculties, and dispo-

sition of action, and maketh both it, and the heart cheer more uncomfortably: and if it rise of the natural melancholy, beyond all likelihood of truth, [it will] frame monstrous terrors of fear and heaviness without cause. (Bright Chap XVIII; 107–8; sigs. G6–G6v)

"If there be excess of the melancholic humor," Pierre La Primaudaye writes in *The French Academie* as translated by Thomas Bowes in 1584, "the natures of such are sad, still, hard to please, suspicious, conceited, obstinate, some more and some less" (Primaudaye II:lxviii, 535).

A second cause—or perhaps consequence—of melancholy is thinking too precisely (too narrowly, too exclusively, too repeatedly) on an event. Hamlet cautions Horatio that "There are more things in heaven and earth, . . . / Than are dreamt of in our philosophy" (1.5.168–69). But to philosophize, Shakespeare's contemporary Montaigne argued, is to learn to die; and Hamlet's thoughts are never far from death—his own or others'—or from death's affiliations as he saw them: incest, corruption, disease, ghosts, the undiscovered country, woman herself. "Get thee to a nunnery," he tells Ophelia; "Why wouldst thou be a breeder of sinners?" (3.1.122–23). Rather than using philosophy to distance himself from the terrors of living, Hamlet exaggerates them, preserving himself through attitudes of cynicism that prolong and even encourage his skepticism (as a student at Wittenberg, known for theology and philosophy, the home of Martin Luther and Dr. Faustus both). Montaigne's long early work, "An Apology of Raymond Sebond," translated in 1603 by John Florio, establishes resonances for Hamlet:

> Who hath persuaded him, that this admirable moving of heaven's vaults, that the eternal light of these lamps so fiercely rolling over his heads, that the horror-moving and continual motion of this infinite Ocean, were established, and continue so many ages for his commodity, and his service? Is it possible to imagine anything so ridiculous, as this miserable and wretched creature, which is not even so much as master of himself, exposed and subject to the offences of all things, and yet dareth call himself Master and Emperor of this Universe? In whose power it is not to know the least part of it? (Montaigne II. xii, p. 258; sig. 23v)

For Hamlet, "all occasions do inform against me" (4.4.9–22):

> To be, or not to be; that is the question:
> Whether 'tis nobler in the mind to suffer
> The slings and arrows of outrageous fortune,
> Or to take arms against a sea of troubles,
> And, by opposing, end them. To die, to sleep—
> No more, and by a sleep to say we end
> The heartache and the thousand natural shocks
> That flesh is heir to—'tis a consummation
> Devoutly to be wished. (3.1.58–66)

This conclusion is good syllogistic reasoning for the student from Wittenberg; when the world is "an unweeded garden / That grows to seed; [where] things rank and gross in nature / Possess it merely [entirely]" (1.2.135–37), the best offense is defense, the only reasonable action is withdrawal: "O that this too too solid flesh would melt, / Thaw, and resolve itself into a dew," or, says the student from Luther's university, grimly, "Or that the Everlasting had not fixed / His canon [theological law] 'gainst self-slaughter!" (1.2.129–32). His sense of annihilation would spread, too, his deepening misogyny attacking Ophelia (3.1) and Gertrude (3.4). The heir of Wittenberg cannot reconcile philosophy and theology; in Shakespeare's culture the one teaching how to die, the other teaching how to attain eternal life.

A third cause of madness in Elizabethan England was demonic possession of the soul. Hamlet's reference to "a special providence in the fall of a sparrow" (5.2.157–58) may be an urgent appeal or final resignation; either way, it questions the basic tenet of the Reformed Church under Luther (and Calvin) in England that a man of faith would personally find salvation in private association with God. It also calls into question the Ghost's claim to have come from a Catholic purgatory—"Doomed for a certain term to walk the night, / And for the day confined to fast in fires / Till the foul crimes done in my days of nature / Are burnt and purged away" (1.5.10-13)—for Hamlet a "poor ghost"; a "perturbéd spirit" (1.5.4; 183). But Hamlet's immediate reaction to a ghost come from purgatory is not to question it, but to recognize it and its tale: "O my prophetic soul!" (1.5.41). Such an assimilation of Catholic belief in a purgatory denied by the Protestant faith would come easily to Shakespeare's neighbors in Warwickshire, where Catholics were thick on the ground, occupying many of the great manor houses and country estates just north and west of Stratford. It might come easily too to Shakespeare's family, where his father was or at the very least had been a practicing Catholic and the Jesuit Robert Southwell, martyred in 1595, was a distant cousin on his mother's side. A belief in purgatory, however, could increase the possibility of demonism. In his foundational *Summa Theologica*, St. Thomas notes that

> There are two ways of understanding a person to leave hell or heaven. First, that he goes from there simply, so that heaven and hell be no longer his place. . . . Secondly, they may be understood to go forth for a time: and here we must distinguish what befits them according to the order of nature, and what according to the order of Divine providence. . . . According to the natural course, the separated souls consigned to their respective abodes are utterly cut off from communication with the living. . . . Nevertheless, according to the disposition of Divine providence separated souls sometimes come forth from their abode and appear to men, as Augustine . . . relates of the martyr Felix who appeared visibly to the people of Nola when they were besieged by the barbarians. It is also credible that this may occur sometimes to the damned, and that for man's instruction and intimidation they be permitted to appear to the living; or again

in order to seek our suffrages, as to those who are detained in purgatory. (Question LXIX)

This ineluctable multiple perspective was underlined by Noel Taillepied's *Treatise of Ghosts* (1588).

> A ghost will naturally, if it is possible, appear to the person whom he has most loved while on earth, since this person will be readiest to fulfill any wish then communicated by the departed. But if it be an evil Spirit, yes, truly he has a thousand subtle fetches and foul tricks, and will again and again deceive. . . . This evil Spirit goes about seeking whom he may devour, and should he chance to find a man already of a melancholic and Saturnian humor, who on account of some great loss, or haply because he deems his honor tarnished, the demon here has a fine field to his hand, and he will tempt the poor wretch to depths of misery and depression. (Taillepied 168–69)

Before such stark alternatives, Hamlet could be seen as rightly confused, wavering between instant acceptance of the Ghost's commands to kill Claudius—"The time is out of joint. O cursèd spite / That ever I was born to set it right" (1.5.189–90)—and his unwillingness to take any shape at face value—"You're a fishmonger" (2.2.175).

Nor, in Shakespeare's time, was the Ghost's command to revenge one death by another clearly right or wrong. In *The Booke of Honor and Armes* (1590), Sir William Segar informs his reader that

> The cause of all Quarrel is Injury and reproach, but the matter of content, is Justice and Honor. For love whereof, we shun no care of mind, loss of wealth, nor adventure of life. Hereof proceedeth of disputation in Schools, pleading in law, war, and all worldly wrangling. For who so is either in deed or opinion, persuaded to have truth and reason on his side, doth not only constantly believe that so it is, but also being thereof denied, holdeth himself injured, and consequently burdened. True it is, that the Christian law wills men to be of so perfect patience, as not only to endure injurious words, but also quietly to suffer every force and violence. Notwithstanding, for so much as none (or very few men) have attained such perfection, the laws of all Nations, for avoiding further inconveniences, and the manifestation of truth, have (among other trials) permitted, that such questions as could not be civilly proved by confession, witness, or other circumstances, should receive judgment by fight and Combat, supposing that GOD (who only knoweth the secret thoughts of all men) would give victory to him that justly adventured his life, for truth, Honor, and Justice. (Segar sigs. A2–A2v)

Thus combat is advisable and readiness is all: "every injurious action not repulsed, is by common consent of all Martial minds holden a thing dishonorable, infamous, and reproachful; it cannot be, but at some times and occasions such questions and quarrels shall arise, as necessarily must receive trial by the Sword" (Segar sig. A2v). Later, however, Segar advises an eye for an eye, tooth for tooth, blood revenge: "for revenge of cowardly and bestial offenses, it is allowable to use any advantage or subtlety, according to the Italian proverb, *Ad vna supercheria, si conviene vn'altra sopercheria, & ad vn tradimento vn altro tridimento* which is, that one advantage requires another, and one treason may be with another acquitted" (Segar 20, sig. D2v).

For women if not for men, suicide was a cultural practice, for "the woman is a weak creature, not endued with like strength and constancy of mind," as the church Homily on the State of Matrimony (1563 et seq.) put it; "therefore they be the sooner disquieted, and they be the more prone to all weak affections and dispositions of mind." Over one-third of all deaths in Shakespeare's day that were thought to be suicides were deaths by drowning. One of many instances but one that could have suggested Ophelia's death was that of Katherine Hamlett, whose body was found in the river Avon one mile east of Stratford eight days before Christmas in 1579, when Shakespeare was fifteen. The incident is recorded in the oath of the jury at the inquest held at Tiddington on February 11, 1580:

> Who say on their oath that the aforesaid Katherine Hamlett, on the seventeenth day of December in the twenty-second year of the reign of the aforesaid lady the Queen, going with a certain vessel, in English a pail, to draw water at the river called Avon in Tiddington aforesaid, it so happened that the aforesaid Katherine, standing on the bank of the same river, suddenly and by accident slipped and fell into the river aforesaid, and there, in the water . . . by accident was drowned, and not otherwise nor in other fashion came by her death.

This historic event reminds us that events can shape or reinforce cultural beliefs and practices. Bullough cites a verse epistle written to James VI of Scotland urging him to revenge the murder of his father Lord Darnley; in this, the ghost of Darnley addresses the King in ways reminiscent of the Ghost of Hamlet Senior to his son:

> Came blameless down to you, Ancestral Shades,
> Believe no crime of me, unless 'tis wrong
> When any husband loves his wife too much.
> And thou my wife, dearer to me than breath,
> Whose heart so changed against me on behalf
> Of a vile rascal pardoned in despite
> Of Lords' just anger and the People's wrongs! (Bullough 125)

Here a regicide is accused of killing the King for the throne and for the Queen, two reasons Hamlet recognizes: for him, King Hamlet was "so loving to my mother / That he might not beteem the winds of heaven / Visit her face too roughly!" (1.2.140-42). Bullough also records other parallels in both the foreign and domestic *Calendar of State Papers* of Elizabeth's reign; but perhaps the manu-script account by the Queen's godson, Sir John Harington, in his *Nugae Antiquae* (c. 1600) concerning Essex gives some sense of how Shakespeare and his early audiences could conceive of Hamlet.

> It resteth with me in opinion, that ambition thwarted in its career, doth speedily lead on to madness; herein I am strengthened by what I learn of my Lord of Essex, who shifteth from sorrow and repentance to rage and rebellion so sud-denly, as well proveth him devoid of good reason or right mind; in my last dis-course [conversation], he uttered such strange designs that made me hasten forth, and leave his absence. . . . The Queene well knoweth how to humble the haughty spirit. The haughty spirit knoweth not how to yield, and the man's soul seemeth tossed to and fro like the waves of a troubled sea. (Harington 225–26)

"'Tis now the very witching time of night," Hamlet remarks after the aborted *Mousetrap*, "When churchyards yawn, and hell itself breathes out / Contagion to this world. Now could I drink hot blood, / And do such bitter business as the day / Would quake to look on" (3.2.358–62).

Written remarks and observed events join in Shakespeare's other plays, which can establish yet another perspective on *Hamlet* for playgoers at Shakespeare's Globe. Nominalism is an issue in *Romeo and Juliet*; melancholy initiates action in *The Merchant of Venice*; the problem of perspectivism under-mines Othello as well as Claudio in *Much Ado About Nothing*; and ghosts rise to haunt Richard III, Julius Caesar, and Macbeth. Willful women—Kate, Lady Macbeth, Volumnia—are seen as dangerous, perverse, even treacherous. And, holding his own mirror up to his own nature, Richard II must shatter it, because the image he sees is one of a shattered soul, while Brutus betrays himself when he accepts Cassius's invitation to be the mirror that informs him of himself: "I, your glass, / Will modestly discover to yourself / That of yourself which you yet know not of" (*Julius Caesar* 1.2.70-72). Hamlet too would learn of himself through his imposed self-reflections in Horatio, Laertes, and Fortinbras. But he neglects Cicero's more insightful comment on such a practice (in *Julius Caesar*): "Indeed it is a strange-disposèd time; / But men may construe things after their fashion, / Clean from the purpose of the things themselves" (1.3.33–35). Yet to understand Denmark as an unweeded garden, a prison, something rotten, is to construe it. Further contextual studies illuminate this play, such as those dis-cussed by Roland Frye, Andrew Gurr, Hiram Haydn, D.G. James, and Bertram L. Joseph.

EARLY CRITICAL REACTIONS: SEVENTEENTH AND EIGHTEENTH CENTURIES

The same implicitly polysemous—and implicitly indeterminate—meanings of *Hamlet* available at its first performances also characterize critical responses for the first two centuries, when critics both defined and attacked the play, developing a sense of Hamlet as tragic, inexcusable, and the object, finally, of sentimentality. Around 1601, Gabriel Harvey wrote in his *Marginalia* that *Hamlet* could please "the wiser sort," while three years later Antony Skoloker pronounced that Hamlet could "please all." Such are the first extant comments, but Harvey and Skoloker were reacting as playgoers, not as readers: the first known instance of a reader's comment belongs to the first important editor of Shakespeare, Nicholas Rowe, in 1709. Rowe concentrates on the character of Hamlet and compares him to Sophocles's Orestes: both are avengers. But Hamlet, he says, is more humane. While each protagonist feels the same respect and admiration for his departed father, and each resolves to kill his father's murderer, Hamlet, unlike Orestes, does not kill his mother, restrained by the Ghost's injunction. The same interest in the protagonist and in his piety is noted the following year in the *Soliloquy, or Advice to the Author* of Anthony Ashley Cooper, earl of Shaftesbury:

> That Piece of his, which appears to have most affected *English* Hearts, and has perhaps been oftenest acted of any which have come upon our Stage, is almost one continu'd *Moral*: A Series of deep Reflections, drawn from *one Mouth*, upon the Subject of *one* single Accident and Calamity, naturally fitted to move Horror and Compassion. It may be properly said of this Play, if I mistake not, that it has only ONE *Character* or *principal Part*. It contains no Adoration or Flattery of the *Sex*: no ranting at *the Gods*: no blustering *Heroism*: nor any thing of that curious mixture of *the Fierce* and *Tender*, which makes the hinge of modern Tragedy, and nicely varies it between the Points of *Love* and *Honour*. (Shaftesbury 1732 ed., I:2575–76)

In 1711 John Dennis remarks that "young Hamlet," like many characters in Shakespeare, has no tragic fault, for his regicide answered a call from Heaven. In *Tatler* 106, Sir Richard Steele talks of *Hamlet* in conjunction with the propriety of a widow's chastity. He notes Hamlet's bitterness over his mother's remarriage, then his indignation, then his rage, in a developing passion that sweeps up the reader:

> The circumstance of time I never could enough admire. The widowhood had lasted two months. This is his first reflection: but, as his indignation rises, he sinks to scarce two months: afterwards into a month: and at last, into a little month: but all this so naturally, that the reader accompanies him in the violence of his passion, and finds the time lessen insensibly, according to the different workings of his disdain. (Steele 1822 ed., II:422)

Not the manipulation of Hamlet's passion but the appearance of the Ghost seems most important to Joseph Addison in 1711, in the April 20 issue of *The Spectator*:

> The Appearance of the Ghost in *Hamlet* is a Masterpiece in its kind, and wrought up with all the Circumstances that can create either Attention or Horrour. The Mind of the Reader is wonderfully prepared for his Reception by the Discourses that precede it: His dumb Behaviour at his first Entrance, strikes the Imagination very strongly; but every Time he enters, he is still more terrifying. Who can read the Speech with which young *Hamlet* accosts him, without trembling?

Such comments were doubtless prompted by Rowe's edition of Shakespeare in 1709, to be followed by those of Alexander Pope in 1723–25 and Lewis Theobald in 1733.

It is Theobald, in fact, who issues the first charges against Shakespeare. He attacks Hamlet's coarse and obscene language and manner, which for Theobald, in an age of neoclassicism, were not merely matters of taste but matters of ethics. During *The Murder of Gonzago*, Theobold remarks, "Hamlet is talking to [Ophelia] in such gross double *entendres*, that she is forc'd to parry them by indirect answers" (*Works* VIII:177), while in *Shakespeare Restored* (1726), he says of Hamlet's line "Do you think I meant country matters?" (3.2.105), "But, indeed, if ever the Poet deserved Whipping for low and indecent Ribaldry, it was for this Passage: ill-tim'd in all its Circumstances, and unbefitting the Dignity of his Characters, as well as of his Audience" (Theobald 86–87). But Theobald merely opened the floodgates for a prolonged attack on the play in the anonymous work entitled *Some Remarks on the Tragedy of Hamlet Prince of Denmark* published in 1736 and widely and commonly attributed to Thomas Hanmer:

> Now I am come to mention *Hamlet*'s Madness, I must speak my Opinion of our Poet's Conduct in this Particular. To conform to the Ground-work of his Plot, *Shakespeare* makes the young Prince feign himself mad. I cannot but think this to be injudicious; for so far from Securing himself from any Violence which he fear'd from the Usurper, which was his Design in so doing, it seems to have been the most likely Way of getting himself confin'd, and consequently, debarr'd from an Opportunity of Revenging his Father's Death, which now seem'd to be his only Aim; and accordingly it was the occasion of his being sent away to *England*. Which Design, had it taken effect upon his Life, he never could have revenged his Father's Murder. To speak Truth, our Poet, by keeping too close to the Ground-work of his Plot, has fallen into an Absurdity: for there appears no Reason at all in Nature, why the young Prince did not put the Usurper to Death as soon as possible, especially as *Hamlet* is represented as a Youth so brave, and so careless of his own Life.
>
> The Case indeed is this: Had *Hamlet* gone naturally to work, as we could suppose such a Prince to do in parallel Circumstances, there would have been an End of our Play. The Poet therefore was obliged to delay his Hero's Revenge; but then he should have contrived some good Reason for it.

Moreover,

> Hamlet's Speech upon seeing the King at Prayers, has always given me great
> Offence. There is something so very Bloody in it, so inhuman, so unworthy of
> a Hero, that I wish our Poet had omitted it. To desire to destroy a Man's Soul,
> to make him eternally miserable, by cutting him off from all hopes of
> Repentance; this surely, in a Christian Prince, is such a Piece of Revenge, as no
> Tenderness for any Parent can justify. To put the Usurper to Death, to deprive
> him of the Fruits of his vile Crime, and to rescue the Throne of *Denmark* from
> Pollution, was highly requisite: But there our young Prince's Desires should
> have stop'd, nor should he have wished to pursue the Criminal in the other
> World, but rather have hoped for his Conversion, before his putting him to
> Death; for even with his Repentance, there was at least Purgatory for him to
> pass through, as we find even in a virtuous Prince, the Father of Hamlet.
> (Hanmer 41)

Apparently unaware of the Elizabethan conventions for revenge tragedy,
"Hanmer" initiated the charge of cruelty that would all but dominate later eighteenth-century criticism. In this, he fails to separate Hamlet from Shakespeare.

John Upton's *Critical Observations on Shakespeare* followed in 1746 and
William Warburton's edition of Shakespeare in 1747, but it is William Guthrie's
An Essay upon English Tragedy in 1747 that develops a substantially new reaction—that the tragic hero should be the common man: "though I have the pre-
possession of a whole age against me," he writes, "there is not the least necessity for the chief personage in a play to have either courage, wisdom, virtue, passion, or any other quality, above what is to be found in his real history, or in common life" (20). For him, Hamlet is just that: in the play Shakespeare

> has supported the character of Hamlet entirely by the force of sentiment, with-
> out giving him any of those strong markings, which commonly form the chief
> modern personage in a tragedy. He has not even made use of those advantages,
> with which the great historian from whom he took his subject might have fur-
> nished him. . . . Where is the poet but Shakespeare who could have worked so
> insipid a character [as found in Saxo] into life by the justness of reflection, and
> the strength of nature, without applying those colours, which an inferior genius
> must have used to mark a principal figure. All we see in Hamlet is a well-mean-
> ing, sensible, young man, but full of doubts and perplexities even after his res-
> olution is fixed. In this character there is nothing but what is common with the
> rest of mankind; he has no marking, no colouring, but its beautiful drawing, per-
> haps, cost Shakespeare more than any one figure he ever attempted. (Guthrie
> 20-21)

In the anonymous *A Companion to the Theatre*, meantime, published in Dublin
in 1751, there is the seed of later criticism about Hamlet's ploy of pretended

madness: he "countefeits a frenzy" so as to "conceal the true Cause of the Horror of his Mind."

Oliver Goldsmith, however, finds cause to criticize the part of Hamlet, especially in the "to be or not to be" soliloquy, in an essay called "The Use of Metaphor" published in *British Magazine* (?1763). In this, he is one of the first to divorce a playtext from performance and consider it wholly as a reader might, testing it solely by its literary value.

> The soliloquy in Hamlet, which we have so often heard extolled in terms of admiration, is, in our opinion, a heap of absurdities, whether we consider the situation, the sentiment, the argumentation, or the poetry. Hamlet is informed by the Ghost, that his father was murdered, and therefore he is tempted to murder himself, even after he had promised to take vengeance on the usurper, and expressed the utmost eagerness to achieve this enterprise. It does not appear that he had the least reason to wish for death; but every motive which may be supposed to influence the mind of a young prince, concurred to render life desirable—revenge towards the usurper; love for the fair Ophelia; and the ambition of reigning. (Goldsmith 316)

Indeed, Hamlet's "whole chain of reasoning . . . seems inconsistent and incongruous."

Samuel Johnson's magisterial edition of Shakespeare in 1765 focuses on a discussion of character, too, and again it is often divorced from the stage: in this, he anticipates the work of William Hazlitt and, in our own day, of Harold Bloom. While he gives greater attention to a discussion of Polonius, it is his remarks on Hamlet, and on variety as a chief attribute of the play, that are historically most important:

> If the dramas of *Shakespeare* were to be characterised, too, and again each by the particular excellence which distinguishes it from the rest, we must allow to the tragedy of *Hamlet* the praise of variety. The incidents are so numerous, that the argument of the play would make a long tale. The scenes are interchangeably diversified with merriment and solemnity; with merriment that includes judicious and instructive observations, and solemnity, not strained by poetical violence above the natural sentiments of man. New characters appear from time to time in continual succession, exhibiting various forms of life and particular modes of conversation. The pretended madness of *Hamlet* causes much mirth, the mournful distract of *Ophelia* fills the heart with tenderness, and every personage produces the effect intended, from the apparition that in the first act chills the blood with horror, to the fop in the last, that exposes affectation to just contempt.
>
> The conduct is perhaps not wholly secure against objections. The action is indeed for the most part in continual progression, but there are some scenes which neither forward nor retard it. Of the feigned madness of *Hamlet* there appears no adequate cause, for he does nothing which he might not have done

with the reputation of sanity. He plays the madman most, when he treats *Ophelia* with so much rudeness, which seems to be useless and wanton cruelty. (303)

Dr. Johnson finds that Hamlet is, throughout the play, more instrument than agent, for he makes no attempt to punish Claudius, and his final regicide is an act not of his making; indeed, "the exchange of weapons is rather an expedient of necessity, than a stroke of art. A scheme might easily have been formed, to kill *Hamlet* with the dagger, and *Laertes* with the bowl." He continues, much in the vein of later eighteenth-century sentimentality,

> The poet is accused of having shewn little regard to poetical justice, and may be charged with equal neglect of poetical probability. The apparition left the regions of the dead to little purpose; the revenge which he demands is not obtained but by the death of him that was required to take it; and the gratification which would arise from the destruction of an usurper and a murderer, is abated by the untimely death of *Opheli*a, the young, the beautiful, the harmless, and the pious. (Johnson 303–4)

In *The Dramatic Censor* of 1770, Francis Gentleman finds "variety" to be, rather, "inconsistency."

> In respect of characters, we are to lament that the hero, who is intended as amiable, should be such an apparent heap of inconsistency: impetuous, tho' philosophical; sensible of injury, yet timid of resentment; shrewd, yet void of policy; full of filial piety, yet tame under oppression; boastful in expression, undetermined in action; and yet from being pregnant with great variety, from affording many opportunities to exert sound judgment and extensive powers, he is as agreeable and striking an object as any in the English drama. (Gentleman 55)

Gentleman admits, however, that such inconsistencies can disappear when the play is put on the stage. Nevertheless, Gentleman's focus became an issue debated throughout the decade. In a letter to Mrs. Montagu sometime in 1772, Dr. James Beattie sees this positively.

> I have often seen Hamlet performed by the Underlings of the theatre, but none of these seemed to understand what they were about. Hamlet's character, though perfectly natural, is so very uncommon, that few, even of our critics, can enter into it. Sorrow, indignation, revenge, and consciousness of his own irresolution, tear his heart; the peculiarity of his circumstances often obliges him to counterfeit madness, and the storm of passions within him often drives him to the verge of real madness. This produces a situation so interesting, and a conduct so complicated, as none but Shakespeare could have had the courage to describe, or even to invent, and none but Garrick will ever be able to exhibit. (Forbes I:283–84)

But the following year, George Steevens, in the first edition of the Steevens-Johnson Shakespeare, is decidedly more negative:

> Hamlet, at the command of his father's ghost, undertakes with seeming alacrity to revenge the murder; and declares he will banish all other thoughts from his mind. He makes, however, but one effort to keep his word . . . defers his purpose . . . he deliberately procures the execution of Rosencrantz and Guildenstern. . . . Their death . . . gives him no concern. . . . He is not less accountable for the distraction and death of Ophelia . . . he kills the king at last to revenge himself, and not his father.
>
> Hamlet cannot be said to have pursued his ends by very warrantable means; and if the poet, when he sacrificed him at last, meant to have enforced such a moral, it is not the worst that can be deduced from the play. (X:343–44)

He adds, by way of apology, "I have dwelt the longer on this subject, because Hamlet seems to have been hitherto regarded as a hero, not undeserving the pity of the audience, and because no writer on Shakespeare has taken the pains to point out the immoral tendency of his character" (X:343–44). The Scotsman William Richardson, a professor of humanities at the University of Glasgow, far removed, geographically and intellectually, from such attacks, defends Hamlet in his *Philosophical Analysis of Some of Shakespeare's Remarkable Characters* (1774) by offering the first psychoanalytical examination of Shakespeare's protagonist. Richardson sees Hamlet as "moved by finer principles" than, say, self-interest, and one whose every act and thought is motivated by "an exquisite sense of virtue, of moral beauty and turpitude." His difficulty is twofold: he is torn between opposing points of view and he thinks and feels more intensely than most men do. His attributes can thus curse him.

> The tendency of indignation, and of furious and inflamed resentment, is to inflict punishment on the offender. But, if resentment is ingrafted on the moral faculty, and grows from it, its tenor and conduct will be different. In its first emotion it may breathe excessive and immediate vengeance. But sentiments of justice and propriety interposing, will arrest and suspend its violence. An ingenious mind, thus agitated by powerful and contending principles, exceedingly tortured and perplexed, will appear hesitating and undetermined. Thus, the vehemence of the vindictive passion will, by delay, suffer abatement; by its own ardour it will be exhausted; and our natural and habituated propensities will resume their influence. (Richardson 130-31)

Richardson's sense of Hamlet as someone too refined to manage the harsh task required of him complements nicely, however, the increasing interest in sentiment and sentimentality and what has been called the "Cult of Sensibility," epitomized in Henry Mackenzie's popular novel *The Man of Feeling*. But Mackenzie remarks, too, on Hamlet, in *The Mirror* for April 22, 1780, noting that Hamlet's "gaiety and playfulness of deportment and of conversation" actually stem from his overall melancholy:

> That sort of melancholy which is the most genuine, as well as the most amiable of any, neither arising from natural sourness of temper, nor prompted by accidental chagrin, but the effect of delicate sensibility, impressed with a sense of sorrow, or a feeling of its own weakness, will, I believe, often be found indulging itself in a sportfulness of external behaviour, amidst the pressure of a sad, or even the anguish of a broken heart. Slighter emotions affect our ordinary discourse; but deep distress, sitting in the secret gloom of the soul, casts not its regard on the common occurrences of life, but suffers them to trick themselves out in the usual garb of indifference, or of gaiety, according to the fashion of the society around it, or the situation in which they chance to arise. The melancholy man feels in himself (if I may be allowed the expression) a sort of double person; one which, covered with the darkness of its imagination, looks not forth into the world, nor takes any concern in vulgar objects or frivolous pursuits; another, which he lends, as it were, to ordinary men, which can accommodate itself to their tempers and manners, and indulge, without feeling any degradation from the indulgence, a smile with the cheerful, and a laugh with the giddy.

There is for Mackenzie an especially provocative example: "The conversation of *Hamlet* with the *Grave-digger* seems to me to be perfectly accounted for under this supposition; and, instead of feeling it counteract the tragic effect of the story, I never see him in that scene, without receiving, from his transient jests with the clown before him, an idea of the deepest melancholy being rooted at his heart. The light point of view in which he places serious and important things, marks the power of that great impression, which swallows up every thing else in his mind, which makes *Caesar* and *Alexander* so indifferent to him, that he can trace their remains in the plaster of a cottage, or the stopper of a beer-barrel."

The canons of good taste likewise governed the relatively sparse French criticism of *Hamlet* in the eighteenth century. The first example, De La Roche in 1717, sees Hamlet as a man of genius but of little taste; for him, Shakespeare has Hamlet speak like a buffoon, both in soliloquies and with the grave-diggers. The Abbé Prévost, writing around 1730, finds a certain aesthetic appeal, despite his French view of the general crudity of English writing. In 1738, Louis Riccoboni, of the Italian theater in Paris, condemns English plays that "have, beyond Imagination, stained their Stage with Blood," while P. A. LaPlace, remarking in 1746 on the "blemishes" in Shakespeare, notes that "beauties" can outnumber them. J. F. Marmontel goes even further the same year, by suggesting that English drama finds its power in resources not allowed the French on the stage, such as (in *Hamlet*) the interview with the Ghost and the fencing match with Laertes. Of all the French critics, however, it is the rationalist Voltaire (in his "Dissertation sur la Tragedie" published in *Semiramia* in 1748) who is the most offended by forthright English style.

Englishmen believe in ghosts no more than the Romans did, yet they take pleasure in the tragedy of *Hamlet*, in which the ghost of a king appears on the stage. . . . Far be it from me to justify everything in that tragedy; it is a vulgar and barbarous drama, which would not be tolerated by the vilest populace of France, or Italy. Hamlet becomes crazy in the second act, and his mistress becomes crazy in the third; the prince allays the father of his mistress under the pretence of killing a rat, and the heroine throws herself into the river; a grave is dug on the stage, and the grave-diggers talk quodlibets worthy of themselves, while holding skulls in their hands; Hamlet responds to their nasty vulgarities in silliness no less disgusting. In the meanwhile another of the actors conquers Poland. Hamlet, his mother, and his father-in-law, carouse on the stage; songs are sung at table; there is quarreling, fighting, killing—one would imagine this piece to be the work of a drunken savage. But amidst all these vulgar irregularities, which to this day make the English drama so absurd and so barbarous, there are to be found in *Hamlet*, by a *bizarrerie* still greater, some sublime passages, worthy of the greatest genius. It seems as though nature had mingled in the brain of Shakespeare the greatest conceivable strength and grandeur with whatsoever witless vulgarity can devise that is lowest and most detestable.

Not surprisingly, Voltaire—the liberal in politics and the conservative in art—is the most acerbic.

If eighteenth-century French criticism concerned itself with decorum, German criticism of the period centered on sentimentality; in this, it anticipates the "Beautiful Soul" of Hegel's *Phenomenology*:

It lives in dread of staining the radiance of its inner being by action and existence. And to preserve the purity of its heart, it flees from contact with actuality, and steadfastly perseveres in a state of self-willed impotence to renounce a self which is pared away to the last point of abstraction, and to give itself substantial existence, or, in other words, to transform its thought into being, and commit itself to absolute distinction. (VI.C.c)

In 1757, Moses Mendelssohn translated the "to be or not to be" speech with a certain morbidity, but it is Goethe's commentary in *Wilhelm Meister's Apprenticeship* (1795–96) that is perhaps most representative and surely the best known:

The time is out of joint, O cursed spite,
That ever I was born to set it right!

In these words, I imagine, will be found the key to Hamlet's whole procedure. To me it is clear that Shakespeare meant, in the present case, to represent the effects of a great action laid upon a soul unfit for the performance of it. In this view the whole piece seems to me to be composed. There is an oak-tree planted in a costly jar, which should have borne only pleasant flowers in its bosom; the roots expand, the jar is shivered.

> A lovely, pure, noble, and most moral nature, without the strength of nerve which forms a hero, sinks beneath a burden which it cannot bear and must not cast away. All duties are holy for him; the present is too hard. Impossibilities have been required of him; not in themselves impossibilities, but such for him. He winds, and turns, and torments himself; he advances and recoils; is ever put in mind, ever puts himself in mind; at last does all but lose his purpose from his thoughts; yet still without recovering his peace of mind.

Projecting his only vibrant emotions onto Hamlet, Goethe may only be more transparent than his predecessors in finding *in* Shakespeare's play what, essentially, he himself brings *to* it. Goethe's late-eighteenth century sense of Hamlet had a considerable influence in the nineteenth century, with some critics' deepened personal responses arguing that the play is too unbearable to perform.

FROM SENTIMENTALISM TO ROMANTICISM: THE NINETEENTH CENTURY

Friedrich Schlegel, in *Die Griechen und die Römer* of 1797, extends Goethe's views by seeing tragedy in the disparity between the nature of man and the world in which he is condemned to live, but his brother, August Wilhelm Schlegel, writing in his *Dramatic Art and Literature* (1809–11), chooses to focus on Goethe in his striking disagreement.

> With respect to Hamlet's character: I cannot, as I understand the poet's views, pronounce altogether so favourable a sentence upon it as Goethe does. He is, it is true, of a highly cultivated mind, a prince of royal manners, endowed with the finest sense of propriety, susceptible of noble ambition, and open in the highest degree to an enthusiastic admiration of that excellence in others of which he himself is deficient. He acts the part of madness with unrivalled power, convincing the persons who are sent to examine into his supposed loss of reason, merely by telling them unwelcome truths, and rallying them with the most caustic wit. But in the resolutions which he so often embraces and always leaves unexecuted, his weakness is too apparent: he does himself only justice when he implies that there is no greater dissimilarity than between himself and Hercules. He is not solely impelled by necessity to artifice and dissimulation, he has a natural inclination for crooked ways; he is a hypocrite towards himself; his far-fetched scruples are often mere pretexts to cover his want of determination: thoughts, as he says on a different occasion, which have
>
> > but one part wisdom,
> > And ever three parts coward.

The finer sensibility advocated by Goethe, however, is what so deeply influences the English Romantics and dominates their criticism throughout the first half of the nineteenth century.

Among the English Romantics, Wordsworth has nothing to say concerning Hamlet, although Keats in one letter, has it "upon the pulses" and in another finds Shakespeare's middle years "all clouded over; his days were not more happy than Hamlet's." In a letter to Fanny Brawne, he compares Hamlet to himself:

> Shakespeare always sums up matters in the most sovereign manner. Hamlet's heart was full of such Misery as mine is when he said to Ophelia: "Go to a Nunnery, go, go!" Indeed I should like to give up the matter at once I should like to die. I am sickened at the brute world which you are smiling with. I hate men, and women more. (ed. Forman, 141–42; 346–47; 503)

Leigh Hunt, however, admires the paradoxes and complications in Hamlet's character that surpass his ability to characterize them:

> It must be the praise of a man, who shall possess a genius capable of more than the art of acting, to personate Hamlet, the gallant, the philosophical, the melancholy Hamlet, that amiable inconsistent, who talked when he should have acted and acted when he should not even have talked, who with a bosom wrung with sensibility was unfeeling, and in his very passion for justice unjust, who in his misery had leisure for ridicule and in his revenge for benevolence, who in the most melancholy abstraction never lost the graces of mind or the elegancies of manner, natural in the midst of error. But let me not attempt to describe the indescribable. (182–83)

Conversely, the three great English Romantic critics of Shakespeare—Lamb, Coleridge, and Hazlitt—alike thought the play difficult or impossible to perform; as Lamb puts it,

> It may seem a paradox, but I cannot help being of opinion that the plays of Shakespeare are less calculated for performance on a stage, than those of almost any other dramatist whatever. Their distinguished excellence is a reason that they should be so. There is so much in them, which comes not under the province of acting, with which eye, and tone, and gesture, have nothing to do. (ed. Lucas, I:98ff.)

When writing his *Tales of Shakespeare* with his sister Mary, Charles Lamb attempted to even out the inconsistencies others found in Hamlet by explaining his delay not as a matter of unmotivated procrastination, but rather as a response to several factors: that Claudius was often with his mother; that to kill his own mother's new husband would fill him "with some remorse"; that it was "odious" to kill a fellow human being; that he was too scrupulous, being unsure of the identity or motivation of the Ghost. All of these earlier thoughts correlate and combine into a more mature portrayal of Hamlet that Lamb would publish in *The Reflector* in 1811, under the title of "On the Tragedies of Shakespeare":

The play itself abounds in maxims and reflexions beyond any other, and therefore we consider it as a proper vehicle for conveying moral instruction. But Hamlet—himself what does he suffer meanwhile by being dragged forth as a public schoolmaster, to give lectures to the crowd! Why, nine parts in ten of what Hamlet does, are transactions between himself and his moral sense, they are the effusions of his solitary musings, which he retires to holes and corners and the most sequestered parts of the palace to pour forth; or rather, they are the silent meditations with which his bosom is bursting, reduced to words for the sake of the reader, who must else remain ignorant of what is passing there. These profound sorrows, these light-and-noise-abhorring ruminations, which the tongue scarce dares utter to deaf walls and chambers, how can they be represented by a gesticulating actor, who comes and mouths them out before an audience, making four hundred people his confidants at once? I say not that it is the fault of the actor so to do; he must pronounce them *ore rotundo*, he must accompany them with his eye, he must insinuate them into his auditory by some trick of eye, tone, or gesture, or he fails. *He must be thinking all the while of his appearance, because he knows that all the while the spectators are judging of it.*

And this is the way to represent the shy, negligent, retiring Hamlet. "I am not arguing that Hamlet should not be acted, but how much Hamlet is made another thing by being acted" (Lamb I:100-01).

This thoughtful Hamlet is maintained for Lamb when he attempts to explain away the prince's words to Ophelia; they are due, he says, to "a profound artifice of love, to alienate Ophelia by affected discourtesies, so to prepare her mind for the breaking off of that loving intercourse, which can no longer find a place amidst business so serious as that which he has to do" (Lamb I:103). Although what results seems monotonal, it is, on later readings, a subtle and engaged character sketch.

"The most influential critic of *Hamlet* that ever lived" is Coleridge, for Paul S. Conklin as for many others, because he "combined a keenly analytical and penetrating mind with romantic tendencies. It was because of his powers of analysis, his ability to take the actual aesthetic data before him and examine them without destroying their essential dramatic integrity, that he achieved results most potent of all romantic critics before and after him" (Conklin 97). For Coleridge himself,

Shakespeare knew the human mind; and its most minute and intimate workings, and he never introduces a word, or a thought, in vain or out of place: if we do not understand him, it is our own fault or the fault of copyists and typographers; but study, and the possession of some small stock of the knowledge by which he worked, will enable us often to detect and explain his meaning. He never wrote at random, or hit upon points of character and conduct by chance; and the smallest fragment of his mind not unfrequently gives a clue to a most perfect, regular, and consistent whole. (ed. Raysor, II:145)

In his critical practice of reading playtexts, Coleridge claims not to have avoid-
ed the works as playscripts, but he treats them as literary texts nonetheless.

> Each scene of each play I read as if it were the whole of Shakespeare's works—
> the sole thing extant. I ask myself what are the characteristics, the diction, the
> cadences, and metre, the character, the passion, the moral or metaphysical
> inherencies and fitness for theatric effect, and in what sort of theatres. All these
> I write down with great care and precision of thought and language . . . and thus
> shall not only know what the characteristics of Shakespeare's plays are, but
> likewise what proportion they bear to each other.

By just such an approach, Coleridge conceives of Hamlet as a man of great and
admirable intellectual power who cannot put his thoughts into action. He cannot
balance the imaginary world and the real one.

> In Hamlet this balance is disturbed: his thoughts, and the images of his fancy,
> are far more vivid than his actual perceptions, and his very perceptions, instant-
> ly passing through the *medium* of his contemplations, acquire, as they pass, a
> form and a colour not naturally their own. Hence we see a great, an almost enor-
> mous, intellectual activity, and a proportionate aversion to real action, conse-
> quent upon it, with all its symptoms and accompanying qualities. This charac-
> ter Shakespeare places in circumstances, under which it is obliged to act on the
> spur of the moment:—Hamlet is brave and careless of death; but he vacillates
> from sensibility, and procrastinates from thought, and loses the power of action
> in the energy of resolve. . . .
>   The effect of this overbalance of the imaginative power is beautifully illus-
> trated in the everlasting broodings and superfluous activities of Hamlet's mind,
> which, unseated from its healthy relation, is constantly occupied with the world
> within, and abstracted from the world without,—giving substance to shadows,
> and throwing a mist over all commonplace actualities. (I:37)

So the *Lectures*. In *Table Talk* for June 24, 1827, Coleridge takes up the matter
again and ends with a surprising revelation:

> Hamlet's character is the prevalence of the abstracting and generalizing habit
> over the practical. He does not want courage, skill, will, or opportunity; but
> every incident sets him thinking; and it is curious, and, at the same time strict-
> ly natural, that Hamlet, who all the play seems reason itself, should be impelled,
> at last, by mere accident to effect his object. I have a smack of Hamlet myself,
> if I may say so. (Coleridge II:150)

His eldest son Hartley, writing for *Blackwood's Edinburgh Magazine* for
November 1828, agrees: Hamlet is "an habitual dweller with his own thoughts—
preferring the possible to the real, refining on the ideal forms of things, till the
things themselves become dim in his sight, and all the common doings and suf-

ferings, the obligations and engagements of the world, a weary task, stale and unprofitable. . . . The death of his father, his mother's marriage, and his own exclusion from the succession—sorrow for one parent, shame for another, and resentment for himself—tend still further to confirm and darken a disposition, which the light heart of happy youth had hitherto counteracted. Sorrow contracts around his soul, and shuts it out from cheerful light, and wholesome air." Thus William Hazilitt's remarks are confirmed: Hamlet for him is "the prince of speculators; and because he cannot have his revenge perfect, according to the most refined idea his wish can form, he declines it altogether," he comments in *The Characters of Shakespeare's Plays* (1817), noting even more dramatically that

> It is *we* who are Hamlet. This play has a prophetic truth, which is above that of history. Whoever has become thoughtful and melancholy through his own mishaps or those of others; whoever has borne about with him the clouded brow of reflection, and thought himself "too much i' th' sun"; whoever has seen the golden lamp of day dimmed by envious mists rising in his own breast, and could find in the world before him only a dull blank with nothing left remarkable in it; whoever has known "the pangs of despised love, the insolence of office, or the spurns which patient merit of the unworthy takes"; he who has felt his mind sink within him, and sadness cling to his heart like a malady, who has had his hopes blighted and his youth staggered by the apparitions of strange things; who cannot be well at ease, while he sees evil hovering near him like a spectre; whose powers of action have been eaten up by thought, he to whom the universe seems infinite, and himself nothing; whose bitterness of soul makes him careless of consequences, and who goes to a play as his best resource to shove off, to a second remove, the evils of life by a mock representation of them—this is the true Hamlet.

For Hazlitt, Hamlet, like himself, did not belong to the stage.

THE LATER NINETEENTH CENTURY

After such influential and penetrating criticism from the Romantic writers, the English Victorian critics had little to say. Matthew Arnold, in the preface to his *Poems* in 1853, links Hamlet with Faust as a representative of the doubt and discouragement of the modern temperament, as opposed to the monumental works of the Greeks. George Henry Lewes, in his 1855 *Life and Works of Goethe*, dismissed the hesitation of the Romantics; *Hamlet* was of interest because it had broad theatrical appeal, he writes, "becoming the most popular play in our language." He goes on,

> It *amuses* thousands annually, and it stimulates the minds of millions. Performed in barns and minor theatres oftener than in Theatres Royal, it is always and everywhere attractive. The lowest and most ignorant audiences delight in it. The source of the delight is twofold: First, its reach of thought on

topics the most profound; for the dullest soul can *feel* a grandeur which it cannot *understand*, and will listen with hushed awe to the out-pourings of a great meditative mind obstinately questioning fate; Secondly, its wondrous dramatic variety. Only consider for a moment the striking effects it has in the Ghost; the tyrant murderer; the terrible adulterous queen; the melancholy hero, doomed to so awful a fate; the poor Ophelia, broken-hearted and dying in madness; the play within a play, entrapping the conscience of the King; the ghastly mirth of the gravediggers; the funeral of Ophelia interrupted by a quarrel over her grave betwixt her brother and her lover; and, finally, the horrid bloody denouement. Such are the fixtures woven in the tapestry by passion and poetry. Add thereto the absorbing fascination of profound thoughts. It may indeed be called the tragedy of thought, for there is as much reflection as action in it; but the reflection itself is made dramatic, and hurries the breathless audience along, with an interest that knows no pause.

Other Victorian critics, each in his way, were less kind. For H. A. Taine (*History of English Literature*, 1863–64), Hamlet "belongs to the sixteenth century" — coldblooded, active during fits of enthusiasm, controlled by occasion. For Edward Dowden (*Shakespeare: A Critical Study of his Mind and Art*, 1875), Hamlet represents Shakespeare in mid-career. "The studious superintendence of the poet over the development of his thought and imaginings, very apparent in Shakespeare's early writings, now conceals itself; but the action of imagination and thought has not yet become embarrassing in its swiftness and multiplicity of direction." Finally, for Swinburne (*A Study of Shakespeare*, 1880), "for all this voice as of one crying in a wilderness, Hamlet will too surely remain to the majority of students, not less than to all actors and all editors and all critics, the standing type and embodied emblem of irresolution, half-heartedness, and doubt." A second provocative thinker, with far more influence deep into the next century was Friedrich Nietzsche. His *Birth of Tragedy from the Spirit of Music* (1870-71) joined the Modern Library texts in 1954 in a translation by Clifton Fadiman. Dividing the impulses of tragedy into the Dionysian and the Apollonian, Nietzsche considers Hamlet as one who resembles the Dionysiac: "both have for once penetrated into the true nature of things they have *perceived*, but it is irksome for them to act."

Indeed, for anything like a fresh and provocative idea—what *Wid's Daily* would call a "modern theory"—we must turn to the lesser-known book by Edward P. Vining, *The Mystery of Hamlet. An Attempt to Solve an Old Problem* (Philadelphia, 1881). Vining finds Hamlet a "bundle of contradictions," for "weak and vacillating as he is, there is yet some quality which forbids that any should despise or condemn him." He goes on to remark that "As Hamlet lacks the energy, the conscious strength, the readiness for action that inhere in the perfect manly character, how comes it that humanity still admires him?" (46). The answer for Vining, if not for his readers at first, is obvious.

> There is not only a masculine type of human perfection, but also a feminine type; and when it became evident that Hamlet was born lacking in many of the elements of virility, there grew up in him, as compensation, many of the perfections of character more properly the crown of the better half of the human race. All mankind has recognized the deep humanity of the melancholy prince, and many have been puzzled to find that they are instinctively compelled to bow before him in admiration, while still finding in him so many faults and weaknesses. The depths of human nature which Shakespeare touched in him have been felt by all, but it has scarcely been recognized that the charms of Hamlet's mind are essentially feminine in nature. (Vining 46–47)

Vining's book is dedicated to the editor of the monumental Variorum Shakespeare, Horace Howard Furness—they both were published by J. P. Lippincott and Co.—but his view formed a foundation for women taking the role of Hamlet.

George Bernard Shaw has also been widely cited, but more for his wit than his ideas. In a 1945 postscript to his 1921 play *Back to Methuselah*, Shaw claims that Shakespeare, in writing *Hamlet*,

> took up an old play about the ghost of a murdered king who haunted his son crying for revenge, with comic relief provided by the son pretending to be that popular curiosity and laughing-stock, a village idiot. Shakespeare, transfiguring this into a tragedy on the ancient Athenian level, could not have been quite unconscious of the evolutionary stride he was taking. But he did not see his way clearly enough to save the tons of ink and paper and years of "man's time" that have been wasted, and are still being wasted, on innumerable volumes of nonsense about the meaning of Hamlet, though it is now as clear as daylight. Hamlet as a prehistoric Dane is morally bound to kill his uncle, politically as rightful heir to the usurped throne, and filially as "the son of a dear father murdered" and a mother seduced by an incestuous adulterer. He has no doubt as to his duty in the matter. . . . But when fully convinced he finds to his bewilderment that he cannot kill his uncle deliberately. . . . In a later transport, when the unlucky uncle poisons not only Hamlet's mother but his own accomplice and Hamlet himself, Hamlet actually does at last kill his enemy on the spur of the moment; but this is no solution of his problem: it cuts the Gordian knot instead of untying it, and makes the egg stand on end only by breaking it.

He then concludes with a Shavian twist designed to call attention to his own cleverness as much as to the text he is examining:

> What happened to Hamlet was what had happened fifteen hundred years before to Jesus. Born into the vindictive morality of Moses he has evolved into the Christian perception of the futility and wickedness of revenge and punishment, founded on the simple fact that two blacks do not make a white. But he is not philosopher enough to comprehend this as well as apprehend it. When he finds he cannot kill in cold blood he can only ask "Am I a coward?" When he cannot

nerve himself to recover his throne he can account for it only by saying "I lack ambition." Had Shakespeare plumbed his play to the bottom he would hardly have allowed Hamlet to send Rosencrantz and Guildenstern to their death by a forged death warrant without a moment's scruple.

In his decidedly personal viewpoint—not to mention an iconoclastic one—Shaw temperamentally belongs more to the nineteenth century than to the twentieth century, despite the time of his writing.

TWENTIETH-CENTURY CRITICISM: THE MODERN PERIOD

Unlike the previous century, the last century was marked largely by careful analytical essays of *Hamlet*, even, as in the case of A. C. Bradley, when they seem widely inclusive, even expansive. What Coleridge was to the nineteenth century, Bradley and, arguably, Freud have been to the modern era. In *Shakespearean Tragedy* (1904), Bradley attempts to reconstruct Hamlet's life by inferring what it was like before King Hamlet's death. In seeking an organic psychological portrait through narrative, through a kind of retelling of the play as biography, Bradley locates an abnormal, even "morbid" melancholy that colors every thought and feeling; it is a melancholy akin to a diseased mental condition that Hamlet fails to understand. Bradley claims that Hamlet's "cloud of melancholy" is caused by "the moral shock of the sudden ghastly disclosure of his mother's true nature" (Bradley 101); watching Gertrude transfer her affections to someone Hamlet considers base forces him to see in her "not only an astounding shallowness of feeling, but an eruption of coarse sensuality." Thus he asks, rhetorically, "Is it possible to conceive an experience more desolating to a man, such as we have seen Hamlet to be?" (Bradley 101–2) Such a method of criticism was directly attacked in 1931 by A. J. A. Waldock in *"Hamlet": A Study in Critical Method*. Taking Bradley on his own grounds, Waldock notes that we need not conclude that a melancholy Dane would be rendered inactive; he might, in fact, do Claudius in more quickly. But Waldock's real objection is to Bradley's method. He argues that "Drama is *not* history," not narrative; rather than rely on inferred and causal events, we need to examine the sequence of words and scenes. One instance for Waldock is 3.3.73–96. Bradley sees Hamlet's pausing before the sight of Claudius at prayer as a pretext to postpone any decisive action, but Waldock argues more compellingly that the words Hamlet uses signify what he is thinking and what he means: he wants to damn Claudius, not risk saving him.

Bradley writes that Hamlet is one "whose conscience secretly condemned the act which his explicit consciousness approved" (Bradley 109); simultaneously, Sigmund Freud was also examining a divided mind needing analysis and perhaps medical treatment. Freud describes his discovery of the unconscious and the initial value of dream analysis in understanding it in *The Interpretation of Dreams* (1900). *Hamlet* is central to his self-analysis of dreams, but his examination draws to a conclusion with his discovery of the Oedipus complex, a psychic phenomenon he links both to his own feelings at the death of his father and the feelings of Oedipus and Hamlet. "The prince of the play, who had to disguise himself as a madman," Freud writes, "was behaving just as dreams do in reality; so we can say of dreams what Hamlet says of himself, concealing the true circumstances under a cloak of wit and unintelligibility: 'I am but mad north-by-north-west'" (480-81). He distinguishes between Hamlet and Oedipus by noting Western civilization's increasing degree of repression in a footnote to *The Interpretation of Dreams* later brought into the body of his text:

> In *Oedipus* the child's wishful fantasy that underlies it is brought out into the open and realized as it would be in a dream. In *Hamlet* it remains repressed; and just as in the case of a neurosis—we only learn of its existence from its inhibiting consequences. . . .
>
> Hamlet is able to do anything—except take vengeance on the man who did away with his father and took that father's place with his mother, the man who shows him the repressed wishes of his childhood realized. (Freud 298–99)

But he had already made this point at greater length in a letter to Wilhelm Fliess dated October 15, 1897:

> Everyone in the audience was once a budding Oedipus in fantasy, and each recoils in horror from the dream fulfillment here transplanted into reality, with the full quantity of repression which separates his infantile state from his present one.
>
> Fleetingly the thought passed through my head that the same thing might be at the bottom of *Hamlet* as well. I am not thinking of Shakespeare's conscious intentions, but believe, rather, that a real event stimulated the poet to his representation, in that his unconscious understood the unconscious of his hero. . . . How does [Hamlet] explain his irresolution in avenging his father? . . . How better than through the torment roused in him by the obscure memory that he himself had contemplated the same deed against his father out of passion for his mother. . . . And is not his sexual alienation in his conversation with Ophelia typically hysterical? . . . And does he not in the end, in the same marvellous way as my hysterical patients do, bring down punishment on himself by suffering the same fate as his father of being poisoned by the same rival? (Freud 272–73)

In his essay "Mourning and Melancholia," Freud distinguishes between the two in ways that suggest Hamlet might be the model for his explanation of melancholia.

> The distinguishing features of melancholia are a profoundly painful dejection, cessation of interest in the outside world, loss of the capacity to love, inhibition of all activity, and a lowering of the self-regarding feelings to a degree that finds

utterance in self-reproaches and self-revilings, and culminates in a delusional expectation of punishment. (Freud 244)

For those in mourning, what is lost is fully conscious; in the case of melancholia the loss is hidden, unconscious. Further, melancholia promotes a harsh self-criticism, criticism of the ego, promoting a derogatory sense of the self because the melancholic identifies the ego with the loved "object" (person) he has lost and so directs toward himself the anger felt at the loss of the beloved. Withdrawing from the desired "object" in the case of melancholia leaves emotional energy that is not displaced onto something new but instead serves "to establish an *identification* of the ego with the abandoned object. Thus the shadow of the object fell upon the ego, and the latter could henceforth be judged . . . as though it were an object, the forsaken object. In this way, the object-loss was transformed into ego-loss." (Freud 249) Hamlet suffers more than one loss, though: his father; his mother; Ophelia; even his school friends all seem to betray him, complicating and intensifying what might otherwise be a less charged, even common human experience. Claudius and Gertrude tell Hamlet that the loss of fathers is common and his mourning unnatural (1.2.68–74; 87–109); as Claudius tells the prince,

> to perserver
> In obstinate condolement is a course
> Of impious stubbornness, 'tis unmanly grief,
> It shows a will most incorrect to heaven,
> A heart unfortified, a mind impatient,
> An understanding simple and unschooled (92–97)

Claudius's bewilderment is understandable, but for Freud the repressed guilt and envy that Hamlet harbors is equally so. A supplementary text by Freud is his essay "On Narcissism: An Introduction," in which he argues that the ego can invest itself libidinally, especially in the two original objects of his desire, himself and the woman who first tends and nourishes him; conversely, prolonged infantile narcissism in an adult can take a person toward homosexuality, perhaps throwing some light on Hamlet's strong feelings for Horatio (and perhaps for Laertes and Fortinbras) and his strong aversion to Rosencrantz and Guildenstern (who seem adequately happy with each other).

The powerful possibilities of Freud's reading of *Hamlet* led to a sequence of psychoanalytic theories that still continues. His disciple Ernest Jones, in *Oedipus and Hamlet* (rev. ed. 1949: 1976), gives the play a detailed reading in light of Hamlet's incestuous desire for his mother and his desire to kill Claudius as a rival for his mother rather than for the throne of Denmark. Otto Rank has objected that if Hamlet were truly driven by instincts of incest, he would have more quickly dispatched with his rival. More recently, Theodore Litz has claimed that the play is not about the Oedipus complex so much as it is about an impossible idealization of the mother:

> *Hamlet* . . . does not, in itself, consider the instinctual nature of the oedipal situation, or require that Hamlet be preoccupied with his hostility to his mother and uncle because of a fixation at the oedipal phase of development. Rather it deals with what a mother's betrayal of her husband can do to a son and with the importance of the parents' relationship with each other and to their child. . . . The play primarily stresses the importance of continuing intrafamilial relationships to a person's emotional stability rather than solely, or primarily, the influence of early childhood relationships on later life. (Litz 1975, 113)

Other recent critics who have drawn individually on Freud's thoughts include Ari Erlich, Norman N. Holland, William Kerrigan, and Arthur Kirsch.

If Freud countered Bradley by using his own medical evidence to explain the facts of the text without creating a prequel to it, then T. S. Eliot began another line of twentieth-century criticism (in response to Bradley's character analysis) by seeing plays as if they were poems. This concept explains his objections to the play in his essay on *Hamlet* (1919); the play fails for the poet Eliot because its presentation lacks an "objective correlative."

> The only way of expressing emotion in the form of art is by finding an "objective correlative"; in other words, a set of objects, a situation, a chain of events which shall be the formula of that *particular* emotion; such that when the external facts, which must terminate in sensory experience, are given, the emotion is immediately evoked. (Eliot 1963, 107–8)

The term "objective correlative" is vague if not awkward, and its portmanteau definition did not help matters; but Eliot likely had in mind the functioning of something akin to a poetic image or symbol. Yet his own explanations seem to emphasize something situational as well: "Hamlet (the man) is dominated by an emotion which is inexpressible, because it is in *excess* of the facts as they appear"; or, again, "Hamlet is up against the difficulty that his disgust is occasioned by his mother, but that his mother is not an adequate equivalent for it; his disgust envelops and exceeds her." G. Wilson Knight was more successful. In his essay on *Hamlet* in *The Wheel of Fire* (1930) entitled "The Embassy of Death," he finds death to be the play's reigning symbol (or, perhaps, its objective correlative). For Knight, Hamlet represents a diseased consciousness in an otherwise healthy world; he brings with him "the poison of negation, nothingness, threatening to a world of positive assertion." (Knight 41) This disease takes two negative forms, "love–cynicism and death–consciousness." (Knight 43) L. C. Knights also argued for the central symbolic order in a work of art in "How Many Children Had Lady Macbeth?" (1933): "In the mass of Shakespeare criticism there is not a hint that 'character' like 'plot,' 'rhythm,' 'construction' and all our other critical counters—is merely an abstraction from the total response in the mind of the reader or spectator" (Knights in *Explorations* 16). The mind unifies the work of art; about this, Knights is the first to be explicit: he says that the play really is "a poem." (Knights in *Explorations* 16) The idea of symbolism as defining and ranking art reaches its apogee with *Shakespeare's Imagery and What It Tells Us* by Caroline Spurgeon (1935). Spurgeon isolated all of the images in any given play and then analyzed the play in terms of what was most dominant. In the case of *Hamlet*, the dominant cluster of images was that of disease.

But Eliot's sense of an organic work of art arranged and controlled by the artist also spawned a line of formalist critics who practiced what came to be called the New Criticism, eschewing history and context to concentrate on the structure and texture of the work in isolation with the help of such concerns as point of view, irony, and rhythm. This practice lies behind the work of the German critic Levin Schücking, who complicates the critical practice of the formalists in *Der Sinn des Hamlet* (*The Meaning of Hamlet*, 1935). He argues (in the 1937 translation by Graham Rawson) that

> The close association, too, of contrasted effects is a distinctive feature of [Shakespeare's] art. It comes out in a tendency to witty exaggeration, particularly in the use of paradox and cryptic utterance—very much a fashion of the time. Tragedy and Comedy are seen side by side, even permeating one another. Both kings and grave-diggers are allowed to speak their minds. The character-drawing of the hero is based—as elsewhere in Shakespeare's plays—entirely on the contrast between his innate capacity and his desires, so that he is torn in two and continually tortured by his conscience. As an example of internal dissension Hamlet has no equal; and it is in this that his ironic wit, which throws such a sparkling light over the whole play, is rooted.
>
> All these qualities belong to the type of art that modern scholarship has termed "literary baroque." There can, in fact, be no doubt that *Hamlet*, like the rest of Shakespeare's work, belongs to this category. (Schücking 8)

In Spain, Salvadore de Madariaga was making similar remarks.

> The speed of [Shakespeare's] creation [in *Hamlet* and elsewhere] is so overpowering that images overtop images in succeeding waves, so that it often happens that five or six lines, through sheer density, become opaque without becoming dark—very much like the white foam of a precipitous torrent which, though itself luminous, allows no light through; while in other passages his thought struggles desperately for freedom, entangled in coils within coils of words and phrases, like a Laocoon. (de Madariaga 129)

The work of Wolfgang Clemen and Maynard Mack illustrated a disciplined formalist approach to *Hamlet*. In *The Development of Shakespeare's Imagery*,

Clemen builds on the sense of disease identified both by Freud and Spurgeon. This is how he moves out from the Ghost's description of being poisoned by Claudius (1.5.60-79):

> A real event described at the beginning of the drama has exercised a profound influence upon the whole imagery of the play. What is later metaphor, is here still reality. The picture of the leprous skin disease, which is here — in the first act — described by Hamlet's father, has buried itself deep in Hamlet's imagination and continues to lead its subterranean existence, as it were, until it reappears in metaphorical form.
>
> As Miss Spurgeon has shown, the idea of an ulcer dominates the imagery, infecting and fatally eating away the whole body; on every occasion repulsive images of sickness make their appearance. It is certain that this imagery is derived from that one real event. Hamlet's father describes in that passage how the poison invades the body during sleep and how the healthy organism is destroyed from within, not having a chance to defend itself against attack. But this now becomes the leitmotiv of the imagery: the individual occurrence is expanded into a symbol for the central problem of the play. The corruption of land and people throughout Denmark is understood as an imperceptible and irresistible process of poisoning. And, furthermore, this poisoning reappears as a leitmotiv in the action as well — as a poisoning in the "dumb show," and finally, as the poisoning of all the major characters in the last act. This imagery and action continually play into each other's hands and we see how the term "dramatic imagery" gains a new significance.

For Mack, in "The World of *Hamlet*," published in *The Yale Review* in 1952, the play's key is not so much in its images as in its structure; and characteristic of the way the play is structured is its basic preoccupation with questions.

> Hamlet's world is pre-eminently in the interrogative mood. It reverberates with questions, anguished, meditative, alarmed. There are questions that in this play, to an extent I think unparalleled in any other, mark the phases and even the nuances of the action, helping to establish its peculiar baffled tone. There are other questions whose interrogations, innocent at first glance, are subsequently seen to have reached beyond their contexts and to point towards some pervasive inscrutability in Hamlet's world as a whole. Such is that tense series of challenges with which the tragedy begins: Bernardo's of Francisco, "Who's there?" Francisco's of Horatio and Marcellus, "Who is there?" Horatio's of the ghost, "What are thou . . . ?" . . .
>
> Thus the mysteriousness of Hamlet's world is of a piece. It is not simply a matter of missing motivations, to be expunged if only we could find the perfect clue. It is built in.

Harry Levin extends Mack's idea into a detailed analysis of classical sources of thought in *The Question of "Hamlet"* (1959).

Psychoanalytic criticism was further theorized by the postmodernist think-ing of Jacques Lacan. In "Desire and the Interpretation of Desire in Hamlet," Lacan distinguishes between the phallus, or lack of power, and the penis; for him, Ophelia is phallic, "exteriorized and rejected by the subject as a symbol signify-ing life" (Lacan 23). Before her as "the Other," Hamlet senses his inferiority in action and in mourning. But mourning—essentially the loss of the phallus—causes Hamlet to strike out, accosting his mother, jumping into Ophelia's grave, killing Claudius. Bert O. States suggests in *"Hamlet" and the Concept of Character* that disjunctions—what deconstructionists term aporias—mark Hamlet's "distinct behavioral keys" (65) of cruelty, generosity, kindness, reflec-tiveness, and melancholy that never cohere but, instead, are extended by his rela-tionships with others, including his Lacanian relationship to Ophelia. Another strand of postmodernist psychoanalytic theory is developed by David Leverenz, who combines Jung's sense of the anima with the developmental psychology of R.D. Laing and D.W. Winnicott. A more contained and focused sense of psy-chology is seen in metadramatic criticism as illustrated in the work of James Calderwood and Kirby Farrell. Expanding on Hamlet's play-within-a-play, they examine ways in which characters write scripts for others, take on postures or roles for themselves, and see themselves as destined to play roles for a provi-dential force or a demonic command.

TWENTIETH-CENTURY CRITICISM: POST-MODERNISM

Formalist criticism, sometimes called modernist criticism, can be fruitfully seen as a reaction against the dominant social and political criticism of the 1930s and 1940s, in which classic literary texts were read as socialist or radical documents, the working-class or bourgeois were made central, and a kind of Marxist class consciousness was in the ascendant. In the 1980s and 1990s, the pendulum swung back the other way. Now it was formalism that was challenged by the use of works beyond the borders of the text (indeed, in the deconstructivist readings of postmodernist thought, literary texts were porous, without boundaries, leaking into the culture as the culture leaked back into them). This led to several strands that can be distinguished, such as feminist criticism, neo-Marxist criticism, New Historicism, and Cultural Materialism.

Deconstructionist criticism insists that works of art are not—and need not be—integrated and organic. Howard Felperin argues in *Shakespearean Representation* for a disjunction that is central to the play: "forms and figures of an older drama stand out from the ... naturalistic surface of the play" (Felperin 377), so that the skeleton of the *ur-Hamlet* keeps intruding, making virtually impossible the need to remember and to tell. In "Telmah," Terence Hawkes argues that there is a recursive structure to the play, its endless repetitions con-stantly invading the linear structure of traditional criticism. In *The Culture of Violence*, Francis Barker notes the "strategic displacement" caused by a loss of cultural memory and the failure of a reliable representation. This analysis broadens and complicates his previous remarks in *The Tremulous Private Body*, which builds on the epistemic shifts, popularized by Michel Foucault in *The Order of Things*, between a feudal theater inherited by the Renaissance and the emergent bourgeois theater in the age of Pepys.

The first feminist treatment of *Hamlet* was an essay entitled "Hamlet's Mother" by Carolyn Heilbrun (1957). Arguing against the grain, as it became known, Heilbrun dismisses much criticism of the play as masculine in perspective and therefore unnecessarily limited. Instead, she points out that reading the play from a feminist perspective suggests that Gertrude is honest, concise, and straightforward in her speech and in her behavior, but her social maneuverability is severely limited. The same is true of Ophelia, whose madness is brought on by the death of her father and the absence of her brother and of Hamlet, and thus of any stable family or personal relationships where she might find guidance or consolation. Both Gertrude and Ophelia are as imprisoned by Denmark as Hamlet feels he is.

In another early and important essay, "A Heart Cleft in Twain: The Dilemma of Shakespeare's Gertrude," Rebecca Smith, in *The Woman's Part* (ed. Carol Ruth Swift Lenz et al., 1980), agrees that "Finding answers . . . about Gertrude is complicated by the fact that in *Hamlet* one hears a great deal of discussion of Gertrude's personality and actions by other characters" (ed. Lenz 196). Gertrude, she notes, appears in half of the scenes in the play, but she is given only 157 lines of a total of 4,042 (3.8 percent). Yet Shakespeare develops her considerably from the role she plays in his sources; "Gertrude's brief speeches include references to honor, virtue, flowers, and a dove's golden couplets; neither structure nor content suggests [the] wantonness" attributed to her by the masculine perspectives in the play (ed. Lenz 200). Rather, what "*her* words and actions actually create is a soft, obedient, dependent, unimaginative woman who is caught miserably at the center of a desperate struggle between two 'mighty opposites,' her 'heart cleft in twain' (3.4.147) by divided loyalties to husband and son" (ed. Lenz 194). King Hamlet implies her innocence in the past; when she acts in the play near the end, it is to restrain both her son and Laertes from harm. When she does confess to "black and grainéd spots" in her "very soul" (3.4.80, 79), Smith writes, it is never clear to what she is referring: "if it is a newly aroused awareness of her adulterate and incestuous relationship, if it is her marriage to a man whom Hamlet so clearly despises, or if it is merely her already lamented o'erhasty marriage." (ed. Lenz 203) Rather, it is part of the mystery that continually lies at the heart of the play.

Carol Thomas Neely turns to Ophelia in *Broken Nuptials in Shakespeare's Plays*. She notes that "Ophelia's movement from submissive daughter to mad prophet reveals the combination of powerlessness and freedom that women in the tragedies achieve by virtue of their isolation from men and their position partly implicated in, partly outside of the violent conflicts of patriarchy," pointing out that

> Until her madness, Ophelia scarcely exists outside of men's use of her. She is not simply driven to this madness but freed for it by her father's death, Laertes's and Hamlet's absence, Claudius's indifference. The madness incorporates and allows expression of the earlier pressures on her: the desired and forbidden loss of chastity, the virtues hypocritically enjoined, the corruption perceived. And even if not fully comprehended by the other characters, her madness influences them. It magnifies Laertes's obsession with revenge, driving him to become Claudius's tool as Ophelia was before him. It draws from Gertrude an uncoerced achnowledgment of her own guilt. The death in which Ophelia's madness culminates repurifies her for Hamlet, freeing him to love her and to achieve his own revenge. (Neely 103)

Her suicide completes her separation from the social roles of daughter, beloved, and subject and from the poison that literally and metaphorically permeates the play; her death prefigures Gertrude's. "The two women break their ties with the corrupt roles and values of Elsinore as Laertes and Hamlet, returning to the castle to seek revenge, move toward accommodation with these values." (Neely 104) Cleansing Elsinore debilitates Hamlet, and he leaves behind him an all-male but therefore also a shrunken world.

Marxist criticism goes back to the works of Karl Marx and the dramatic theory and practice of Bertolt Brecht; in England, it began with Christopher Caudwell's *Illusion and Reality*:

> Marlowe, Chapman, Greene, but above all Shakespeare, born of bourgeois parents, exactly express the cyclonic force of the princely bourgeois will in [their] era, in all its vigour and recklessness. Lear, Hamlet, Macbeth, Antony, Troilus, Othello, Romeo and Coriolanus, each in his different way knows no other obligation than to be the thing he is, to realise himself to the last drop, to give out in its purest and most exquisite form the aroma of self.

But these writers' energy comes from their illusion of life, rather than its possibilities; Shakespeare naturally wrote tragedies (Caudwell 74–75). In Marxist criticism, characters are described and analyzed in terms of the state apparatus of power and the ideologies behind them. To open up those ideologies—systems of belief which no one really escapes—Terence Hawkes's essay called "Telmah" reverses the conventional reading of *Hamlet* as he does the play's title, seeing Claudius as a worthy opponent of Hamlet. This leads to a larger claim: "I propose: the sense of the text as a site, or an area of conflicting and often contradictory potential interpretations, no single one or group of which can claim 'intrinsic' primary or 'inherent' authority, and all of which are always ideological in nature and subject to extrinsic political and economic determinants" (Hawkes 330). In his *William Shakespeare* published in the following year, Terry Eagleton claims Hamlet has no "new bourgeois way of thinking" (Eagleton 72, 74).

His "self" consists simply in the range of gestures with which he resists available definitions, not in a radical alternative beyond their reach. It is thus wholly parasitic on the positions it refuses. . . . Hamlet is a radically transitional figure, strung out between a traditional social order to which he is marginal, and a future epoch of achieved bourgeois individualism which will surpass it. But because of this we can glimpse in him a negative critique of the forms of subjectivity typical of both these regimes. . . . What it is to be a subject, in short, is a political problem for Hamlet, as it has once more become a political problem for us. (Eagleton 72, 74)

In a sense, feminist and neo-Marxist critics practice a kind of deconstruction because they focus largely on parts of a play and do not feel the need to account for all of it. But deconstruction has its own conventional practices, beginning with the location of discrepancies, or aporias, where disjunctions signal some difficulty in the conception or the execution of the work of art. New Historicism and Cultural Materialism can fragment a text in other ways. For New Historicists, such as Stephen Greenblatt or Louis Montrose, Steven Mullaney or Leonard Tennenhouse, works of art are cultural artifacts, texts that are different than, but not necessarily superior to, other texts of a culture such as sermons or regulatory statutes or popular pamphlets. Cultural Materialists would go even farther, seeking in the material practices of a culture analogues to a literary text that help to place the text in its own time and give it new and significant meaning, much as we have cited perspectival texts earlier in this introduction. Richard Corum begins *Understanding "Hamlet"* (1998) by noting that whereas modern critics often think of Polonius as a foolish character, he would hardly be considered so in Shakespeare's day. By citing the *realpolitik* popularized in Shakespeare's England by Machiavelli's *Prince*, he notes "how Polonius's actions are designed to further his own interests and yet not seem in the least to be doing so" (Corum 3).

Technically, there is no upward social mobility in a hierarchical society since everyone is in (and can only be in) their proper place, yet Claudius has in effect married up, and this has (or could be seen as having) opened up new possibilities for those willing to take risks. Polonius—clever, intelligent, and ambitious—is rushing to exploit this new situation to better his children's circumstances, most particularly by deciding to plot a marriage between Ophelia and Hamlet despite the danger such an ambition entails. But how to succeed in a situation where visible pushing would cost him his job if not his life? By what indirect method . . . will he find this "direction" out? (Corum 3–4)

At the time Shakespeare was writing *Hamlet*, Robert Cecil, not unlike Polonius in position, was Principal Secretary to Elizabeth I but, knowing her reign was drawing to an end, was already maneuvering himself into the favor of James VI of Scotland as her likely successor. Cecil never acted as foolishly as Polonius acts, but New Historicists and Cultural Materialists alike might argue that

Polonius has chosen this way to keep his own power play secretive or, more cynically, that such maneuvering *might* appear foolish to those outside the court and without courtly ambition. Psychoanalytic criticism was further theorized by the postmodernist thinking of Jacques Lacan.

As Goldsmith took issue with Addison, Shaw with the Coleridges, and Waldock with Bradley, so the healthy critical disagreements today generate new criticism and new insights. "To call the text 'a site of struggle' is perhaps to use a melodramatic term for the obvious," Cedric Watts writes, but

> the value of a good literary work lies in its renewable excess: the interpretations
> will always be exceeded by the text's potential meanings, which are clarified yet
> adulterated by rational discourse. (Watts xlviii)

Throughout its critical history, *Hamlet* has generated criticism that arises from the play's text and, directly or indirectly, leads back to it.

HAMLET ON STAGE

Recent attempts to see a play like *Hamlet* as a constituent in an active culture has put greater emphasis on performance of the play, but as we have seen, Gabriel Harvey and Antony Skoloker were already practicing that in the early 1600s. "*Hamlet* is Shakespeare's most frequently performed play" (Tardiff 1); the archives of the Royal Shakespeare Company list 77 productions between 1872 and 1998. Indeed, the critical history of performances of *Hamlet* has a long and distinguished pedigree, parallel to that of literary criticism, that includes operas, ballets, travesties, films (seventeen of them early silent productions), radio and television versions, and such affiliated works as Tom Stoppard's play *Rosencrantz and Guildenstern Are Dead* and Kenneth Branagh's film *In the Bleak Midwinter* (or, more suggestively, the film entitled *The Last Action Hero*).

The first extant performance is that recorded by a ship's captain, William Keeling, aboard his ship the *Dragon* off Sierra Leone on a voyage to the East Indies in 1607. Keeling records in his diary the following year that "I envited Captain Hawkins to a ffishe dinner, and had Hamlet acted abord me: which I permitt to keepe my people from idlenes and unlawful games, or sleepe" (Hapgood 8). But the original Hamlet in Shakespeare's company (the Lord Chamberlain's Men, later the King's Men) was likely their lead actor, Richard Burbage. In the anonymous "Funerall Ellegye on ye Death of the famous Actor Richard Burbedge," the author notes that "Oft have I seen him, leap into the Grave / Suiting the person, which he seem'd to have / Of a sad Lover." Burbage died in 1619, but there is also an earlier comment by John Raynold in *Dolarnys Primerose*, published in 1606, that when Burbage's Hamlet confronted Yorick's skull "He held it still, in his sinister [left] hand, / He turn'd it soft, and stroakt it with the other, / He smil'd on it." It is traditionally thought that, in the early productions by Shakespeare's company, Shakespeare himself played the Ghost of

King Hamlet, following Nicholas Rowe's comment of 1709. After Burbage's death, the role of Hamlet was taken by Joseph Taylor and, according to John Downes in *Roseius Anglicanus* (1708), the role was handed down from actor to actor in what was Shakespeare's company, well after the theaters reopened in 1660 following the civil wars:

> The tragedy of *Hamlet*; Hamlet being performed by Mr. Betterton, Sir William [Davenant] (having seen Mr. Taylor of the Black-Friars Company act it, who being instructed by the author Mr. Shakespeare) taught Mr. Betterton in every particle of it; which by his exact performance of it, gained him esteem and reputation, superlative to all other plays. . . . . No succeeding tragedy got more reputation or money to the company than this. (Tardiff, 9)

In fact, Thomas Betterton's Hamlet dominated his fifty-year acting career. In 1740, Colley Cibber reports in *An Apology for the Life of Mr. Colley Cibber* the electrifying effect Betterton could have:

> You have seen a Hamlet perhaps, who, on the first appearance of his father's Spirit, has thrown himself into all the straining vociferation requisite to express rage and fury, and the house has thundered with applause; though the misguided actor was all the while (as Shakespeare terms it) tearing a passion into rags— I am the more bold to offer you this particular instance because the late Mr. Addison, while I sat by him to see this scene acted, made the same observation, asking me, with some surprise, if I thought Hamlet should be in so violent a passion with the Ghost, which, though it might have astonished, it had not provoked him? —for you may observe that in this beautiful speech the passion never rises beyond an almost breathless astonishment, or an impatience, limited by filial reverence, to enquire into the suspected wrongs that may have raised him from his peaceful tomb and a desire to know what a spirit so seemingly distressed might wish or enjoin a sorrowful son to execute towards his future quiet in the grave? This was the light into which Betterton threw this scene; which he opened with a pause of mute amazement, then rising slowly to a solemn, trembling voice, he made the Ghost equally terrible to the spectator as to himself, and in the descriptive part of the natural emotions which the ghastly vision gave him, the boldness of his expostulation was still governed by decency, manly, but not braving, his voice never rising into that seeming outrage or wild defiance of what he naturally revered. But alas! to preserve this medium, between mouthing and meaning too little, to keep the attention more pleasingly awake by a tempered spirit than by mere vehemence of voice, is of all the master-strokes of an actor the most difficult to reach. In this none yet have equaled Betterton. (ed. Low, I:100-02)

Indeed, Barton Booth remarked that "When I acted the Ghost with Betterton, instead of my awing him, he terrified me." The force of Betterton's acting seems to have been caught in a cruder and simpler German adaptation of the play, apparently based on Q1, which omits the soliloquies, the graveyard scene, and the report of Ophelia's death but adds vulgar buffoonery: the Ghost strikes the ears of the sentry; bandits fire on Hamlet; but he drops to the ground and they kill each other.

Betterton was succeeded by David Garrick, who first played on the London stage in 1741; he played the role from 1742 until his retirement in 1776. Like Betterton, Garrick also acted Hamlet with forceful energy; in Smollett's original version of *Peregrine Pickle*, it is said that "his fist [shook] with all the demonstrations of wrath at his mistress" and he "behave[d] like a ruffian to his own mother" (Smollett chap. 55). Garrick's Hamlet was resolute; the actor omitted the "How all occasions do inform against me" speech and other lines suggesting Hamlet's doubt, and reinforced his decisiveness in his loyalty to his father. Near the end of Garrick's career, the German scientist and philosopher Georg Lichtenberg visited England and left this report:

> the theatre is darkened, and the whole audience of some thousands are as quiet, and their faces as motionless, as though they were painted on the walls of the theatre; even from the farthest end of the playhouse one could hear a pin drop. Suddenly, as Hamlet moves towards the back of the stage slightly to the left and turns his back on the audience, Horatio starts, and saying, "Look, my lord, it comes," points to the right, where the ghost has already appeared and stands motionless, before anyone is aware of him. At these words Garrick turns sharply and at the same moment staggers back two or three paces with his knees giving way under him; his hat falls to the ground and both his arms, especially the left, are stretched out nearly to their full length, with the hands as high as his head, the right arm more bent and the hand lower, and the fingers apart; his mouth is open: thus he stands rooted to the spot, with legs apart, but no loss of dignity, supported by his friends, who are better acquainted with the apparition and fear lest he should collapse. His whole demeanour is so expressive of terror that it made my flesh creep even before he began to speak. . . . What an amazing triumph it is. (eds. Mare and Quarrell 9–11)

As the author of "A Poetic Epistle from Shakespear in Elysium to Mr. Garrick" in 1752 puts it, "SHAKESPEARE revives! in GARRICK breathes again!"

The first Russian adaptation of the play, *Gamlet*, opened in 1748 at the Imperial Theatre in St. Petersburg. Ten characters reduced the play using the rules of neoclassicism, reporting events off stage and eliminating the Ghost, whose command was reported by Hamlet. There were no traveling troupe of actors, no play-within-a-play, no gravediggers, and no fencing match. Polonius helps Claudius and Gertrude to kill King Hamlet, but when Gertrude repents the deed, Polonius joins Claudius in planning to murder Gertrude and Hamlet, marrying Ophelia to Tsar Claudius. But Ophelia rebels, proclaiming her everlasting love for Hamlet, and Polonius also condemns her to death. Prince Hamlet, however, with the support of the people, defeats fifty mercenaries; Hamlet himself kills Claudius but spares Polonius (who nevertheless commits suicide, cursing both Hamlet and his daughter). Following neoclassical practice, the tyrant is defeated and the son triumphs as legitimate ruler. But the last lines are given to Ophelia, who concludes, "And I will go to pay my final debt to nature"; it is unclear whether she refers to burial rites for her father or her own death. There is no hint of marriage for Hamlet and Ophelia at the close.

The first recorded performance in the German states is in Vienna on January 16, 1773, followed by performances in Biberach later that year, in Pressburg in 1774, in Prague and Salzburg in 1775, in Pest and Innsbruck in 1776, and in an adaptation by Schröder in Hamburg in 1776 and in Berlin in 1777: one critic called it "Hamlet-fever." Within a few years, *Hamlet* was performed in every sizable town. A concurrent adaptation by Heufeld has been described by Paul S. Conklin.

> He shortened the action considerably. Rosencrantz and Guildenstern are made into one person. Ophelia does not go mad. There are no trip to England, no grave-diggers, no appearance at the end of Fortinbras. Laertes and the duel are omitted. The king is stabbed by Hamlet. The queen drinks poison and admits her guilt before she dies. Hamlet, on the other hand, does not die, but is victorious over his enemies. The object seems to have been to make the play a "family tragedy." In Schröder's adaptation of 1776 many of Heufeld's changes were kept. As in Heufeld, there were no chuchyard scene, no duel and the prince was victorious and alive as the play closed. (Conklin 102)

Schlegel's more authentic translation in blank verse was finally first performed in 1799.

In 1790, a free German prose translation was made topical by the poet, critic, and translator Ferenc Kazinczy, whose central purpose was to organize a nationalist revival of Hungarian language and literature. According to Zednek Stríbrny,

> Kazinczy introduced topical allusions from the very first scenes, which were dominated by the Ghost, representing not only the old King of Denmark but also the venerable past of Hungary destroyed by the usurping Habsburgian Claudius. Prince Hamlet was shaped by a number of cuts into an active and determined hero overcoming all obstacles by his will to revenge his adored father. His soliloquies were the only remnants of the hesitant, philosophizing bent of his mind. After killing Oldenholm (=Polonius), the Prince turned to Gusztáv(=Horatio) and insisted: "Let's not waste time, Gusztáv, but take revenge for my murdered Father!" Bringing about a reconciliation with his repenting mother as well as with Laertes, he executed his revenge, addressed the court with "You that look pale and tremble at this chance, report me and my cause aright to Denmark," and ascended the throne to prove most royally. In this way, Hamlet's succession was turned into an assertion of a just world order in which private losses were compensated by political success and the young hero,

succeeding his murdered father, revived the spirit of the whole nation. (Stríbrny 62)

Kazinczy's preface underscored his intention:

Who would not cry with joy when our destroyed, trampled-on Nation raises its head from the dust once again, and returning to its language, dress and mores, it will once again be what our Ancestors were, it will be what half a year ago the faint hope would not have believed; a free nation,—a Nation having its own constitution, language, and dress,—a Nation every member of which is born to carry a sword, and is a ready defender of his Country and his King. (Stríbrny 62)

This version of *Hamlet* was finally succeeded by a new translation by Peter Vajda in 1839.

In England, Garrick was succeeded in the role of Hamlet by John Philip Kemble. While less energetic than Betterton or Garrick, Kemble was histrionic in his own way: he sought applause, according to the *Morning Chronicle* of October 6, 1783, "by starting, stamping, by grimace and tricks" (Hapgood 18). His performance was noted for its affectations; he had scenes especially painted for the play. Hazlitt found Kemble's "distinguishing excellence" in "the seizing upon some one feeling or idea, in insisting upon it, in never letting it go, and in working it up, with a certain graceful consistency" (Hapgood 19).The consistency caused Kemble to fail in Hazlitt's view; the variety of Hamlet's moods he presented "in one undeviating straight line" (Hapgood 19). Despite this neoclassic presentation, Charles Lamb found in Kemble "pointed and witty dialogue" and "the playful courtbred spirit in which he condescended to the players in Hamlet" (Hapgood 19–20), and the German critic Ludwig Tieck noted that "What Kemble brought prominently out was the sad, the melancholy, the nobly suffering aspect of the character" as "he bore himself like a man of high blood and breeding." So too the high praise of Mary Russell Mitford: "John Kemble is the only satisfactory Hamlet I ever saw—owing much to personal grace and beauty—something to a natural melancholy, or rather pensiveness of manner—much, of course, to consummate art." Kemble's brother Charles was less successful in the part, but he interpreted Hamlet as actually mad. His daughter has recorded her impressions of him.

I have acted Ophelia three times with my father, and each time in that beautiful scene where his madness and his love gush forth together like a torrent swollen with storms, that bears a thousand blossoms on its stormy waters, I have experienced with such deep emotion as hardly to be able to speak. The exquisite tenderness of his voice, the wild compassion and forlorn pity of his looks, bestowing that on others which of all other he most needed: the melancholy restlessness, the bitter self-scorning: every shadow of expression and intonation was so full of the mingled anguish that the human heart is capable of enduring, that my eyes scarce fixed on his ere they filled with tears, and long before the scene was over, the letters and jewel-cases I was tendering to him were wet with them. (Conklin 120)

But both Kembles were overshadowed by their successor, Edmund Kean.

Kean first appeared in London as Hamlet in 1814, a thoughtful, brooding Romantic Hamlet playing at the Whig Drury Lane rather than the Tory Covent Garden where Kemble had performed. Hazlitt was far more impressed: "Mr. Kean has introduced in this part a *new reading*, as it is called, which we think perfectly correct. In the scene where he breaks from his friends to obey the command of his father, he keeps his sword pointed behind him, to prevent them from following him, instead of holding it before him to protect him from the Ghost" (eds. Archer and Lowe 12–13). He was not frightened by the Ghost. "He seemed to me," wrote James Hackett,

> more ably to illustrate the soul of Hamlet than any actor whom I have seen in the part; its intellectuality and sensitiveness were wrought into transparent prominency: every particle of its satire was given with extraordinary pungency; its sentiment was on each occasion very impressively uttered, and the melancholy was plaintively toned and sympathy-winning; the action was full and natural and never ungraceful, the passion heart-stirring, and the poetry was read with correct emphasis and a nice ear to rhythmical measure. (Conklin 123)

Robert Hapgood suggests that "much of the impetus for this view came from Continental Europe," especially Goethe, and that "in the course of the nineteenth century 'Hamletism' became not only a private malady but a general condition with political implications. In "The American Scholar" (1837) Emerson felt his generation 'infected with Hamlet's unhappiness'" (Hapgood 23–24). Employing the Romantics' taste for the vivid bit, Kean was (like Kemble) not past his own staged gestures, as Hazlitt makes evident in his review of March 14:

> Both the closet scene with his mother, and his remonstrances to Ophelia, were highly impressive. If there had been less vehemence of effort in the latter, it would not have lost any of its effect. But whatever nice faults might be found in this scene, they were amply redeemed by the manner of his coming back after he has gone to the extremity of the stage, from a pang of parting tenderness to press his lips to Ophelia's hand. It had an electrical effect on the house. It was the finest commentary that was ever made on Shakespeare. (Hapgood 14)

It was also premeditated art. Kean told Garrick's widow, "There is no such thing as impulsive acting; all is premeditated and studied beforehand" (Hapgood 25).

Kean died in 1833. He was followed in the role of Hamlet by William Charles Macready, who headed both of the patent theaters (Covent Garden from 1837 to 1839 and Drury Lane from 1841 to 1843). He was more subdued than

Kean, presenting a subtler progression of feeling from an initial optimism to one restless, impatient, ironic, and misanthropic, to (in the end) one with a calming trust in events. In the final act, he attempted to portray, as he himself remarked, "the resignation of a generous nature when the storm has spent itself" (Hapgood 28). But he also wrote in his diary that he found it difficult to display "the ease and dignified familiarity, the apparent levity of manner, with the deep purpose that lies beneath. . . . I almost despair of moderately satisfying myself" (Hapgood 28). Pavel Mochalov performed Hamlet at the Moscow Small (Maly) Theatre in 1837, influencing the critic Vissarion Belinsky, who saw eight performances. Belinsky's interpretation in his 1838 essay on *Hamlet* is likely derived from Mochalov; not unlike Macready, Belinsky sees the role of Hamlet in Hegelian terms moving from youthful idealism through its antithesis, disintegration, to a synthesis in the recognition of truth.

In America, Edwin Booth played Hamlet with considerably subdued refinement, restoring the scene of Claudius praying. According to the New York *Herald* on November 28, 1864, his portrayal was "of a reflective, sensitive, gentle, generous nature, tormented, borne down and made miserable by an occasion . . . to which it is not equal." Another review in that paper, on January 6, 1870, noted much improvement: "He has now a delicacy of touch and a finish of execution that betray in every line a thorough knowledge of the workings of the human mind" (Hapgood 7). For critic Charles Clarke, Booth played "a man of first-class intellect but second-class will" (Hapgood 33). He staged *The Murder of Gonzago* with such success that he was rendered helpless; he even softened his remarks to Rosencrantz and Guildenstern, Polonius, Gertrude, and Osric. Part of his motivation in his portrayal was his deep love for his father; when Booth's wife died in 1863, he took up spiritualism and received messages from his father as well as his wife. The miniature he wore during the closet scene with Gertrude was one of his own father and he thought he heard his father's voice in that of the Ghost.

Henry Irving introduced the "psychological Hamlet," according to the *Academy* for September 18, 1897. Eden Phillpotts found in Irving a "man of rare intellect confronted with just those problems that his supreme order of intelligence is powerless to solve," "the threat of madness hovering nearer and nearer" a "psychical torment" for him (Hapgood 37). *Macmillan's Magazine* reported in 1874 that his pronunciation of lines could be idiosyncratic and his walking eccentric, "between a stagger and a slouch" (240; Hapgood 39). Clement Scott agreed writing for the London *Daily Telegraph* November 2, 1874.

> We in the audience see the mind of Hamlet. We care little what he does, how he walks, when he draws his sword. We can almost realise the workings of his brain. His soliloquies are not spoken down at the footlights to the audience. Hamlet is looking into a glass, into "his mind's eye, Horatio!" His eyes are fixed apparently on nothing, though ever eloquent. He gazes on vacancy and communes with his conscience. Those only who have closely watched Hamlet

through the first act could adequately express the impression made. But it has affected the whole audience—the Kemble lovers, the Kean admirers, and the Fechter rhapsodists. They do not know how it is, but they are spell-bound with the incomparable expression of moral poison.

But Irving was not all thought.

Determined not to be conquered by his predecessors, he made a signal success in the play scene. He acted it with an impulsive energy beyond all praise. Point after point was made in a whirlwind of excitement. He lured, he tempted, he trapped the King, he drove out his wicked uncle conscience-stricken and baffled, and with an hysterical yell of triumph he sank down, "this expectancy and rose of the fair State," in the very throne which ought to have been his, and which his rival had just vacated. It is difficult to describe the excitement occasioned by the acting in this scene. When the King has been frighted, the stage was cleared instantaneously. No one in the house knew how the people got off. All eyes were fixed on Hamlet and the King; all were forgetting the real play and the mock play, following up every move of the antagonists, and from constant watching they were almost as exhausted as Hamlet was when he sank a conqueror into the neglected throne.

At one point Scott interjects, "If Hamlet is to be played like a scholar and a gentleman, and not like an actor, this is the Hamlet"; he concludes, "The Hamlet of Henry Irving is a noble contribution to dramatic art." To play Ophelia to Irving's Hamlet, Ellen Terry visited a madhouse where she saw a girl "very thin, very pathetic, very young" who gazed vacantly at a wall; "Suddenly she threw up her hands and sped across the room like a swallow" in a movement "as poignant as it was beautiful" (*Lectures* 122). Terry's delicacy played to Irving's thoughtfulness; in Terry's judgment, Ophelia had from the start "an incipient insanity"; "there is something queer about her, something which explains her wits going astray later on" (110; Hapgood 39). Ophelia was for Terry "Shakespeare's only timid heroine . . . her brain, her soul and her body are all pathetically weak" (165–66; Hapgood 39). The *Daily Chronicle* for December 31, 1878, reported that the flowers Terry carried in the mad scene were "one moment heedlessly crushed, and the next smothered with kisses" (Hapgood 40).

Conversely, the subsequent Hamlet of Johnston Forbes-Robertson was "genial," with "so much sweetness and light" that he was "infinitely more human and more lovable" (*The Illustrated London News* September 18, 1897 CXI: no 3048 p. 375). Max Beerbohm found him "In face, and in voice, and in manner . . . a heaven-born Hamlet" (Hapgood 43). He was praised for his careful elocution, his voice compared to a cello or (for Shaw) to a bass clarinet. Shaw saw Forbes-Robertson at the Lyceum Theatre in London, and reviewed the play for the London *Saturday Review*, on October 2, 1897.

[T]his is not a cold Hamlet. He is none of your logicians who reason their way through the world because they cannot feel their way through it: his intellect is the organ of his passion: his eternal self-criticism is as alive and thrilling as it can possibly be. The great soliloquy—no: I do NOT mean "To be or not be be": I mean the dramatic one, "O what a rogue and peasant slave am I!"—is as passionate in its scorn of brute passion as the most bull-necked affirmation or sentimental dilution of it could be. It comes out so without violence: Mr. Forbes-Robertson takes the part quite easily and spontaneously. There is none of that strange Lyceum intensity which comes from the perpetual struggle between Sir Henry Irving and Shakespeare. The lines help Mr. Forbes-Robertson instead of getting in his way at every turn, because he wants to play Hamlet, and not to slip into his inky cloak a changeling of quite another race.

He adds that

Mrs. Patrick Campbell's Ophelia is a surprise. The part is one which has hitherto seemed incapable of progress. From generation to generation actresses have, in the mad scene, exhausted their musical skill, their ingenuity in devising fantasies in the language of flowers, and their intensest powers of portraying anxiously earnest sanity. Mrs. Patrick Campbell, with that complacent audacity of hers which is so exasperating when she is doing the wrong thing, this time does the right thing by making Ophelia really mad. (Shaw 364–65)

The close of the nineteenth century was marked by several distinguished performances on the Continent. The Italian Tomasso Salvini's Hamlet of 1875 followed the Romantic tradition by displaying "the power of thought over action," according to the December 1907 issue of *Putnam's* (355; Hapgood 45). The French poet Mallarmé saw Jean Mounet Sully play Hamlet in France in 1896:

[M]ad, yes, in outward appearance, whipped as he is in both directions by his duty; but oh! nonetheless, his eyes are still upon an image of himself within, and this he keeps intact—like an Ophelia still undrowned!—always prepared to get his balance back again. Jewel intact in the midst of chaos. (60; Hapgood 46)

The mature Sarah Bernhardt first played Hamlet in Paris in 1899, arguing that a mature woman could act Hamlet better than a young man since the character had the mind of a man forty years old; "The woman more readily looks the part, yet has the maturity of mind to grasp it" she told *Harper's Bazaar* for December 15, 1900. She thought Hamlet "not a weak or languid person" but "manly and resolute" and one who withdraws from Claudius at prayer "not because he is vacillating and weak, but because he is firm and logical" and determined to send him to hell. Seeing Bernhardt, the American actress Elizabeth Robins witnessed "a high spirited, somewhat malicious boy" (*North American Review*, December 1900, 909), although some reviewers objected to a woman of 54 playing a boy of 20, "an elderly lady encased in black silk tights" (Hapgood 47). "As a *tour de force* Mme. Sarah Bernhardt's Hamlet was found to be interesting; as a *succes de curiosité* it was found to attract the town," the review in the *Times* of London on June 13, 1899 begins (Hapgood 7); but Max Beerbohm spoke for many by commenting in *The Saturday Review* of London on June 17, 1899, that "I cannot, on my heart, take Sarah's Hamlet seriously" (87: 2277, p. 747).

The elder son of Sir Henry Irving (H. B. for Henry Brodribb) opened the new century as Hamlet at the Adelphi Theatre in London on April 8, 1905, where Beerbohm saw him with some disgust, as he reported to *The Saturday Review*.

> In the past twenty years or so, the tendency in performing *Hamlet* has been, ever more and more, to present a sensible, realistic, modern drama of psychology, and to let the poetry shift for itself. The Ghost, as being a sort of detached figure, is still allowed to drag poetry in, speaking his lines sonorously and with rhythm. But the days of his privilege are surely numbered. Let's make the most of them.

In this production, Beerbohm found one exception in the performance of Claudius.

> A slight shelter is kindly provided for me by Mr. Oscar Asche. He, as King Claudius, does remember that Shakespeare wrote that part in blank verse—does speak rhythmically, and with reverence for sound, and does comport himself with a large tragic dignity: But the rest! Really, "the rest is silence"—for any pleasure afforded by it to the human ear. Miss Maud Milton, as Queen Gertrude, talks in easy conversational style, exactly as though Queen Gertrude were gossiping across a teacup. It is a wonderfully natural performance; but poetry, tragedy, queenliness, are quite out of it.

So the realistic Irving.

> I cannot acclaim this Hamlet as ideal—cannot even accept it as satisfactory. A thoroughly modern Hamlet, a round-the-corner Hamlet; a Prince (if Prince he be) not of Elsinore, but of Bernstoff; a Hamlet who breaks up his sentences into prose, squeezing the words together, or stretching them interminably out, with no reference at all to their rhythm, and often muttering them inaudibly, on the assumption that they are so familiar to us all that they need not be re-communicated; a Hamlet, in fact, without style—this is not the Hamlet for me. (Beerbohm 147–52)

Realistic theater succeeding the Romantics in the age of Freud was perhaps going too far.

For a brief interval, experimental directors shifted attention from players to productions. William Poel designed four of them. Arguing that "[i]t is the play as an epitome of life which is interesting in the mind of Shakespeare, and not the career of one individual" (Hapgood 56), Poel returned to Elizabethan staging with a thrust platform, no scenery, a boy playing Ophelia, and the text of Q1. In 1914, he mounted a production as he imagined Elizabethans would have seen their Queen, Burghley, Ralegh, and Essex. Gordon Craig, meanwhile, worked toward abstract stage designs. Stanislavsky invited Craig to co-direct *Hamlet* at the Moscow Art Theatre in 1911–12 but from the start the two disagreed (See Laurence Senelick's *Gordon Craig's Moscow "Hamlet"*). Stríbrny notes that "Craig stressed the mystic symbolism of the tragedy, conceiving it as a dream of the supersensitive Prince who is alienated from both the evil court and from action. Stanislavsky demanded from Hamlet and the other actors his own style of Chekhovian poetic realism, rich in atmospheric and psychological suggestion based on inner experience" (Stríbrny 55). Craig's conception won, and Hapgood notes that

> His vision of the falsity and corruption of the Danish court was effectively con-
> veyed by the tarnished gold costumes and decor. It is true that his intended
> effects were not always accomplished in exactly the way he envisaged. He had
> pictured the entire court covered by a single golden cape, with the characters'
> heads protruding through holes in it. When this proved impracticable,
> Stanislavsky had individual mantles made that, when spread, gave "the impres-
> sion of a monolithic golden pyramid." (Hapgood 57)

To insure fluid action, Craig introduced high vertical screens that were moved into various Cubist patterns to indicate the battlement, court, bedroom, and graveyard. "The final scene showed Hamlet dreaming, in the approach of death, the arrival of Fortinbras with his soldiers who filled the stage, lowering their white banners on the dead body and happy face 'of the great cleanser of the earth who had at last found the secrets of life on earth in the arms of death'" (Stríbrny 55).

John Barrymore's Hamlet opened at the Sam H. Harris Theater in New York in 1922 and moved to the Haymarket in London in 1925. Barrymore stressed the prince's masculinity and his athletic ability; Douglas Fairbanks helped him to choreograph the fencing match. But reports of his performance varied. The *New York Tribune* for January 14, 1923, found him "a great gentleman . . . full of con-sideration for others" (Hapgood 60, while *Time and Tide* for February 27, 1925, found him "plausible, natural, and credible to the modern mind" (Hapgood 61). Shaw wrote a letter to the actor noting that "Shakespeare is the worst of bores" unless acted "on the line and not between the lines" (Shaw, *Shaw on Shakespeare*; Hapgood 60), calling attention to Barrymore's pronounced pauses (95, 97). But the young Orson Welles remembered Barrymore's Hamlet as "ten-der and virile and witty and dangerous" and Margaret Webster saw "a tragic yearning, a terrible sense of waste and despair, and moments, especially with Ophelia, of great tenderness" (Hapgood 60). That same year in England, 1925, an ensemble cast brought a modern-dress production of the Birmingham

Repertory Theater to London in which the King wore a white tie and waistcoat and the courtiers wore monocles and smoked cigarettes. The project had Poel's approval, especially because, as one admirer put it, this "was not a play about one person nor a play about six of them, but a play about twenty people, each as vitally interesting as the other" (Hapgood 63). On August 26, 1925, however, the *Manchester Guardian* thought that the play "missed the actuality of youth at odds with the universe and turned ugly in its anger" and Ivor Brown thought the "snarling prince" to be "the first heart-break Hamlet I have seen!" To the young John Gielgud it was "[u]nspeakable" (Hapgood 63–64).

Nikolai Akimov directed for the experimental studio of the Moscow Art Theatre (MAT) an avant-garde production in 1921 that was "a zany play of political intrigue and struggle for the throne of Denmark." According to Stríbrny,

> The Prince soon turned out to be a clever manipulator, as he himself, speaking into an earthen jar, pretended to be his father's Ghost in order to win adherents for his conflict with Claudius. Horatio was an accomplice to this deception, shouting at Marcellus in imitation of the Ghost: "Swear." When Horatio overdid it the fourth time and there was a danger that even the simple-minded soldier might guess what was really cooking, Hamlet gave Horatio a kick and calmed him down with "Rest, rest, perturbèd spirit" (1.5.183). During his central soliloquy, Hamlet sat in a tavern with a tall tumbler of wine in front of him and a paper crown on his head, indicating that his real question was whether to be or not to be king. His pretended madness came into full view in a market place where he paraded in a nightshirt, a paper rose in his hand, and a frying pan ornamented with a carrot on his head, leading a suckling-pig on a string. A dissipated Ophelia, apparently in allusion to Chekhov's Okhemlia in *The Cherry Orchard*, became so drunk that her drowning appeared pretty natural. Grotesque features were enriched with incidental music by Dmitri Shostakovich, for instance in the scene of Hamlet's conversation with his fellow students Rosencrantz and Guildenstern, whom he reproached with trying to play on him as a pipe (3.2.322–41). When he, in a farcical gag, pressed the pipe to his bottom, shrill sounds of a piccolo, bass, and drum mocked at a simple-minded proletarian song celebrating the victory of the Soviet troops over the Chinese in 1929. (Stríbny 83–84)

"The question for us now," Stríbrny asks, "is how far the whole production went in its satirical reflection of the Soviet political scene. Since Lenin's death in 1924, a merciless fight for the post of general secretary of the Soviet Communist Party had been raging, and Stalin was getting rid of rivals with Machiavellian deception and Tamberlanian ruthlessness. Almost unavoidably, Akimov's grotesque production was attacked by Communist critics and soon removed from the repertoire despite the fact that crowds of Muscovites were spending hours in ticket lines to see it and one New York critic called it 'the best show in Europe'" (Stríbrny 84). Akimov moved the show to Leningrad where the party secretary was Sergei Kirov, Stalin's chief rival.

With no rivals, Betterton played Hamlet for nearly half a century, Garrick for thirty-four years; but in the twentieth century, John Gielgud played Hamlet in six different productions over a span of sixteen years. He first appeared at the Old Vic in 1930 at the age of twenty-six, an "angry young man of the twenties," he has remarked, disgusted at the rottenness in the state of Denmark (Hapgood 65). His was a Hamlet "never seeking to noblify, never understressing the quick bitterness and brutality of this crawler between heaven and earth," the *Graphic* pronounced on June 14, 1930; on June 1, the *Sunday Pictorial* reported he was a prince "who has bad dreams" (Hapgood 65). In 1934 Gielgud directed himself as a more intellectual Hamlet. The anonymous reviewer for the London *Times* for November 15 was exceptional in his warm approval: "Hamlet is not a flaunting part, though it is often so treated; it is not designed to provoke hot tears and shouting but to penetrate the soul by way of the intellect; and the first merit of Mr. Gielgud's interpretation is that it does not throw up passionate mists with which to conceal confusions. From the chill, ironical menace of its opening to the fierce attack of the play-scene and the terrible rage at the burying of Ophelia it pursues its argument with a brilliant lucidity. Nothing is smudged or doubtful; everything is as decisive as the line in the pencil-drawing of a master" (12). But Gielgud achieved far less success in this version, returning to his original interpretation when directed by Guthrie McClintic in an American production in 1936. Yet this too did not fare well. Joseph Wood Krutch wrote in *The Nation* for October 24, "*Hamlet* is set in the middle of the seventeenth century. Unimportant as the fact may at first sight seem, it is a symbol of all that is unsatisfactory and bitterly disappointing in the long-awaited interpretation of John Gielgud. *Hamlet* is a Gothic play not a courtly one" (143:17 p.500). Ivor Brown thought the 1939 production, first at Elsinore Castle and then in London, was the best, inspired by Harley Granville-Barker's preface to the play. "The play itself," the *Observer* reported on July 2, "gains in excitement by the earthy vigour of the prince, who seems not so much a moody creature hampered in his task by delicate sensibilities, as a man of strong conflicting passions whose irresolution depends not on lack of will but on the clash of powerful motives" (*Observer* 13; Hapgood 66). Amidst the horrors of World War II and London blitzes, Gielgud took the role again in 1944; in 1945, he toured the Far East in his sixth and last production, with makeshift stagings for audiences that had never seen the play. Throughout all of them, he recalled in *Early Stages*, he sought to give his characterization a straight through-line: "one must concentrate, take care not to anticipate, not begin worrying beforehand how one is going to say it, take time, but don't lose time, don't break the verse up, don't succumb to the temptation of a big melodramatic effect for the sake of getting applause at the curtain" (Gielgud 112).

Throughout his career, Gielgud was known for the musical quality of his voice; "When Gielgud speaks the verse, I can hear Shakespeare *thinking*," the American director Lee Strasberg is said to have remarked. (Hapgood 67) Richard Burton also varied his interpretations of the role, often spontaneously, on the stage. His Hamlet was decisive, purposeful, and vengeful when Burton first took the part in Edinburgh in 1953; when the production moved to London's Old Vic, he made his "uncomplicated prince" one of "dash, attack, and verve, not pausing to worry about psychology," according to the *Daily Express* on September 15, 1953 (Hapgood 71). Winston Churchill thought Burton's Hamlet "as exciting and virile as any I can remember" (*Playboy*, September 1963, 54; Hapgood 71) But when he came to New York in 1964, Burton was a prince of "tempestuous manliness," said the *New York Times* on April 16, with "all the stops out" (Hapgood 71).

"The most overtly oppositional *Hamlet* in the whole Warsaw Pact bloc was produced in Cracow in 1956," Stríbrny writes.

> The director Roman Zawistowski cut the text into a clear and sharp version, concentrated practically on one issue: politics. The production was full of pain and hatred against Stalinist oppression and surveillance. "Watch," "enquire," and "prison" were the words most insistently addressed at the audience. Prince Hamlet was a young, charismatic rebel, "rid of illusion, sarcastic, passionate and brutal," "wild and drunk with indignation." The simplification of his character and of the whole play made it frighteningly straightforward and effective. At Elsinore, every curtain was hiding a spy, everything was corroded by suspicion and fear. Hamlet feigned madness in order to deceive the tyrant and to show that politics itself was madness, when it was destroying all feelings of love and friendship. Above all, the mask of madness served him to brace himself for the decisive fight with the oppressor. His wit and bravery were rewarded by a magnificent funeral: his body was carried high by Fortinbras's captains in reverence of the hero whose death was not a defeat. (Stríbny 100-01)

Josef Svoboda designed two modern productions of *Hamlet* for the Prague National Theatre in 1959–66 and in 1982–88; both are legendary. In the first, black plastic material covered twenty tall vertical panels that shifted rapidly into different scenes while dimly reflecting halberds, swords, cups, or bodies in motion; this alienating world was mysteriously lit until whirling spotlights were fixed on the Ghost as a pair of eyes high up on a black background. Hamlet's chief soliloquy was done in silhouette. In Svoboda's second production, stepped platforms were surrounded by black velvet drapes where the full space was deferred until the ending when Claudius, groping for aid at Hamlet's attack, tore the drapes down and died among their folds. Prague's most significant production of *Hamlet* was at the Balustrade Theatre in 1978, Stríbrny notes,

> under the direction of Evald Schorm, who used the heavily abridged and garbled text of the First Quarto to produce a swiftly moving play with striking effects. The first surprise came with the Ghost, whose creaking armour and heavy bandages soaked in blood pointed to a travesty of the Elizabethan "bloody tragedy." This impression was strengthened by the rudimentary setting of white vertical panels spattered with blood. It gradually dawned upon the

audience that the whole play was meant to oscillate between farce and tragedy. . . .

Young Hamlet, in black jeans and sweater, behaved in quite a calm manner, but spoke daggers most of the time. His final act of revenge received a surprising support: during his duel with Laertes, the grave-diggers reappeared to take hold of King Claudius, tossing him back and forth and eventually presenting him to victorious Hamlet as the final target. Even more surprisingly, the gravediggers continued to dominate the whole ending of the play. They were not presented as sturdy, staunch representatives of the people but as modern circus clowns in white face with glaring red plastic balls for noses; they wore the black rubber boots and gloves, long rubberized aprons, and paramilitary peaked caps of a sanitation unit. One of them dragged the corpses of Ophelia and Polonius back on stage, adding them to the dead bodies of the King, the Queen, Laertes, and Hamlet himself. The other gravedigger, softly whistling and humming to himself with malicious relish, pulled down a military camouflage net, which had been suspended above the stage from the beginning, and carefully spread it over all the dead bodies, dusting them with disinfectant powder. (Stríbny 118)

Another postmodern production opened in 1964 at Taganka, a studio theater in Moscow. This time Hamlet wore a turtleneck and slacks, played a guitar, and chanted "To be or not to be" as a rock song. The gravediggers, now Russian peasants drinking vodka, appeared at the opening of the play, and the grave from which they took real earth and skulls remained onstage throughout the performance. In this production, a coarse woolen curtain suspended from a pivot and track moved about to change scenes, even at one point turning into Claudius' throne. At the end of the play, the curtain swept up all of the corpses and actors and threatened to advance into the audience: "The long shadows of Stalin's criminal dictatorship and Brezhnev's aggression," writes Stríbrny, "were falling on the stage." (Stríbny 120) But Stríbrny finds "the most subversive Shakespeare production" in Bucharest just before the fall of the Berlin Wall (Stríbny 134); it transferred to London in 1990. The soldiers' bitter complaints about the cold were ironic, since the play was performed in unheated theaters. The Ghost did not appear, but his voice was heard, accompanied by two searchlights sweeping the sky; Hamlet pronounced his soliloquies in prison, sitting rigidly in a chair under a spotlight. At the close, Fortinbras arrived as a new military dictator surrounded by secret agents, including Rosencrantz and Guildenstern, who, "With a vengeance, . . . returned to fortify the new regime of oppression and deceit." (Stríbny 135)

In Japan, thirteen staged adaptations of Hamlet—five in Tokyo, four in Osaka, two in Kyoto, and others in Kobe and Hakata—preceded the first full translation produced in Tokyo by Bungei Kyokai (Literary Arts Association) in 1907. This production, directed by Shoyo Tsubouchi, grew out of playreading clubs (the Rodoku-kai) he had founded and starred Shunsho Doi as Hamlet and Biyo Mizuguchi as Gertrude. *The Mousetrap* was staged as a Noh Play, but this attempt to situate the play within classical Japanese culture failed to work: no aristocratic Japanese would sleep alone in a garden without his attendants at hand. The second Bungei Kyokai production at the Imperial Theatre in Toyko in May 1911 was far more successful. The theater, which could accommodate 1,700 people, recorded 91 percent capacity audiences over a seven-day run. Tsubouchi again cast a more mature Doi as Hamlet and, in the first modern production to use actresses in a culture that had banned them from 1629 until the 1870s, the young Sumako Matsui as Ophelia. This time Doi's performance was much more inward-looking, especially during the soliloquies. Koreya Senda played the title role in 1938 for the New Tsukiji Theatre Company (Shin-Tsukijiza), in a Marxist-influenced production that emphasized the play's three political rebellions and its corrupt king.

In considerable contrast, Yukio Nimagawa's production in 1978 used the Dolls Festival held each March for the play-within-a-play in an attempt to bridge European and Asian cultures. More recent productions have developed this idea, resulting, for instance, in *Kanadehon Hamlet* by Harue Tsutsumi, which was produced by Kiyama Jimusho in 1992 and 1994. In this version, according to Akihiko Senda,

> The play is set in Tokyo in 1897. A stage rehearsal of *Hamlet* is now going on at the Shintomi-za, an actual Kabuki theatre, for the next day's opening. This is to be Japan's first production of *Hamlet* in translation, planned by Kan'ya Morita, the owner of the theatre. However, knowing nothing about Western drama, the Kabuki actors are at a loss with *Hamlet* and try to put it on the stage in the familiar style of *Kanadehon Chushingura* (a popular Kabuki play first staged in 1748). . . . *Kanadehon Chushingura* dramatises an actual revenge accomplished by forty-seven samurais in Tokyo (or Edo) in 1702, and the play, needless to say, exists independently of *Hamlet*. However, the point suggested in Tsutsumi's play, that these two popular pieces, representing the Japanese and the European drama respectively, share common elements to an unexpectedly great extent seems to give us hints regarding what is shared by dramatic masterpieces that have been favoured by audiences for centuries. (Senda in Sasayama et al. 35–36)

In 1989 in England, Michael Billington noted in the *Guardian* for November 21 that "*Hamlet* is a profoundly political play, one that deals . . . with the whole question of the governance of society." He might have had in mind the Peter Hall production for the Royal Shakespeare Company in 1965 when, in addressing the company, Hall remarked, "For our decade I think the play will be about the disillusionment which produces an apathy of the will so deep that commitment to politics, to religion or to life is impossible. . . . [Hamlet] is always on the brink of action, but something inside him, this disease of disillusionment, stops the final, committed action" (Hapgood 75). Tyrone Guthrie had cast both Laurence Olivier and Alec Guiness in oedipal productions, but Hall cast twenty-four-year-old David Warner as Hamlet. Hall thought Warner "completely expressed the spirit of the young of that period, gentle but dangerous" (Hapgood 77), while Harold Hobson wrote in the Sunday *London Times* for August 22, 1965, that Warner would "wave his arms like a scythe, howl to the moon, and go after the king at a most unrefined gallop"; yet "He is [also] spare, controlled, deadly, and most royally confident . . . in a word, most princely, most exalted, judging as well as being judged" (*Sunday Times*, August 22, 1965). Brewster Mason played Claudius as a smooth if corrupt administrator and Tony Church played Polonius as a "shrewd, tough, establishment figure" (*The Times*, August 20, 1965). (Later, Church told the scholar Stanley Wells that Hall "had in mind both Lord Burleigh and Mr. Macmillan, chief ministers of the two Elizabeths" (Hapgood 77).

Also in 1989, director Ron Daniels took the Royal Shakespeare Company's touring production to Newcastle-upon-Tyne, to Manchester, and to the Broadmoor Hospital for the criminally insane. Antony McDonald's set was out-of-kilter; Mark Rylance, who played Hamlet, called it "a palace tilting into the ocean" (Hapgood 83), but it mirrored a deranged prince out of joint with his surroundings and contrasted with the loving embrace King Hamlet has for Gertrude. Rylance's soliloquies appealed to the audiences; in the first of them, "he cannot bear to look us in the eye as he speaks," *Plays and Players* reported in June 1989; "He does not turn towards us until he speaks of his father: 'So excellent a king,' he explains, holding out a photograph of his father. He speaks directly to us, his face pleading for us to agree" (Hapgood 83). But Claudius and Gertrude have no use for him; isolated, he appears slumped in a black coat, with his suitcase packed for Wittenberg. Later, he is frenzied when with Ophelia, and when he repeatedly stabs Polonius behind the arras. The *Manchester Guardian* recounted on April 28, 1989, that his "antic disposition" turned to a kind of madness as he banged his head against the wall; on December 28, 1989, the paper reported that Rylance "was able to capture every aspect of a person's slip into the world of psychopathic, manipulative paranoia. . . . Many of us here in Broadmoor are able to understand Hamlet's disturbed state of mind because we have experienced such traumas" (Hapgood 84). Speaking of Hamlet at the play's end, Rylance remarked that "[h]e comes to some kind of peace, and I guess that's part of the reason that makes it a tragedy. He's actually reached the state of a prince at the time that he dies, and you should feel he would make a wonderful king" (Hapgood 84).

But actors have testified that the role of Hamlet is a demanding one. Michael Pennington has noted that playing Hamlet "will take the actor further down into his psyche, memory and imagination" than he has been (Hapgood 86). Olivier warned that the part can "cast you into the depths of despair. Once you have played it, it will devour you and obsess you for the rest of your life. It has me. I think each day about it" (Hapgood 86). Taking the role, Daniel Day-Lewis prophesied, "I think this is the year of my nervous collapse. Hamlet's a hard part to live with. It conjures up demons in you. . . . This has certainly taken me closer to the abyss than anything else. And I've discovered fears in myself, or generated fears, I never knew before—and once they're there, they're very difficult to put away again" (*Daily Mail*, September 13, 1989; Hapgood 86). In fact, he withdrew from the part in the middle of its run to be replaced by Ian Charleston, who played the role while dying of AIDS. According to the *Independent* of March 17, 1989, Ben Kingsley became physically ill: "At the centre of the play when you're exhausted, battling with it physically and intellectually, sweat pouring into your eyes and you're wondering if anything is achieved, the 'to be or not to be' soliloquy coincides with your sensibilities" (Hapgood 86). In fact, his director, Buzz Goodbody, committed suicide shortly after the previews began. "Buzz got me through Hamlet," Kingsley told *Time Out*; "For some reason, having examined all the implications of it at a high emotional and intellectual level, she didn't get herself through *Hamlet*" (*Time Out* January 30, 1976; Hapgood 87). In 1988, Kenneth Branagh "felt crushingly the weight of the ghosts of other performances." (*Shakespeare Bulletin*, Fall 1994, 6). But "[i]t is in adaptations that the disintegrated self of the hero has been pushed to the extreme," Hapgood comments;

> there was a spate of them in the 1960s. In *Hamlet Collage* (1965) Charles Marowitz set out to ridicule the Prince as "the supreme prototype of the conscience-stricken but paralysed liberal," making him the laughing stock of the other characters; the play ends with their corpses mocking him "with jeers, whistles, stamping and catcalls." In Joe Papp's *Naked Hamlet* (1968) the final duel is reduced to a game of Russian roulette; when Hamlet happens to shoot Claudius the moment is played for laughs: his attendants topple over one after the other but the King does not accept that he has been shot dead until Hamlet proves it to him by showing him a copy of the play. In Tom Stoppard's *Rosencrantz and Guildenstern Are Dead* (1967) Shakespeare's conflicted hero is displaced to the sidelines in favour of a totally divided protagonist, a pair out of Beckett, whose identities are confused and whose destinies are completely out of their control and in any case inconsequential. (Hapgood 88–89)

"Shakespeare's play does flirt with absurdity," Hapgood concludes, "but thus far stage interpretations of the role have not succumbed to it; on the contrary, the threat of utter futility has been seen as part of the sea of troubles against which the Prince must finally take arms." (Hapgood 89)

The new century opened with Mark Rylance returning to the role of Hamlet in a production at the new Globe Theatre in London, where he had just been reappointed as Artistic Director. Writing in the *TLS* for July 7, 2000, Eleanor Margolies found much of the presentation too obvious, but she appreciated the conclusion of the performance:

> After this *Hamlet*, there is a solemn Jig. The actors enter from the central doors, each carrying a skull on a stick. They beat their staves on the stage as they turn.

They seem to grow in stature, and their faces, looking straight out, drained of their roles, are compelling. Here, at last, is a stage picture that is emblematic of tragedy, and movement that exploits the particular qualities of the Globe theatre. It is the best moment of the evening: clear but strange, addressed to the audience, but not insisting on a single meaning. (21)

Virginia Mason Vaughan was more sympathetic. For her, Mark Rylance's Hamlet, compared to others, "was much less intellectualized and much more a prisoner of volatile emotions"; he "was genuinely upset, desperately sorry, that he had mistakenly killed Polonius." He also showed "genuine affection" for Ophelia as early as 1.2.

The emotions he showed in the nunnery scene thus had a foundation in his earlier actions. But the most unusual choices had to do with the soliloquies. Most contemporary actors view these as interior monologues, the subconscious mind at work. Mark Rylance addressed the rhetorical questions in the soliloquies not to himself but to the Globe audience, whom he could see. Thus when he asked, "Who calls me villain?" it was a genuine question seeming to call for an answer. He even repeated, "Who? who" a couple of times trying to evoke more response from the audience.[5]

The ritual dance at the end of the production thus summed up, and distanced, the audience while bringing them back to many conditions of the play's original production.

HAMLET ON FILM

"*Hamlet* is the world's most filmed story after *Cinderella*," Luke McKernan and Olwen Terris write.

The figure of Hamlet, his agonised choices, his revenge and his fate (not to mention the literary kudos) have attracted filmmakers and actors from 1900 onwards, when Sarah Bernhardt became the first person to play the Dane on film. Since then he has been played by a woman three more times (Asta Nielsen, Joy Caroline Johnson and Fatma Girik), and the men have included Georges Melies, Sir Johnston Forbes-Robertson, John Barrymore, Jack Benny, Laurence Olivier, Maurice Evans, Hardy Kruger, Maximilian Schell, Christopher Plummer, Richard Burton, Innokenti Smoktunaowsky, Nicoll Williamson, Richard Chamberlain, Derek Jacobi, Mel Brooks, Mel Gibson, and Arnold Schwarzenegger. He has been animated at least twice, portrayed as twins (Anthony and David Meyer) and turned into a cowboy (*Johnny Hamlet* and *Lust in the Sun*). India, Ghana, Japan, the USSR, Brazil, Turkey, Greece and Denmark have all produced their versions of the story.[6]

To this Ann Thompson adds *The Bad Sleep Well*, a somber Japanese film with Toshiro Mifune as Hamlet (Thompson 216).

Of all of these films, the most influential was Laurence Olivier's black-and-white film of 1948. The initial voice-over claims "This is the tragedy of a man who could not make up his mind," yet Olivier's Hamlet is, if oedipal in the closet scene, also decisive. The atmosphere, opening on the cliffs, is decidedly Gothic; as Hapgood describes it, "the castle has huge rooms, winding staircases, dark corridors and long vistas through receding archways; its towering battlements look dizzyingly down on a beating tide; and through its mists a spectral ghost appears, its sepulchral voice seemingly muffled by cerements. It is a haunted place where secrets are concealed yet gradually revealed, although the reasons for the Prince's inaction remain a puzzle. It is as if he were under a spell" (Hapgood 68). Although Olivier's filmed Hamlet is much more subdued than his athletic stage performance, it draws nevertheless on it as well as other stage productions: in the byplay of Laertes and Ophelia as Polonius lectures them; in Hamlet's carrying the sword before him as a cross as he follows the Ghost; in Gertrude's denial of Claudius after the closet scene; and in the omission of Fortinbras. The film plays openly and deliberately for mood and for image, as in the highly suggestive bedcoverings that undulate in the meeting between Hamlet and Gertrude.

An equally atmospheric but more original and stunning black-and-white film of *Hamlet* is that by the Russian director Grigori Kozintsev released in 1964, based on the recent translation, after the death of Stalin, by Boris Pasternak. Here too is a dark castle with a rocky coast, but Kozintsev is more concerned with the process of time. Three layers of time are actually fused: the earlier time of the Ghost; the Renaissance time of Hamlet's humanist Wittenberg and Claudius's corrupt anti-humanism; and the present time of the film, with allusions to Hitler's Holocaust and Stalin's Gulag. The dramatic opening shows Hamlet hurriedly riding horseback over the moors and heath and over a massive drawbridge into Elsinore Castle which then entraps him. The court is luxurious, but Hamlet disappears before he is first addressed by Claudius. For there is no room here for individual answers; the men and women of the court are treated like puppets, as later Ophelia will be tightly wound up in an imprisoning dress in preparation to meet Hamlet. Such images are memorable. The only warmth in the film comes in Hamlet's friendship with Horatio and in the visit by the strolling players. The film ends when Hamlet's corpse is held aloft by Fortinbras's company and, taken with a funeral march into a crowd of commoners on the road leading down from the castle, is swallowed up by them.

Franco Zeffirelli's film with Mel Gibson as Hamlet (1991) was limited by contract to run 135 minutes, but this need to cut the script works to Zeffirelli's advantage. The film borrows heavily from Olivier's filmed interpretation—Gibson too is an athletic Hamlet and his encounter with Gertrude is decidedly Freudian. But Zeffirelli has made a career of adapting films to the values of his audiences, holding his mirror up to their nature, and his *Hamlet* omits Fortinbras as it omits all of the politics; rather, the film depicts a family tragedy. His opening shot makes this clear; rather than setting it on the ramparts at Elsinore, he creates a scene in the castle's crypt where only the immediate family (including Claudius) pay their last respects to King Hamlet in his coffin. Other scenes are transposed. An especially successful instance shows Polonius spying on Ophelia at her sewing when Hamlet happens on her and hears her singing the obscene lyrics, transferred from the mad scene, and backs off abashed. The scene not only gives Polonius a fresh plan to have Claudius spy on the lovers, but it gives Hamlet stronger reasons for the nunnery speech. The journey to England is done in swift fragments. Finally, Claudius conspires with Laertes after the death and burial of Ophelia, a consequence of her death as well as that of Polonius. The final scene, in which the principals all lie dead with no Fortinbras to come as *deus ex machina*, takes the attention back to the opening scene of mourning.

Kenneth Branagh hoped for twenty years to play Hamlet in his own film; *In the Bleak Midwinter* (American title: *A Midwinter's Tale*) made in 1993, is exploratory toward that end. The story is about a poor troupe of actors, like the players in *Hamlet*, putting on their own *Hamlet* in a small, poor village at Christmastime. In retrospect, *In the Bleak Midwinter* establishes the relevance of Shakespeare in two ways: by connecting the players' roles to their own lives, it suggests the immediacy of characters in Shakespeare's play; and by showing the power of theater to restore communal bonding in the town of Hope, it shows how theater can transport playgoers out of the dark and cold world in which they live.

Branagh's four-hour, uncut *Hamlet* (1995) is set in the nineteenth century, but its relevance to the decay of the House of Windsor, then under media exposure and attack following the death of Princess Diana, is clear. In public life there is no privacy left, something caught best when Hamlet delivers his soliloquy is a hallway of mirrors as Polonius and Claudius spy on him. "I wanted it to be a very glamorous court," Branagh has said, "a very glamorous-looking place, somewhere where you could understand the fascination of the nation. Which I think is in tune with some part of Shakespeare's interest in it which was to look at the very private lives of very public individuals. If you like, these people could be stepping out of the pages of a nineteenth-century *Hello!* magazine."[7] The film is notable for its flashbacks, as with the story of Priam and Hecuba, where nothing is left unimagined and unexposed. Indeed, even the developing court intrigue gives way to cut-in scenes of Fortinbras's awesome army marching toward Elsinore (shot at Blenheim Place, the Churchill family home outside Oxford). Indeed, "Blenheim Palace enables in the film one further analogy," Julie Sanders writes,

> hinted at in a throwaway comment in Russell Jackson's production diary. He calls Blenheim, in an entry reflecting on artificial snow put down for filming, a "formidable Winter Palace." This evocation of a building seminal to late nineteenth- and early twentieth-century Russian history is more telling than the light-hearted context of Jackson's comment suggests. One of this century's most poignant, and indeed romanticized, images of the fall of monarchy is the mur-

der of Tsar Nicholas II and his family and aides in 1918 by the advancing Russian revolutionaries. That brutal act came, however, in the wake of the Romanov family's own tyrannies against the Russian people (not least the 1905 St. Petersburg [then Petrograd] massacre of protestors in the snow outside the Winter Palace). The recent ceremony held over their corpses, identified through DNA testing, and the controversies it provoked, indicate the political confusions these events still generate, echoing, in its problematic and sometimes diffuse mobilization of popular and political sentiment in the former Soviet Union, the complex impact of Diana's funeral. The British Royal Family is closely related to the Romanovs, and this lends poignancy to these embedded allusions in Branagh's film. (eds. Burnett and Wray 154–55)

Branagh ends the film not with the tribute to Hamlet's corpse, but with Fortinbras's troops destroying the memorial to King Hamlet. The image is a powerful one and is held on the screen, but its significance is not clear: It may be the desecration of the past, the ruthless takeover of a new regime, or the displacement of one tyrant by another. But the film is made to comment on the church as well as the state in the recurring use of the confessional. Sanders remarks that "[i]t is in and around this ecclesiastical site that Polonius interrogates his daughter about her relationship with Hamlet: poignantly, it is also against the screen of this space that Ophelia will hurl herself when she learns of her father's death. . . . Here, too, Claudius delivers his 'O my offence is rank' soliloquy. . . and Hamlet imagines killing him. . . . The privacy of personal faith and space is denied in this secular, corrupt community." (eds. Burnett and Wray159) Just as Shakespeare wrote *Hamlet* when the succession of Elizabeth I was an important issue, so Branagh uses his Hamlet in a parallel way to inquire into the political society of the present day.

Through the years there have also been burlesques of *Hamlet*, beginning in the eighteenth century. In the earliest days of British film, Cecil Hepworth's *Hamlet* of 1913 was followed by the parody *Oh'phelia and 'Amlet* (1919). The era of silent film had more travesties than serious films concerning Hamlet: *When Hungry Hamlet Fled* (United States, 1915), *Pimple as Hamlet* (Britain, 1916), *Colonel Heeza Liar Plays Hamlet* and *Hamlet Made Over* (both United States, 1916). Olivier's widow, Joan Plowright, shows the Olivier film of *Hamlet* in *The Last Action Hero* before Arnold Schwarzenegger parodies the play (and the film). As if in response, the Reduced Shakespeare Company's five-minute stage version borrows from cinema by speeding it up to forty-five seconds, and then playing it backwards. But Hamlet may have received its widest and largest audience in the late twentieth-century Disney film *The Lion King*. In this adaptation, a young lion cub approaches maturity to take over his pride when his wicked uncle convinces him that he is responsible for his father's death, usurping the cub and sending him into depression. He is saved by a wise old prophet (the Ghost) who urges him to seek vengeance on his uncle, revealed as his father's actual murderer, and to resume the throne. The wicked uncle is actually killed by vicious hyenas, leaving the cub free to take up his role as leader. The moral for children may be twofold: growing up means standing for what is right and proper and accepting responsibility. Thus Hamlet holds its various meanings not only for all times, but for all ages too.

NOTES

I am grateful for use of the collections of documents and books at the British Library, the Shakespeare Birthplace Trust Library, and the library of the Royal Shakespeare Company, on which I have drawn liberally, as well as compilations that have preceded this one, particularly those by Geoffrey Bullough, Paul S. Conklin, Richard Corum, Peter Davison, Anthony Dawson, David Farley-Hills, Paul Gottschalk, Robert Hapgood, Harold Jenkins, John Davies Jump, Bernice Kliman, W. Thomas MacCary, Michael E. Mooney, Zednek Stríbrny, Stanley Wells, and Claude Williamson.

1. Peter Hall, quoted in Roger Manvell, *Shakespeare and the Film* (South Brunswick and New York: Barnes, 1979), 134.

2. H. H. Furness, at an address to the Phi Beta Kappa Society, Harvard University, 1908.

3. Chris Rohmann, "Assaults on *Hamlet*," *The Valley Advocate* (April 6, 2000), 23.

4. Elvis Mitchell, "A Simpler Melancholy," *The New York Times*, May 21, 2000, II:1.

5. In private correspondence with the editor on 26 August 2000.

6. Luke McKernan and Olwen Terris, *Walking Shadows* (London: British Film Institute, 1994); Jack Benny and Mel Brooks delivered only Hamlet's "to be or not to be" soliloquy (in part) in a comedy entitled *To Be or Not To Be*. Quoted by Ann Thompson in "Asta Nielson and the Mystery of *Hamlet*" in *Shakespeare the Movie*, ed. Lynda E. Boose and Richard Burt (London: Routledge, 1997), 215.

7. Kenneth Branagh quoted in Julie Sanders, "The End of History and the Last Man: Kenneth Branagh's *Hamlet*" in *Shakespeare, Film, and Fin de Siecle*, ed. Mark Thornton Burnett and Ramona Wray (London: Macmillan Press Ltd., 2000), 153.

WORKS CITED

Barker, Francis. *The Tremulous Private Body: Essays on Subjection*. London: Methuen, 1984.

Barker, Francis. *The Culture of Violence: Tragedy and History*. Chicago: University of Chicago Press, 1993.

Branagh, Kenneth. *Hamlet by William Shakespeare: Screenplay, Introduction, and Film Diary*. New York: W. W. Norton Co., 1996.

Bullough, Geoffrey, ed. *Narrative and Dramatic Sources of Shakespeare*, 7 vols. London: Routledge and Kegan, 1973.

Calderwood, James L. *To Be and Not to Be: Negotiation and Metadrama in Hamlet*. New York: Columbia University Press, 1983.

Conklin, Paul S. *A History of "Hamlet" Criticism 1601-1821*. rep. London: Frank Cass and Co, Ltd., 1967.

Corum, Richard. *Understanding "Hamlet."* Westport, Conn.: Greenwood Press, 1998.

Davison, Peter. *"Hamlet": Text and Performance*. London: Macmillan, 1983.

Dawson, Anthony B. *Hamlet: "Shakespeare in Performance."* Manchester: Manchester University Press, 1995.

Erlich, Avi. *Hamlet's Absent Father*. Princeton: Princeton University Press, 1997.

Farley-Hills, David, ed. *Critical Response to Hamlet 1600-1900*, 4 vols. New York: AMS Press, 1995-<c1999>.

Farrell, Kirby. *Play, Death, and Heroism in Shakespeare's Plays*. Chapel Hill: University of North Carolina Press, 1989.

Frye, Roland Mushat. *The Renaissance Hamlet: Issues and Responses in 1600*. Princeton: Princeton University Press, 1984.

Gielgud, John. *Early Stages*. rev. ed. London: Heinemann, 1974.

Gottschalk, Paul. *The Meanings of "Hamlet": Modes of Interpretation Since Bradley*. Albuquerque: University of New Mexico Press, 1972.

Greenblatt, Stephen. *Renaissance Self-Fashioning: From More to Shakespeare*. Chicago: University of Chicago Press, 1980.

Gurr, Andrew. "Hamlet's Claim to the Crown of Denmark," *Critical Essays on "Hamlet,"* ed. Linda Cookson and Brian Loughrey. Harlow, Essex: Longman, 1988.

Hall, Peter. *Theatre at Work: Playwrights and Productions in Modern British Theatre*, ed. Charles Marowitz and Simon Trussler. London: Methuen, 1967.

Hapgood, Robert, ed. *Hamlet, Prince of Denmark*. New York: Cambridge University Press, 1999.

Hawkes, Terence. "Telmah" in *Shakespeare and the Question of Theory*, ed. Patricia Parker and Geoffrey Hartman. New York: Methuen, 1985.

Haydn, Hiram. *The Counter-Renaissance*. New York: Charles Scribner's Sons, 1950.

Heilbrun, Carolyn. *Hamlet's Mother and Other Women*. New York: Columbia University Press, 1990.

Holland, Norman N. *Psychoanalysis and Shakespeare*. New York: McGraw-Hill, 1964, 1966.

James, D. G. *The Dream of Learning*. Oxford: Clarendon Press, 1951.

Jenkins, Harold. "Introduction" to *Hamlet*, Arden Edition. London: Methuen, 1982.

Joseph, Bertram L. *Conscience and the King*. London: Chatto and Windus, 1953.

Jump, John Davies, ed. *Shakespeare: Hamlet: A Casebook*. London: Macmillan, 1968.

Kerrigan, William. *Hamlet's Perfection*. Baltimore: Johns Hopkins University Press, 1994.

Kirsch, Arthur. *The Passions of Shakespeare's Tragic Heroes*. Charlottesville: University of Virginia Press, 1990.

Kliman, Bernice and Paul Bertram, eds. *The Three-Text Hamlet: Parallel Texts of the First and Second Quartos and First Folio*. New York: AMS Press, 1991.

Kott, Jan. *Shakespeare Our Contempory* trans. Boleslaw Taherski. Garden City: Doubleday, 1964.

Lacan, Jacques. "Desire and the Interpretation of Desire in Hamlet" trans. James Hulbert. *Yale French Studies* 55/56, 1997.

Leverenz, David. "The Women in Hamlet: An Interpersonal View," *Signs* 4, 1978.

MacCarey, W. Thomas. *Hamlet: A Guide to the Play*. Westport, Conn.: Greenwood Press, 1998.

Madariaga, Salvatore de. *On Hamlet*. London: Hollis and Carter, 1948.

Montrose, Louis. *The Purpose of Playing: Shakespeare and the Cultural Politics of the Elizabethan Theatre* . Chicago: University of Chicago Press, 1996.

Mooney, Michael E. *Hamlet: An Annotated Bibliography of Shakespeare Studies 1604-1998*. Asheville, NC: Pegasus Press, 1999.

Mullaney, Steven. *The Place of the Stage*. Chicago: University of Chicago Press, 1988.

Neely, Carol Thomas. *Broken Nuptials in Shakespeare's Plays*. New Haven: Yale University Press, 1985.

Nietzsche, Friedrich. *The Birth of Tragedy from the Spirit of Music* in *The Philosophy of Nietzche*, trans. Clifton Fadiman. New York: Modern Library, 1954.

Sasayama, Takashi, J. R. Mulryne, and Margaret Shewring, eds. *Shakespeare and the Japanese Stage*. Cambridge: Cambridge University Press, 1988.

Senelick, Laurence. *Gordon Craig's Moscow "Hamlet": A Reconstruction*. Westport, Conn.: Greenwood Press, 1982.

Shaw, George Bernard. *Shaw on Shakespeare*, ed. Edwin Wilson. New York: Dutton, 1961.

States, Bert O. *"Hamlet" and the Concept of Character*. Baltimore: Johns Hopkins University Press, 1992.

Stríbrny, Zednek. *Shakespeare and Eastern Europe*. Oxford: Oxford University Press, 2000.

Tardiff, Joseph C. and Elizabeth Morrison, eds. *Shakespearean Criticism* Vol. 21. Detroit: Gale Research Inc., 1993.

Tennenhouse, Leonard. *Power on Display: The Politics of Shakespeare's Genres*. New York: Methuen, 1986.

Terry, Ellen. *Four Lectures on Shakespeare*. London: M. Hopkinson, 1932.

Updike, John. *Gertrude and Claudius*. New York: Alfred A. Knopf, 2000.

Wells, Stanley, ed. *Shakespeare in the Theatre: An Anthology of Criticism*. Oxford: Oxford University Press, 2000.

Williamson, Claude C.H., ed. *Readings on the Character of Hamlet 1661-1947*. London: Allen & Unwin, 1950.

Part I
Tudor–Stuart *Hamlet*

Shakespeare at Work: The Invention of the Ghost

E. PEARLMAN

Any moderately knowledgeable Londoner who in 1599 or shortly thereafter had set out for the Globe to see a performance of the new and revised *Hamlet* could safely assume that the play would give prominence to its very famous ghost. While crossing the Thames by bridge or by wherry, he might anticipate that sometime early in the play the Ghost would let loose a high-pitched blood-curdling shriek, "Hamlet, revenge," or perhaps, "Hamlet, revenge my griefs"[1]—the celebrated (if even then somewhat dated) lament was so fabled a piece of theatrical extravagance that even a refurbished *Hamlet* would dispense with it only reluctantly. Such a playgoer might think himself aggrieved, at first, to discover that the re-imagined apparition failed to utter the outbursts of ghosts of *Hamlet*s past. And although he might be temporarily solaced that the new Ghost retained some features that harked back to ancient Seneca, he would shortly come to realize that almost his every expectation about this new Ghost's nature—when the phantom would appear or not appear, what he would say or not say (or shriek or not shriek), what he would look like, and even the very essence of his putative being—would defy both formula and precedent. Yet a playgoer might in the course of the afternoon come to acknowledge that although the Ghost declined to gratify old expectations, he pleased and startled the audience with newer and more sophisticated joys. A person who might have entered the Globe complacently would return home knowing full well that the Ghost had simultaneously shocked, teased, chastened, and befuddled him—exactly the same reaction, history shows, that the Ghost has provoked in strenuous critics for four hundred years.[2]

Shakespeare's radical re-invention of the Ghost, and most specifically his staging of the first meeting between the Ghost and Hamlet, is one of the stellar triumphs of the Elizabethan theater. It is almost impossible to exaggerate how startling and original the Ghost must have seemed to its first audiences. Although over the course of the centuries the scene's impact has been diluted by imitation and by familiarity, it still provokes a powerful response. In its own time, when ghosts were still ghosts and the play was newly mounted, it would have been a truly spectacular *coup de théâtre*. Although there is no early account of the play in performance, the first encounter between Ghost and Hamlet continued to generate its extraordinary emotional force well into the eighteenth century, when it was still thought by some to be the greatest scene ever written. The tradition that had begun with Burbage playing Hamlet (Shakespeare himself personating the Ghost) and had been sustained by Taylor, Betterton, and Robert Wilks found its fruition in David Garrick's playing (most familiar to moderns from Benjamin Wilson's famous portrait of the horror-stricken actor). Lichtenberg's detailed account of Garrick in action hints at the power that would have transfixed the very earliest audiences.

> As Hamlet moves towards the back of the stage . . . Horatio starts, and saying: "Look, my lord, it comes," points to the right, where the ghost has already appeared. . . . At these words Garrick turns sharply and at the same moment staggers back two or three paces with his knees giving way under him . . .; thus he stands rooted to the spot. . . . His whole demeanor is so expressive of terror that it made my flesh creep even before he began to speak. . . . At last he speaks, not at the beginning, but at the end of a breath, with a trembling voice: "Angels and ministers of grace defend us!" words which supply anything this scene may lack and make it one of the greatest and most terrible which will ever be played on any stage. (Lichtenberg, p. 15–16)

The emotion for which Garrick aimed is a "terror" so powerful that it made Lichtenberg's "flesh creep." It is the "most terrible" (terrifying, in contemporary idiom) scene that can possibly be played. While the Ghost who in the early 1590s shrieked "Hamlet, revenge" had already become just slightly ludicrous or a trifle campy, the new ghost, Shakespeare's Ghost, could still a century and a half after its creation "chill . . . the blood with horror" (as Samuel Johnson feelingly observed [Johnson, p. 112]). The question, then: by what means did Shakespeare transform a somewhat old-fashioned shrieking ghost into a vision as haunting and fearful as Garrick (and Burbage, presumably even more so) managed to portray?

Shakespeare's earlier forays into ghostmanship, it must be acknowledged, were not especially innovative and do not hint at the triumph he would achieve at the end of the century. In *Richard III*, George of Clarence describes his nightmare encounter with spirits. It is a detailed and leisurely narrative, gorgeous in its own terms, but nevertheless an elaboration of a technique that Shakespeare would soon overleap. Borrowing from the ancient epics, Clarence tells how the "sowre Ferry-man" helped him across the "Mellancholy Flood" where he entered "unto the Kingdome of perpetuall Night" (1.4.46–47; TLN 881–883).[3] There he confronted the ghost of Henry VI's son Edward, whose murder by the Yorkists

(Clarence himself a willing co-conspirator) Shakespeare had dramatized in the antepenultimate scene of *3 Henry VI*. Edward's ghost, as Clarence says, was

> A Shadow like an Angell, with bright hayre
> Dabbel'd in blood, and he shriek'd out alowd
> *Clarence* is come, false, fleeting, perjur'd *Clarence*,
> That stabb'd me in the field by Tewkesbury,
> Seize on him Furies, take him unto Torment.
> (1.4. 53–56; TLN 889–893)

The Vergilian setting, together with the ghost's normative and inherited properties (his bloody appearance, his high-pitched noise, his league with other spirits, and most particularly his slightly hysterical diction), offer a nice epitome of the characteristics that audiences had every reason to expect of such spirits (and, it may be supposed, of the older *Hamlet*'s ur-ghost), but it is far wide of the Ghost with whom Shakespeare would in a few years thrill his audience.

There are other noteworthy old-style ghosts in *Richard III*. In restless sleep during the night before the climactic battle at Bosworth, Richard of Gloucester finds himself stalked by an almost endless parade of wraiths. First the spirit of Prince Edward (he of the bloody bright hair), then Edward's father the pious and feckless King Henry VI, then drowned Clarence, followed by Rivers, Grey, Vaughan, Hastings, and the famous tower princes, then Richard's wife Anne, and last of all Gloucester's noble henchman Buckingham one after another arise from death to praise Richmond and to heap their curses upon Richard. Each of the ghosts in turn directs the same formulaic malediction at the usurper: "despair and die." It is a long and consequently predictable series that makes use of reiteration and ritual rather than novelty or surprise for its dramatic power. For Shakespeare, the ghosts in *Richard III* were both a precedent to be honored and a noose to be slipped. A trace of Buckingham's stylized repetitions ("Dreame on, dreame on, of bloody deeds and death;/ Fainting dispaire; dispairing yeeld thy breath" [5.3.72–73; TLN 3631–32]) survives in the later Ghost's melodramatic refrains (both "Adue, Adue, Hamlet: remember me" [1.5.91; TLN 777]) and the slightly antique "Oh horrible, Oh horrible, most horrible" [1.5.80; TLN 765]). Yet even though the Ghost in *Hamlet* utters an occasional atavistic line, his impact is far greater and he himself more immediate and engaging than his counterparts in *Richard III*, for the ghosts who haunt Gloucester are not much to be distinguished from the familiar creatures of Elizabethan convention. Shakespeare, it is clear, still had a good deal of thinking and rethinking ahead of him.

The great emancipating moment in the re-invention of the Ghost in *Hamlet* seems to have occurred, surprisingly enough, while Shakespeare was engaged in writing *Julius Caesar*—a play that, it has been well established, is very closely linked to *Hamlet* in chronology and design. How many years (or months) intervened after Shakespeare had done with *Julius Caesar* and before he turned his now-accomplished hand to his next tragedy cannot be established with certainty, but it could not have been many. *Julius Caesar* was in performance in September, 1599, when Thomas Platter heard it at the Globe, and *Hamlet* was by most reckonings composed during 1600 and 1601 and perhaps even earlier (it is possible that the great revision might have been in an early phase of composition even before Shakespeare brought *Julius Caesar* to completion)[4] However long (or short) the interval between the two works, the Roman play did not slip easefully from Shakespeare's consciousness, but continued to reverberate while he composed the Danish tragedy. Perhaps *Julius Caesar* remained in suspension in the playwright's faculties because of the very general similarity of the plots of the two plays: the assassinated Julius, the assassinated King Hamlet; the long travail of Anthony the protegé and young Hamlet the son to make amends for their "fathers'" deaths; the rivalry of Brutus and Cassius in the one play and the rivalry of Hamlet and Laertes in the other. And then there are additional links between the two plays, the oddest of which is Polonius's (or John Hemmings's) curious intimacy that he himself acted the part of Julius Caesar once, and that "*Brutus* kill'd me" (3.2.100; TLN 1959). Even more pertinent is the parallel between the brooding Hamlet and the brooding Brutus (both proper names, curiously enough, translate as "stupid"). There is a sense that the whole burden of *Hamlet* is to explore what Brutus terms the interval between "the first motion" and the "acting of a dreadfull thing" when "the state of a man . . . suffers then / The nature of an Insurrection" (2.1.63–64, 67–69; TLN 683–4; 688–690).

Just as Hamlet is visited by a wraith, so too is Brutus. But the ghost in *Julius Caesar* is unlike any whom Elizabethan playgoers had yet encountered. To create this revolutionary specter, Shakespeare rejected the long theatrical tradition that governed the ghosts who bedeviled Richard, and turned instead to a distinctly separate literary legacy. He imitated a passage in which the historian Plutarch, attempting to demonstrate that the gods were offended by Caesar's assassination, paused in his narrative to spin a truly fabulous yarn.

> Brutus . . . thought he heard a noise at his tent-door, and looking towards the light of the lamp that waxed very dim, he saw a horrible vision of a man, of a wonderful greatness and dreadful look, which at the first made him marvelously afraid. But when he saw that it did him no hurt, but stood by his bedside and said nothing; at length he asked him what he was. The image answered him: "I am thy ill angel, Brutus, and thou shalt see me by the city of Philippes." Then Brutus replied again, and said: "Well I shall see thee then." Therewithal the spirit presently vanished from him. (*Julius Caesar*, ed. Dorsen, *Appendix A*, p. 157)

This gem of a story set Shakespeare's imagination ablaze and freed him to set aside views about ghosts that had hitherto been held sacrosanct. Plutarch's spirit may have had a "dreadful look," but he is not cloaked in supernatural trappings. On the contrary, he possesses an appealing, matter-of-fact, almost ghost-next-door quality. He is not bloody, he does not shriek, he does not deal in hyperbole or injunction (no "Despair and die"), and he speaks in relaxed tones and in quotidian language. And yet, Shakespeare certainly noticed, he makes his point without recourse to the gadgetry of stage ghosts, for even the stoical Brutus was (at least at first) "marvelously afraid."

Shakespeare was clearly dazzled by the novelty of Plutarch's spirit, for while it was not his habit to re-use dialogue that he encountered in his reading, he took the unusual step of incorporating the anecdote with only minor alterations into *Julius Caesar*:

> *Brutus.*   Art thou any thing?
> Art thou some God, some Angell, or some Devill,
> That mak'st my blood cold, and my haire to stare?
> *Ghost.* Thy euil spirit *Brutus.*
> *Bru.* Why com'st thou?
> *Ghost.* To tell thee thou shalt see me at Philippi.
> *Brut.* Well: then I shall see thee againe?
> *Ghost.* I, at Philippi.
> *Brut.* Why I will see thee at Phillipi then.
> (4.3.278–86; TLN 2292–2300)

In the process of transforming Plutarch's "horrible vision" into a wraith of his own, Shakespeare learned many valuable lessons. Among the most obvious (though not the most important) was the realization that to smuggle a ghost onto the stage could be more startling than to contrive a spectacular entrance. Brutus's ghost appears silently, without drums and trumpets: in just the same way, it will be remembered, the ghost who terrified Garrick had made his entrance in advance of the moment that the actor first noticed him.

Shakespeare also appropriated some of the language he invented in *Julius Caesar* for re-use in *Hamlet*. In the Roman play, the specter (it is only in a Folio stage direction that he is identified as *"the Ghost of Caesar"*) caused Brutus's "blood [to become] cold, and [his] haire to stare." Shakespeare expanded Brutus's confession into the Ghost's brag that if he chose, he could "freeze [Hamlet's] young blood . . . / And [make] each particular haire to stand on end, / Like Quilles upon the fretfull Porpentine" (1.5.16, 19–20; TLN 701; 703–4) Brutus's "cold" transmutes into Hamlet's more frigid "freeze," and "start" reappears as "stand on end," while the homely simile about the porcupine adds a touch drawn not from supernatural but, most suitably, from natural history.

Shakespeare also took careful note of the fact that Brutus's ghost not only shuns oratory, but is in fact hesitant to speak at all: in Plutarch's story, he "stood by [Brutus's] bedside and said nothing" until Brutus "asked him what he was." In *Julius Caesar*, the specter is granted only two short sentences and a sum of twelve words. From this close-mouthedness, Shakespeare learned that it was utterly superfluous for the Ghost to produce the hitherto mandatory myth-encrusted narrative about life in the underworld. Here it should be recalled that when the ghost of Don Andrea (who is thought to be the nearest surviving cousin

to the old *Hamlet*'s ghost) launched *The Spanish Tragedy*, he embarked on a stu-
pendous monologue about existence on the other side. After he was killed, Don
Andrea's spirit proclaims to the audience, his "soule descended straight / To
passe the flowing streame of Acheron" (*Induction* 18–19); once there, the audience is informed, the "Feriman of Hell" took him to "fell Avernus' ougly waves"
(29) where after lengthy consultation the judges Minos, Acacus, and
Rhadamanth sent him on to "Pluto's Court / Through dreadfull shades of ever
glooming night" (55–56). Like an eager tourist, Don Andrea returned with tall
(but hallowed) tales of "the deepest hell . . . Where bloudie Furies shakes their
whips of steele . . . / Where usurers are choakt with melting golde" (Kyd, *Works*
64–67). It is a great set piece of a speech, an epic and spacious unfolding of classical motifs. Shakespeare might have taken the challenge and attempted to surpass Kyd—for to do so was entirely within his capabilities—but instead he chose
to follow Plutarch and to build upon the innovations that he had himself pio-
neered in *Julius Caesar*. It is therefore entirely purposeful that the Ghost in
Hamlet specifically repudiates a confirmed practice of Kyd and other
Elizabethan playwrights:

> But that I am forbid
> To tell the secrets of my Prison-House,
> I could a Tale unfold, whose lightest word
> Would harrow up thy soule, freeze thy young blood,
> Make thy two eyes like Starres, start from their Spheres,
> Thy knotted and combined locks to part,
> And each particular haire to stand on end
> Like Quilles upon the fretful Porpentine.
>   (1.5. 13–20; TLN 698–705)

The Ghost's claim that he is "forbidden" to speak is simply Shakespeare's bold
pretext (such an interdiction is nowhere else on record) to avoid the vein that Kyd
had already searched with Don Andrea and he himself had exhausted with
Clarence. The important lines might even encrypt some sort of apology to an
expectant and disappointed auditory. Shakespeare elected to bypass the recitation
and instead turned directly to the effects that the suppressed narrative would or
should provoke in Prince Hamlet (and, less explicitly, in the audience, who in the
course of the Ghost's speech are lessoned as to how their eyeballs and hairs
should react to such ghostly narratives). The playwright has created an instance
in which a species of aposiopesis—not telling the story—becomes far more chill-
ing than the tale itself. Shakespeare had learned from Plutarch that the engen-
dering of horror depends less on what is explicit than on what is implied; he followed the ancient writer because he did not want to repeat himself (or compete
with himself) and because he did not want to weary his audience with a recapit-
ulation of things familiar. It was a daring move; and it is worth noting that
Shakespeare made his next ghost more daring still, for when the murdered

Banquo takes his seat at the table he is so reluctant to speak that he utters nary a word (although he does nod and shake his gory locks).

Having profited from his encounter with Plutarch, and having experimented with a new style of spirit in *Julius Caesar*, Shakespeare then proceeded to revise and reinvent the theatrical ghost. He created the Ghost in *Hamlet* by the simple expedient of systematically overturning, one after another, almost every characteristic of which such spirits had traditionally been comprised. For example: all but one of the Elizabethan theater's ghosts who had called for revenge (Corineus in *Locrine* the exception) had stood outside of the play and had served rather as a prologue or chorus than as a participant in the action. The prologue ghost was also a feature in plays of Seneca that were easily accessible to Shakespeare both in Latin and in Thomas Newton's 1581 collection of translations called *Seneca, His Tenne Tragedies*. In *Hamlet*, the Ghost is not only very much a part of the action, but he deliberately countermines the expectation that he should appear only as prologue or epilogue or between the acts, and each of his surprising manifestations is designed to overturn such complacent assumptions. Shakespeare plays a complicated hand in the first act of *Hamlet* where the problem of getting the Ghost on the stage (as has been frequently discussed) exercises a considerable portion of the playwright's ingenuity. Just as dazzling is the Ghost's abrupt reappearance in the closet scene where Shakespeare redoubles the novelty by rendering him visible to Hamlet but invisible to Gertrude. And inasmuch as previous revenge ghosts had made it their frequent habit to reappear at the conclusion of the play to summarize and to gloat, unsuspecting audiences would have been just as defeated in their expectations by the Ghost's absence at the end of the play as by his unanticipated appearances at the beginning and in the middle. Shakespeare assuredly recognized that a final bow by the Ghost would have made *Hamlet* a far more ordinary and conventional work than he purposed. When no ghost returns to provide closure and to moralize, there can be no pious tribute to the power of the supernatural—and therefore the ending of the play remains, in structural terms, resolutely secular. Horatio's judgement that flights of angels will sing Hamlet to his rest may very well be correct, but it is an opinion that is not to be confirmed by epilogue or chorus.

Shakespeare also made an effort to reform the language of the Ghost, for previous ghosts had been not only voluble but florid. Those members of the audience whose expectations were not governed by "Hamlet, revenge," or by Don Andrea might have thought back to the ghost of Gorlois in *The Misfortunes of Arthur*, a play composed by Thomas Hughes and a consortium of young wits in the late 1580s. Here is a taste of proper ghostspeak in the decade before *Hamlet*:

> Since thus through channells blacke of *Limbo* lake,
> And deepe infernall floude of *Stygian* poole,
> The gastly *Carons* boate transported backe

> Thy ghost, from *Plutos* pittes and glowming shades,
> To former light once lost by Destnies doome: . . .
> Now (Gorlois) worke thy wish, cast here thy gaule,
> Glutte on reuenge: thy wrath abhorrs delayes.[5]

Did the ghost in the earlier *Hamlet* indulge himself with such fearsome tirades? The revised *Hamlet*'s Ghost speaks in a spacious dialect of his own, but one that is not nearly so swollen or purplish. In fact, he delivers some parts of his tale in a diction transparent enough to have jolted audiences who were raised on Gorlois and Don Andrea.

> Sleeping within mine Orchard,
> My custome alwayes in the afternoone;
> Upon my secure hower thy Uncle stole
> With iuyce of cursed Hebenon in a Violl,
> And in the Porches of mine eares did poure
> The leaperous Distilment. (1.5.59–64; TLN 744–49)

As if the rejection of rhetorical display were not a sufficient surprise, the fact that this particular Ghost stoops to mention his commonplace habit of napping daily in his own garden (rather than, say, slumbering in ghastly Charon's boat) is a revolutionary subtlety.

Another convention overthrown by Shakespeare at Plutarch's prompting is the idea that a ghost should get right to work and tell his grisly tale. Once again acting contrarily, the Ghost in *Hamlet*, like Brutus's specter, is skittish and reluctant to speak. He slips away once and again and in fact must be begged to tell his tale. And so it is at first Bernardo and Horatio, not the Ghost, who assail our ears. Despite Horatio's enthusiastic encouragement ("Speak to me . . . Speak to me . . . O speak . . . Speak of it, stay and speak" [1.1.129, 132, 135, 138; TLN 132, 135, 137, 142]), the intransigent Ghost refuses to open his mouth. Instead (and another shock) the Ghost substitutes what seems to be a portentous visual sign ("*It spreads his arms*") for the long-delayed narrative. This action has been interpreted variously and may possibly have symbolic or religious significance, but its primary effect is to provoke the audience to additional eye-rubbing and wonderment. And again, after the intervening events at the Danish court, when the Ghost returns to the stage he first "beckons," and then with "courteous action . . . wafts" (i.e. waves) Hamlet on (61–62; TLN 644, 647). These very specific gestures are not accidental or casual but are part of the strategy of subverting audiences' expectations—in this case, by substituting movement for oratory. Having dispensed with the loquacious and ready speaker, Shakespeare makes his Ghost prolong and postpone, communicate with arms and hands rather than language, and respond elusively to requests for verbal communication. Even a modern audience finds its curiosity piqued by so bashful a Ghost, but an Elizabethan audience would have been orders of magnitude more engaged and intrigued by his stubborn unghostlike silence. When, after all of this carefully contrived and elaborate preparation, the Ghost finally deigns to begin, the first words with which Shakespeare provides him are as wondrous a stroke as anything the tragedy offers: the exceedingly simple and restrained, "Marke me" (1.5.2; TLN 683). With these monosyllables, Shakespeare demonstrates utter confidence in his craft; after so much dallying, and with the audience so thoroughly wrought to bend an ear to the merest sound to which the Ghost might give voice, "Marke me" is a magnificent (and insufficiently appreciated) stroke of art. The two short words are almost comic in their superfluity; Shakespeare can indeed rest assured that both Hamlet and the audience will pay the Ghost close attention. And when this Ghost finally does tell his story, it might not be evident to moderns that compared to the contemporary norm, he is moderately laconic. The ghost of Don Andrea utters a full eighty-five lines before he yields the podium; *Hamlet*'s Ghost's lengthiest speech is fifty-six lines long (in the course of which he puts forth a full measure of essential exposition), and he produces these lines only after reiterated entreaties.

Still another effort to counter the prevailing norms of ghostly tradition is Shakespeare's attentive registering of the Ghost's quite natural physical appearance. It would appear that previous ghosts had made it their practice to advertise an otherworldly look, even if their otherness was signified only by fairly simple insignia—the "fowle sheet, or a leather pelch" satirized in *The Warning for Fair Women*,[6] perhaps, or the flour that seems to have been used to turn the actors' faces a ghastly white. Shakespeare not only shuns the opportunity to employ such distancing artifices, but he goes out of his way to make his Ghost appear to be very much of the world of everyday Denmark. It is no accident that the audience is apprised that the Ghost wears "the very Armour he had on, / When th'Ambitious Norwey combatted" (1.1.60-61; TLN 76–77)—as if he were merely completing an action left unfinished at his death.

When Hamlet cross-examines Horatio and Marcellus, each successive revelation of the Ghost's costume, habit, or complexion would have struck the audience with a force of novelty that moderns must be prompted to appreciate:

Ham.	Arm'd say you?
Both.	Arm'd, my Lord.
Ham.	From top to toe?
Both.	My Lord, from head to foote.
Ham.	Then saw you not his face?
Hor.	O yes, my Lord, he wore his Beaver up.
Ham.	What, lookt he frowningly?
Hor.	A countenance more in sorrow then in anger.
Ham.	Pale, or red?
Hor.	Nay very pale.
Ham.	And fixt his eyes upon you?
Hor.	Most constantly. (1.1.226–235; TLN 421–432)

The minute discussion of the Ghost's clothing and expressive face, while along the way exhibiting Hamlet's very natural suspicions, specifically responds to the costuming of previous ghosts, and perhaps in particular to the convention that at least some of these spirits had worn eerie masks (as seems to be the case of the apparition in the old *Hamlet*, who was distinguished by a "pale . . . vizard"). Even in the later closet scene, Shakespeare insists on differentiating his new ghost from the strangely-costumed "sheeted dead": "My father in his habite, as he lived" (TLN 2518; 3.4.135). Moreover, in both these passages and throughout, Shakespeare turned away from the use of special effects. When the chain of ghosts appeared to Richard before Bosworth, "the Lights burne blew" (TLN 3642; 5.3.184) (an allusion to the folk belief that candles dim in the presence of the supernatural). Even in *Julius Caesar*, when the evil spirit appears, the "Taper burnes . . . ill" (TLN 2288; 5.3.184). In other plays, the advent of a ghost had been announced when "little Rosen flasheth forth,/ Like smoke out of a Tabacco pipe or a boyes squib" (*Warning*, 1.1. 59–60); there is not the least glimmer of any such stuff in *Hamlet*.

Natural appearance and costuming was probably reinforced by a similarly realistic tone of voice. Pre-*Hamlet* ghosts, it would appear, seem to have spoken in a tone of voice that was a conventionalized sign of the supernatural. They scream like an oyster wife, or they come "whining . . . like a pigge halfe stickt" (*Warning* 1.1.54, 56). In *Julius Caesar* (in the first part of the play, long before the advent of the innovative spirit who appeared to Brutus), it is reported that "Ghosts did shrieke and squeale about the streets" (TLN 1011; 2.2.24)—a sentiment repeated and re-written in *Hamlet* (Q2 only) as "the sheeted dead / Did squeake and gibber in the Roman streets" (B2v). The high-pitched tones of such spirits were still on Shakespeare's mind even as late as 1611, when (in *The Winter's Tale*) the presumed ghost of Hermione disappears from Antigonus's view as "with shriekes / She melted into Ayre" (TLN 1478–79; 3.3.36–37). Audiences would have anticipated that the Ghost, if he did not squeak or gibber, would at least recite his lines in some sort of high treble. But there is not the slightest hint that the reimagined Ghost engages in such an affectation and every sign points to the fact that when Shakespeare the actor delivered the Ghost's first lines, he spoke in a standard baritone. As if the Ghost's long-awaited "Marke me" were not surprise enough, his words would have been even more startling to an audience that consciously or unconsciously awaited some sort of atonal falsetto. Altogether, the specter who had been prompted by Plutarch and realized in *Julius Caesar* liberated Shakespeare to create a ghost who was not of the prologue but of the play, who was stripped of special effects, no longer voluble or oratorical (no mythological catalogue), devoid of mask or unusual costume or of peculiar tonality. The Ghost in *Hamlet* is no longer an alien being rooted in ageless theatrical tradition; he has been reimagined as a fellow creature who just happens to be a spirit. For the Ghost, simply to be ordinary is extraordinary. The Ghost of Hamlet is no less of this world than any other character in the play, and yet he is set apart because his every word and gesture challenges the deeply-held conviction that by rights he ought to be different. Shakespeare's reimagining of the Ghost is a triumph of art that is all the more impressive for its near invisibility.

Yet Shakespeare was not satisfied merely to reinvent the Ghost's appearance and patterns of speech; he also decided to engage his audience intellectually by casting doubt on the very nature of his specter. Once again he found his inspiration in *Julius Caesar*. Brutus had asked the ghost an important question (and one that is a contribution not of Plutarch but of Shakespeare himself). "Art thou," he inquired, "some God, some Angell, or some Devill." It is an odd inquiry for a play set in antique Rome, for the concepts "angel" and "devil" are not properly germane to the world of Brutus and Cassius (Shakespeare no stickler for scholarly accuracy in such matters). Devil or angel had not been a subject of concern either in *Richard III* or in earlier Elizabethan plays. Stage ghosts had always been vaguely classical visitors of indifferent theology and indefinite origins (and the underworld from which they emerged a confounding of Hades, hell, and elysium). Nor had Shakespeare made much of the matter in *Julius Caesar*, in which the vision had neatly sidestepped the cross-examination ("thy evill Spirit *Brutus*") and by doing so set the question of his place of residence aside. Although Shakespeare did not dwell on the ghost's nature in *Julius Caesar*, he must have been struck by its grand implications and possibilities, because in *Hamlet* he returned to the subject in full force, and by doing so he introduced a dimension into the play that surely startled early audiences and has cast a deep shadow over modern criticism. When Hamlet comes face to face with the Ghost for the first time, he recalls and varies Brutus's formula of "some God, some Angell, or some Devill."

> Be thou a Spirit of health, or Goblin damn'd,
> Bring with thee ayres from Heaven, or blasts from Hell,
> Be thy intents wicked or charitable. . . .
> (1.4.40-42; TLN 625–7)

What had been merely a fleeting suggestion in *Julius Caesar* has been transformed into a major subject of consideration in *Hamlet*.

Unlike Brutus's spirit, Hamlet's Ghost directly and unequivocally answers the crucial question. He has been, he testifies,

> Doom'd for a certaine term to walke the night
> And for the day confin'd to fast in Fiers,
> Till the foule crimes done in my dayes of Nature
> Are burnt and purg'd away.
> (1.5.10-13; TLN 694–97)

And while this answer has generated some resistance among commentators, it is clear that the Ghost claims to dwell in a purgatory of the sort that adherents of the reformed religion were instructed (and perhaps believed) was a Catholic fiction. No other Elizabethan stage ghost had ever laid claim to such a habitation.[7] Yet Shakespeare's intent was not theological but theatrical: to extract the Ghost from some literary never-never land and place him where every hearer's father or grandfather might be imagined to abide. Still unsatisfied even with so stunning an innovation, Shakespeare decided to strike out in a direction of even greater challenge. So the Ghost confesses to his horrified son that at the moment of his murder he was unprepared for death and died "unhouzzled, disappointed, unnaneld" (TLN 762; 1.5.71)—that is to say, unshriven and without the benefit of the church's last rites. Once again Shakespeare has overleaped expectations, for surely no audience was in 1600 prepared to hear a theatrical ghost lament the state of his immortal soul because of his neglect of familiar rituals. The Ghost's very human claim to the ceremonial emollients that should be available to every suffering mortal completes the process that makes the Ghost simultaneously more familiar and more profound; more familiar in costume and language and other external features and at the same time a suffering fellow creature who returns from a known and definable otherworld. Shakespeare has invented a ghost with whom Hamlet, although terrified, feels genuine empathy. His very plain but heartfelt "Alas, poore Ghost" would have been ludicrous if it had been addressed to a pre-Shakespearean spirit; in this play, his "alas" is an unobtrusive but glorious measure of the playwright's achievement.

Yet even in the midst of these triumphs of theatrical expertise, Shakespeare left one brief sequence (whether a remnant or an innovation is impossible to determine) that has thoroughly boggled commentary. The "cellarage scene" in which the Ghost repeatedly urges Horatio and Marcellus to "Swear" to silence is a corner of the play that is without parallel (the disembodied voice in Marston's *Antonio's Revenge* is of an entirely different character) and stands beyond the ken of commentary. There is no satisfactory explanation for the Ghost's decline from the massive dignity of his statement of grievances in order to make flippant game with Hamlet and his companions. Why does the scene so abruptly plummet down from high seriousness to grotesquerie? It is one of those inexplicable moments in Shakespeare's work—like the clown Peter's (or the actor Will Kemp's) improvisations on "Hearts ease" and "silver sound" in *Romeo and Juliet* (;4.5.96–141; TLN 2681–2722), or the Fool's tetrameter prophesies in *King Lear* (3.2.75–95; TLN 1736–49). The Ghost in the cellarage is perhaps most closely linked to the poignant but mystifying scene in *Antony and Cleopatra* when *Musicke of the Hoboyes is under the Stage* and, it is reported, "the God *Hercules*, whom *Anthony* loved, / Now leaves him" (4.3.11 s.d., 16–17; TLN 2482, 2491–92). Criticism tends to turn away from such puzzling moments. But surely any interpretation of the Ghost in the cellarage must recognize that in making the Ghost, Shakespeare regularly aimed to defeat his audience's expectations. Revenge ghosts were not comic; if they happened to exit through a trap door, they did not wail from under the stage; nor do they demand that human mortals swear them allegiance. While the true meaning of the cellarage scene may be unrecoverable because it appeals to Elizabethan sensibilities that moderns do not share, it is obvious that once again Shakespeare aimed for the novel, the original, and the shocking. An appreciation of Shakespeare's craftsmanship and of the fact that theatricality and surprise were always the playwright's first priority should serve to temper the excesses of pneumatological, psychological, and latterly cultural criticism that the scene has provoked.

NOTES

1. Thomas Lodge, *Wits Misery* (1596), p. 56; Samuel Rowlands, *The Night Raven* (1620), *sig* D2.

2. *Hamlet* is the recipient of endless commentary and the first Ghost scene is no exception. The foundation for study of the Ghost was laid in two still-valuable articles by F. W. Moorman: "The Pre-Shakespearean Ghost" *MLR* 1 (1906), 85–95, and "Shakespeare's Ghosts" *MLR* 1 (1906), 192–201. Among latter commentary, the following have been most relevant to this study: J. Dover Wilson, *What Happens in Hamlet* (London, 1935); Eleanor Prosser, *Hamlet and Revenge* (Stanford: Stanford University Press, 1967); Charles S. Hallett and Elaine S. Hallett, *The Revenger's Madness* (Lincoln: Nebraska University Press, 1980); Roland Mushat Frye, *The Renaissance Hamlet* (Princeton: Princeton University Press, 1984); Arthur McGee, *The Elizabethan Hamlet* (New Haven: Yale University Press, 1987); Stanley Wells, "Staging Shakespeare's Ghosts," in *The Arts of Performance and Early Stuart Drama* ed. M. Biggs (Edinburgh: Edinburgh University Press, 1991); Robert S. Miola, *Shakespeare and Classical Tragedy: The Influence of Seneca* (Oxford: Clarendon, 1992).

3. Quotations from Shakespeare's plays are drawn from the facsimile of *The First Folio of Shakespeare* ed. Charlton Hinman (New York: Norton, 1968) and are identified by Hinman's through line numbering (TLN) as well as by the lineation in *William Shakespeare: The Complete Works,* ed. Alfred Harbage (Baltimore: Penguin, 1969).

4. In the matter of chronology, I follow Harold Jenkins's new Arden edition (London: Methuen, 1982): "as it has come down to us it belongs to 1601; but . . . the essential *Hamlet* . . . was being acted on the stage just possibly even before the end of 1599 and certainly in the course of 1600" (13).

5. *The Misfortunes of Arthur* ed. B. J. Corrigan (New York: Garland, 1992), Appendix A 1–5; 8–9.

6. Ed. C. D. Cannon (The Hague: Mouton, 1975), l. 55.

7. Cf. Prosser, *Hamlet and Revenge* (Stanford: Stanford University Press, 1967): "In only one instance in Elizabethan and Jacobean plays (and nowhere, so far as I have read, in popular literature) is there even a hint that a ghost may have returned from Purgatory. That play, of course, is Hamlet" (105).

WORKS CITED

Cannon, C. D., *ed. Warning for Fair Women*. The Hague: Mouton, 1975.

Kyd, Thomas. *The Works of Thomas Kyd,* ed. F. S. Boas. Oxford: Clarendon, 1901.

Mare, Margaret and W. H. Quarrell, ed. and trans. *Lichtenberg's Visits to England, as Described in His Letter and Diaries*. Oxford: Clarendon, 1938.

Prosser, Eleanor. *Hamlet and Revenge*. Stanford: Stanford University Press, 1967.

Wimsatt, W. K., ed. *Samuel Johnson on Shakespeare*. New York: Hill and Wang, 1960.

Shakespeare, William. *Julius Caesar*, ed. T. S. Dorsch. Cambridge: Harvard, 1955).

Hamlet's Neglect of Revenge

R. A. FOAKES

Hamlet has commonly been regarded as a revenge tragedy, its early impact being marked by works that capitalized on its success, like John Marston's *Antonio's Revenge* and the anonymous *Revenger's Tragedy*, possibly written by Thomas Middleton. In the twentieth century, critics from A. C. Bradley, writing in 1904, to the editors of the three editions that appeared in the 1980s, all have had much to say about Hamlet's "task" or "duty" to carry out his revenge. Hamlet could be seen as having to deal with "the predicament, quite simply, of a man in mourning for his father, whose murder he is called on to avenge" (Jenkins 126). Hence a central concern for many critics has been the question of why Hamlet delays or avoids taking his revenge on Claudius. He might be seen as pathologically disabled by his speculative intellect and sensitivity in a world of action, handicapped by weakness of character (Dover Wilson), tainted by a "fatal aestheticism" (Nevo 162), or inhibited by the inescapable condition of man (Mack); in any case, and for whatever reason, he has been regarded as a failure in his "evasion of the task imposed on him" (Dodsworth 297). All such accounts of the play have taken for granted that the play's central concern is the need for Hamlet to carry out the Ghost's demand for revenge, and his inability to act has been related to the condition of "Hamletism," a condition that seemed to define the disillusion, cynicism, or despair that marked a century in which two world wars were fought, and in which the new-media technologies of the film and television made all too familiar the horrors of Nazi gas chambers, of atomic bombs, and of the resurgence of genocide .

Yet, as John Kerrigan observes, "Hamlet never promises to revenge, only to remember"(126) [1]—that is, to remember the Ghost, and to memorize his "commandment" (1.5.102). On reflection, Hamlet reasonably resists the demand for revenge by a questionable Ghost that appears strangely in armor, and that may come from the hell symbolized by his voice from the "cellarage" under the stage. Hamlet later identifies revenge with the figure of Pyrrhus taking vengeance for the death of Achilles by "mincing" the limbs of Priam—this is the horrid image that appalls Hamlet (2.2.513–14). Indeed, revenge is not the dominant concern in *Hamlet*, as comparison with *The Revenger's Tragedy* shows. This play adapts to new uses one of the property skulls thrown about in the gravedigger scene in *Hamlet* first by displaying it as an emblem of murder and of revenge to come, and then as a means of poisoning the Duke in a kiss. From the opening moment, the action is thus determined by Vindice's cry:

> Vengeance, thou murder's quit-rent, and whereby
> Thou show'st thyself tenant to Tragedy,
> O, keep thy day, hour, minute, I beseech,
> For those thou hast determined!   (1.1.39–42)

The play looks ahead to vengeance being "paid" as a requital for murder, not only for the rape and murder of Gloriana by the Duke, but for the rape and Lucretia-like suicide of Antonio's wife, a "religious lady" (1.1.111), by the Duchess's youngest son. Most of the male characters in the play are caught up in a desire for revenge of some kind, since the law, as administered by the Duke, is corrupt, and the first act ends with a group swearing on their swords to revenge the death of Antonio's wife if "Judgment speak all in gold" (1.4.61). Vindice claims a high moral ground in his missionary zeal to "blast this villainous duke-dom vexed with sin" (5.2.6), but his long obsession with obtaining revenge contaminates him, so that he is shown taking increasing pleasure in torture and murder. He becomes morally indistinguishable from other revengers in the masque of four revengers followed by "the other masque of intended murderers" in act 5, where all look alike and could substitute for one another. The play closes on a Christian moral pattern in which all of the guilty, including Vindice and his brother Hippolito, meet with retribution finally, so that Antonio is left in charge at the end, and can cry "Just is the law above!" But the action throughout is also self-consciously theatrical, as Vindice contrives plots and stages his own scenarios and plays within the play.

In so doing, Vindice often includes the audience in his denunciations of luxury, wealth, ambition, and lust, so that the unnamed court in the play may reflect the licentiousness and corruption perceived by spectators as present at the court of James I and in Jacobean London. The opening scene looks ahead to the completion of revenges, and the action presses forward, stressing the present tense. "Now" is the most frequently occurring adverb in the play, giving a sense of urgency as well as a sense of immediate relevance to the world of the audience (McMillin 282–3):

> Now 'tis full sea abed over the world;
> There's juggling of all sides. Some that were maids
> E'en at sunset are now perhaps i' th' toll-book.
> This woman in immodest thin apparel

> Lets in her friend by water; here's a dame,
> Cunning, nails leather hinges to a door
> To avoid proclamation; now cuckolds are
> A-coining, apace, apace, apace . . . (2.2.136–43)

The play thus speaks home to a London audience through images such as that of the woman letting in her friend by water (the Thames?), and by various forms of direct address. The Italianate setting permits the audience to associate the depiction of intrigue, lust, and murder with a foreign country, but at the same time to enjoy the frisson of recognizing satirical relevances to their own city and court. As in *Hamlet*, the protagonist is something of a misogynist, for whom women may represent an ideal of virtue, as embodied in his sister, Castiza (signifying Chastity), but more commonly are seen as a source of corruption, of the wealth and sex that fascinated people then as now: "were't not for gold and women, there would be no damnation" (2.1.257).

The opening of this play, which has no ghost, is dominated by the displayed skull of a victim of murder, whereas in *Hamlet*, by contrast, the early scenes are dominated by the Ghost, and Yorick's skull, handled by Hamlet, is seen only in act 5, where it recalls the Ghost in serving as a reminder of the past, a remembrance of Hamlet's childhood. In *The Revenger's Tragedy,* most of the characters are engaged in a feverish pursuit of pleasure, sex and power,

> Banquets abroad by torchlight, music, sports,
> Bare-headed vassals that had ne'er the fortune
> To keep their own hats on, but let horns wear 'em;
> "Nine coaches waiting,—hurry, hurry, hurry!" (2.1.203–6)

When Vindice broods on his world as he contemplates the skull of Gloriana again in act 3, he questions this pursuit of luxury and pleasure, seeing the court as absurdist and the people in it as mad:

> Surely we are all mad people, and they
> Whom we think are, are not . . . (3.5.80–81)

He is right to include himself, and yet he speaks as the one rational character who is capable of reflecting on the conduct of others, and who is therefore able to manipulate them and control events. In Shakespeare's play the situation is reversed, as Hamlet himself feels estranged to the point of madness in a court that is going about its orderly business as usual. These differences relate to a more fundamental dissimilarity between the plays, for Hamlet is not in control, but rather is being watched and monitored in a court run with some efficiency by Claudius. Hamlet thinks of himself as subject to the whims of unstable Fortune, or assaulted by her "slings and arrows," which tend to disable the "discourse of reason."[2] As noted earlier, his neglect of revenge has troubled many interpreters of the play, who tend to see Hamlet as "a man with a deed to do who for the most part conspicuously fails to do it" (Jenkins 139–40, Foakes 35–40). Hence the long tradition of regarding Hamlet as irresolute, paralyzed in will, unhealthy, morbid, neurotic, a dreamer who appears a very disturbing figure in the context of Western ideologies that value men of decision and action who are ready to do their duty. It should not surprise that many actresses have taken on the role, and that Hamlet has been appropriated critically as "sensitive, intellectual, and feminine" (French 158, Foakes 24–6, Thompson and Taylor 42–50).

The idea that Hamlet fails to carry out an appointed task or duty is based on his encounter with the Ghost of his father in act 1, and our understanding of this encounter relates to the presentation of the Ghost in the opening scene. There the Ghost appears as a "warlike form," in "the very armor he had on / When he the ambitious Norway combated," according to Horatio, who speaks as if he had witnessed the battle with his own eyes. Not until near the end of the play does it emerge that the old King fought old Fortinbras thirty years previously, on the very day Hamlet was born (5.1.147), so that Horatio, his fellow-student, and presumably about the same age as Hamlet, cannot have seen old Hamlet at that time. This inconsistency is not noticed in performance, nor often in reading, and seems designed to establish an image of old Hamlet as a warrior king. Shakespeare had recently worked on *Julius Caesar*, which could have influenced his use of classical names in *Hamlet*, such as Horatio, Marcellus, Claudius, and Laertes, and also his references to Caesar and the classical deities, but this classical contextualization goes deeper. In the Quarto, Horatio recalls in this scene the apparitions that preceded the fall of Julius Caesar in "the most high and palmy state of Rome," thereby associating old Hamlet directly with ancient Rome, but these lines were omitted from the Folio, possibly cut in performance because they do not advance the action, or alternatively because they mislead by suggesting the Ghost is merely a portent of disasters to come. However, the passage shows how Shakespeare's mind was working to create a complex idea of the Ghost. He is represented as not only a sort of epic figure, at once associated with ancient history, with old battles fought against Norway, and with heroic values, but also as someone known to Horatio, and connected to a present moment when it seems that history may repeat itself in an invasion of Denmark by young Fortinbras.

The Ghost probably startled the first audience to see *Hamlet* staged by its appearance in armor—the only ghost in early modern English drama to be so costumed (Prosser 120, 255). With his "martial stalk" he seems to emerge from an ancient time when fighting was the normal way to conduct affairs, and this "portentous figure," as he is called by Barnardo, is linked by Horatio with the portents and ghosts or "sheeted dead" that squeaked and gibbered in the streets of Rome before the assassination of Julius Caesar (1.1.113–25). Yet he is also old Hamlet to the life, so that Horatio reports to Hamlet, "I think I saw him yesternight" (1.2.189), his beard grizzled "as I have seen it in his life" (1.2.240). By this time, Hamlet has already, in his "O that this too too sullied flesh would melt" soliloquy, compared his father with Hyperion the sun-god and with Hercules (1.2.140, 153), so enhancing his association with the classical world. The Ghost who interviews Hamlet late in act 1 in effect becomes the living man again, gesturing, passionate, bearded, armed, and carrying his marshal's truncheon, an actor visibly turning into Hamlet's father when he begins to speak. He carries the authority not only of a "supernatural being, King and father"(Hibbard 185), but also of the martial heroes of the classical world. But Hamlet has responded to the appearance of the Ghost with his cry,

> Angels and ministers of grace defend us!
> Be thou a spirit of health or goblin damned,
> Bring with thee airs from heaven or blasts from hell,
> Be thy intents wicked or charitable,
> Thou comest in such a questionable shape
> That I will speak to thee.   (1.4.39–44)

All those forms of authority are thus put in question in relation to a Christian pattern of values, and the Ghost is "questionable" not only as inviting question, but also as doubtful, of uncertain origin.[3] Furthermore, the Ghost's first words suggest he has come from Hell ("sulphurous and tormenting flames") or Purgatory (where his "foul crimes" are to be "burnt and purged away"),[4] and his intents appear to be wicked rather than charitable. When he addresses Hamlet directly, he speaks in the voice of a Senecan revenger, invoking classical values again in calling on Hamlet to "Revenge his foul and most unnatural murder" (1.5.25).

> *Hamlet*   Murder?
> *Ghost*   Murder most foul, as in the best it is,
>   But this most foul, strange and unnatural.
> *Hamlet*   Haste me to know't, that I, with wings
>   As swift as meditation or the thoughts of love
>   May sweep to my revenge.   (1.5.26–31)

Hamlet's immediate reaction to the Ghost's words is often taken as signifying an acceptance of a duty to revenge: "He now also has his directive, a commission that is also a mission. His reaction to the Ghost is like a religious conversion" (Edwards 39, 45). Hamlet's first response, however, is spoken in the context of the Ghost's Christian qualification of his Senecan call for revenge: in condemning murder as "most foul" at the best, he thus exhorts Hamlet to kill his murderer and at the same time denounces the idea of revenge killing (Alexander 45–46).

As the Ghost continues with his long account of Gertrude transferring her affections to Claudius, and of Claudius poisoning him, his emphasis is on the sinful nature of these events and on the horrible effects of the poison on his body. The Ghost is troubled with a moral disgust on the one hand, and a physical revulsion on the other, and the two meet in his sermonizing about Gertrude's behavior:

> So lust, though to a radiant angel linked,
> Will sate itself in a celestial bed
> And prey on garbage   (1.5.55–57)

The moral and physical disgust associated with lust and garbage is seen also in the Ghost's horror both at the appearance of his body, covered by the poison with a "loathsome crust," and at being denied the sacraments at his death. This talking Ghost becomes flesh, a living actor, in his anxiety about what happened to his body, and in his outrage at the idea that the "royal bed of Denmark" should become "[a] couch for luxury and damned incest" (1.5.83). The Ghost's moral outrage, expressed in Christian terms, echoes that expressed by Hamlet in his first soliloquy in 1.2, who, like his father, thinks of the marriage of Claudius and Gertrude as incestuous (1.2.157); the Ghost adds adultery as a further charge (1.5.41). Both also have a kind of voyeuristic horror in imagining what goes on in the "incestuous sheets" of the "royal bed."

In the Ghost's long narrative the idea of revenge becomes diluted, and almost lost, especially as he ends by telling Hamlet to leave his mother to her conscience and to heaven. His final imperative is "Remember me," and this is what catches Hamlet's attention:

> Remember thee?
> Ay, thou poor ghost, whiles memory holds a seat
> In this distracted globe. Remember thee?
> Yea, from the table of my memory
> I'll wipe away all trivial fond records,
> All saws of books, all forms, all pressures past
> That youth and observation copied there,
> And thy commandment all alone shall live
> Within the book and volume of my brain,
> Unmixed with baser matter   (1.5.95–104)

Hamlet indeed dwells above all on remembering the Ghost, and wiping away all other records he has kept in the notebook of his memory . But what does he mean by the "commandment" he wants to register there? The Ghost's imperatives have shifted from "Revenge" (25) through "bear it not" (81) and "Taint not thy mind" (85) to "Remember me" (91). The word "commandment" incorporates "command," appropriate to a figure appearing as a great warrior and wielding a marshal's truncheon, and this is how Hamlet recalls this moment later in 3.4, when he expects the Ghost, appearing for the third time, to chide him for neglecting to carry out his "dread command." In 1.5, however, "commandment" had a much more immediate sense for Shakespeare and his audience, one derived from its use in the Bible, specifically in relation to the ten commandments given by God to Moses, which were by law inscribed or hung on the walls of parish churches in England. Prominent among them is the injunction, "Thou shalt not kill,"[5] so that the term in itself contains the contradictory impulses that characterize both the Ghost and Hamlet, namely a quasi-Senecan desire for revenge, and a Christian inhibition against taking life.

In his study *Pagan Virtue*, John Casey argues that "we inherit a confused system of values; that when we think most rigorously and realistically we are 'pagans' in ethics, but that our Christian inheritance only allows a fitful sincerity about this" (Casey 225–6). He observes that our society admires qualities derived from the ancient Greeks and Romans, what he calls the "irascible" virtues, "pride and shame, a sense of the noble, a certain valuing of courage and ambition," as against compassion, meekness, pity, and love, qualities that we associate with Christ. He thinks *King Lear* shows that Shakespeare was confused, that the play "uncomfortably combines, without reconciling, 'pagan' and Christian elements" (Casey 212, 225). I think what *Hamlet* demonstrates is that Shakespeare was fully aware of the differences between these inherited sets of values and used them in establishing the character and dilemma of his protagonist. Hamlet sees his father in ideal terms, associating him with classical deities and heroes, Hyperion, Jupiter, Mercury, and Hercules. Old Hamlet is established for us in the opening scene by Horatio as a warrior who challenged old Fortinbras to single combat and killed him, and Hamlet's remarks about his father confirm this image of a hero from the past, possessing "An eye like Mars to threaten and command" (3.4.57). Old Hamlet represents martial honor, is associated with the irascible virtues, and is distanced into something of a mythical figure—doubly distanced in the past history of Denmark, and by association with the classical world.

Hamlet is represented as a student, whose training in the classics is reflected in his language, in his image of his father, and in other ways, as when he invites the players to rehearse a speech describing the death of Priam based on the *Aeneid*. For Hamlet, his father is measured against the heroes of the Trojan war. In challenging old Fortinbras, old Hamlet behaved like the heroes of the *Iliad*, making courage a prime virtue, and courting death in war: "[I]n heroic societies life is the standard of value. If someone kills you, my friend or brother, I owe you their death and when I have paid my debt to you their friend or brother owes them my death" (MacIntyre 117). In that simpler world of masculine values, revenge could be seen as a virtuous act, but this is not the world invoked in the Player's speech narrating the revenge taken for the death of his father Achilles by Pyrrhus, whose "roused vengeance" drives him to butcher the old king, "mincing" his limbs in full view of Queen Hecuba. The speech brings out the full horror of what Pyrrhus does, insuring that, in spite of the classical imagery, and the attribution of blame to Fortune, as though it is Priam's bad luck to suffer thus, the "hellish" (2.2.463) deed of the black and bloody murderer is condemned.

Hearing this speech prompts Hamlet to a tirade against himself, first for not having spoken out, like the player, and then for doing nothing but unpacking his heart with words. He does not threaten direct action against Claudius,[6] and slides from cursing into reflection; though "prompted" to revenge, as for the moment he claims, "by heaven and hell" (2.2.584), he goes on to question whether the Ghost may be "a devil" tempting him to damnation. So he shifts from a heroic stance applauding the idea of revenge to a Christian anxiety about the nature of the Ghost, and ends by deciding to try to "catch the conscience of the king," using the New Testament term that specifically signifies a consciousness of sin, and might suggest that Hamlet relates Claudius to those sinners who condemned the woman taken in adultery and were "convicted by their own conscience" (John, 8.9).

Hamlet's shift from Thyestean revenge to Christian conscience parallels the Ghost's turn away from his demand for revenge to his call to Hamlet to leave Gertrude to her conscience. The Ghost does not represent the simple heroic warrior Hamlet imagines, but a more complex figure who defines virtue not in terms of a heroic code but in relation to lust. In the *Iliad,* women are taken by the victors in battle as spoils of war, but the Christian morality that the Ghost preaches is focused on sexual relations, and he is especially outraged by thoughts of incest and adultery, as if he has in mind Christ's sermon on the mount, "whosoever looketh on a woman to lust after her hath committed adultery with her already in his heart" (Matthew 5.28). The Ghost's concern here in 1.5 in turn echoes Hamlet's thought in his first soliloquy, where he, too, is already tainted in his mind by his disgust with sullied flesh, and by his mother's marriage to Claudius. Indeed, he begins by rejecting suicide because "the Everlasting" has "fixed / His canon 'gainst self-slaughter" (1.2.131–2), apparently recalling the sixth of the ten commandments, "Thou shalt not kill." When Hamlet modulates in his "O, what a rogue and peasant slave am I" soliloquy from cursing and shouting for vengeance into worrying that the Ghost may be a devil, he again seems trapped in the conflict between the heroic ethos exemplified for him by the image he has of his father, and the Christian values the Ghost and he also share, and which are assumed as a common frame of reference by the other characters.

Hamlet takes the performance of *The Mousetrap* as causing Claudius, "frighted with false fire," to reveal his guilt when he suddenly calls for lights and leaves the stage, though it may well be, as Guildenstern reports, that Claudius is angered and frightened by something else: He has heard Hamlet identify the murderer in the play as "nephew to the king" (3.2.244),—pointing threateningly to himself as a potential murderer of his uncle. However that may be, Hamlet seems prepared to act in "the witching time of night" (3.2.358) as he goes to "speak daggers" (3.2.365) to his mother and encounters Claudius at prayer.

Claudius has just admitted to the audience his offense in a reference to the first murderer, Cain:

> It hath the primal eldest curse upon 't,
> A brother's murder. (3.3.37–38)

Inevitably, it seems, Hamlet is inhibited from carrying out a murder that would be analogous, the killing of a blood relative, now that he has the perfect opportunity. It is, of course, ironic that his chance comes when Claudius is kneeling, as if he were a silent embodiment of contrition, so that Hamlet is stymied by the thought that his uncle might go to heaven rather than to hell if he is killed while praying. Whenever Hamlet reflects upon revenge, he cannot carry it out because the very idea clashes with his awareness of biblical injunctions against taking life.

What happens when Hamlet comes into the presence of his mother in 3.4 is therefore crucial in the action of the play. He forces her to sit down, physically handling her in a way that makes her cry out, fearing he may murder her, and in response to her shout, "Help, ho!," a voice is heard from behind an arras or curtain, "What ho! Help!" Hamlet does not identify the voice, but draws his sword and stabs it through the curtain.

It is the first time he has not paused to reflect, and his act seems spontaneous. When Gertrude asks what he has done, he replies, "Nay, I know not. Is it the King?" Hamlet has worked himself up in preparation for the "bitter business" of his verbal attack on his mother, and, concentrating with all his force on the harsh things he has to say to her, he cannot bear to be interrupted. His reaction to the discovery that he has killed Polonius is callous, since all his attention is concentrated on forcing Gertrude to share his disgust with her marriage to Claudius, and persuading her to forego

> the rank sweat of an enseamed bed,
> Stewed in corruption, honeying and making love
> Over the nasty sty. (3.4.92–94)

She has risen to see what Hamlet has done, as he presumably draws the arras and reveals the body, and, bidding a quick farewell to Polonius as a "wretched, rash, intruding fool," he turns back to her, once again making her sit down and listen to him. What has he done? It is not premeditated murder, or a *crime passionel*, since his passion is directed against his mother in the scene, and he does not know whom he has stabbed. It is not an accident, though there is an accidental aspect to the deed in that stabbing blindly through an arras might merely wound rather than kill. Hamlet hopes he may have killed the King, but really has no idea who is hiding. One might argue that he transfers his anger with his mother momentarily to the figure behind the arras, or that his frustration in passing up the chance to kill Claudius at prayer causes this sudden act of violence, but there is no adequate explanation for why Hamlet behaves as he does. His killing of Polonius is best thought of as a lashing out, a spontaneous act that may in some way release pent-up feelings and frustrations associated with his uncle, his mother, Ophelia, and the general state of affairs in Denmark, but it remains in the end inexplicable. It is a primal act of violence.[7]

Hamlet continues for about 150 lines to excoriate his mother in his anxiety to persuade her not to sleep with her present husband, Claudius, and ends by pleading,

> Forgive me this my virtue;
> For in the fatness of these pursy times
> Virtue itself of vice must pardon beg . . .   (3.4.152–54)

His words, with their generalizing stress on gross physicality in the overtones of "fatness" and "pursy" or flabby recall the Ghost's confidence in generalizing about his "virtue":

> But virtue, as it never will be moved,
> Though lewdness court it in a shape of heaven,
> So lust, though to a radiant angel linked,
> Will sate itself in a celestial bed,
> And prey on garbage.   (1.5.53–57)

Like his father's, Hamlet's "virtue" is focused in his horror at her sexual behavior, and, as if to pull him back from his obsession with sex, the Ghost returns, seen only by Hamlet, to whet his "blunted purpose," and remind him of more important matters. In the first Quarto the stage direction calls for the Ghost to enter "in his night gown," not in the armor he wore in act 1, as if the actor who played in this shortened version adapted his costume to a bedchamber, and there may have been deliberate irony in so clothing the Ghost when his words are more appropriate to a warlike figure, since they serve to remind Hamlet about revenge. Since the Queen does not see the Ghost, the audience may think it is a hallucination perceived only by Hamlet, confirming his eccentric behavior, which Gertrude regards as madness and so reports to Claudius in the next scene (4.1.7). The ironies are compounded in Hamlet's speeches, which are rational except for their obsessive concern with sex, which is morally disgusting to him in a way that the killing of Polonius is not. Polonius is dismissed and then forgotten for 120 lines, after which Hamlet rewrites what he has done by appointing himself as heaven's agent of punishment:

> For this same lord,
> I do repent. But heaven hath pleased it so

> To punish me with this and this with me,
> That I must be their scourge and minister. (3.4.172–75)

Here Hamlet abandons all of his earlier wrestlings with conscience and with the biblical injunction against killing. He casually pushes responsibility away from himself with no remorse, treating the corpse with a mocking detachment as he makes his exit, lugging "the guts into the neighbor room." Has the body of Polonius, bloodied from the sword-thrust, been visible on stage throughout the scene? If so, it would serve as a reminder of the disparity between Hamlet's fixation on sex and his lack of concern about a man he has killed.

Hamlet has accused his mother of making "sweet religion" into a "rhapsody of words," or meaningless medley, which is, ironically, what he now does himself by claiming to be the instrument of providence. Gertrude tells Claudius that Hamlet weeps for what he has done (4.1.27), but the Hamlet we see again in the following scenes seems unconcerned, as he puts on his antic disposition in mockingly talking to Rosencrantz and Guildenstern and then to the King about what he has done with the body of Polonius.

After his sudden act of violence his attitude to the idea of killing and death changes rapidly, the biblical commandments are forgotten, and he openly promises that Claudius will soon follow Polonius on his way to heaven or hell (4.3.35–37). At this point Hamlet is dispatched to England, and is offstage for about five hundred lines, while the action focuses on Ophelia and Laertes. When we see him again, in the graveyard scene, he is brooding over skulls on the leveling that death brings. He links the first skull thrown up by the Gravedigger to Cain: "How the knave jowls it to the ground, as if 'twere Cain's jawbone, that did the first murder" (5.1.76–77). Whereas Claudius sees himself as Cain committing a "brother's murder," Hamlet refers only to the primal act of murder, something he repeated in killing Polonius. The scene points up his casual attitude to death since he stabbed through the arras, while also marking his acceptance of the idea of his own death and its insignificance in relation to that of Caesar or Alexander the Great. But then comes the great shock of discovering that Ophelia is dead, and he realizes that the gravediggers have been preparing for the burial of her body. This is the only death that moves him, not to a recognition that he might be to blame for her suicide, but rather to anger at the ostentatious grieving of Laertes: "the bravery of his grief did put me / Into a towering passion" (5.2.79–80).

Hamlet has no compunction about sending Rosencrantz and Guildenstern to their deaths in England ("They are not near my conscience," 5.2.58, F only), and now accepts (also in lines found only in F) the idea of killing Claudius, "is't not perfect conscience, / To quit him with this arm?" (5.2.67–68). This passage from "To quit him . . ."(5.2.68–81) may have been omitted by accident or cut in performance because it makes Hamlet's intentions too explicit, but it is revealing, especially in the use of the word "conscience" in a sense that conflicts with biblical usage, as in 1 Timothy 1.5 (Geneva text): "the end of the commandment is love out of a pure heart, and of a good conscience, and of faith unfeigned"—in biblical terms, it is not possible to kill with a good conscience.[8] After he stabs Polonius, Hamlet increasingly displays a sardonic acceptance of the idea of death, and learns to distance himself from what he has done by claiming he is an agent of providence, and that his conscience is untroubled. By openly showing his hostility to Claudius, he has insured that sooner or later they will clash as "mighty opposites" (5.2.62), and he resigns himself to providence in the knowledge that death awaits him: "If it be now, 'tis not to come. If it be not to come, it will be now" (5.2.220–22). What he has done has made him ready to accept his own death ("The readiness is all."), but still not dedicated to revenge. It is only after he has his own death wound that he turns the poisoned weapon on Claudius, not in a plotted revenge, but in a spontaneous act of retaliation.

In neglecting his revenge, Hamlet is not "stifled by remembrance" (Kerrigan 186) so much as by his inheritance of conflicting classical and Christian values. The heroic code he associates with his father urges him to action, while the Christian code that is given lip-service in Claudius's Denmark condemns revenge and inhibits him from murder most foul. A ruler, however bad, may be God's "minister" in punishing the evil subjects do, according to St. Paul, as "a revenger to execute wrath upon him that doeth evil" (Romans 13.4), and the people must accept this, "for conscience sake."[9] Hamlet is not the king, but he claims the prerogative of a ruler in the role of "scourge and minister" after killing Polonius. From this point on, he likes to associate his actions with Providence, whereas earlier he had seen himself as subject to Fortune, contrasting himself with Horatio, the embodiment of Senecan stoicism. As long as he contemplates the idea of revenge, Hamlet cannot sustain resolution, finding "conscience does make cowards of us all" (3.1.82), and it is his exploration of this issue that makes the "To be or not to be" soliloquy so central in the play.

Only in his last soliloquy, omitted from the Folio text, does he find in Fortinbras an inspiring warrior image resembling that of his father, marching off to fight a war merely for honor, who might prevent Hamlet from "thinking too precisely on the event" (4.4.41) if it were not that this encounter occurs as he is on his way to England; furthermore, this soliloquy is present only in Q2, not in the Folio or Q1, and was probably omitted in performance not only because it duplicates Hamlet's self-denunciation in his earlier soliloquy, "O what a rogue and peasant slave am I," without advancing the action, but also because the momentum of that action has already shifted toward a final showdown with Claudius consequent upon the killing of Polonius and the open hostility to the King shown by Hamlet. Another self-questioning soliloquy is unnecessary (Foakes 92–94). Fortinbras resembles old Hamlet as a warrior prince, but now he is not, as Horatio supposed in the opening scene, aiming to attack Denmark to recover lands old Hamlet fought to win, but setting off for Poland to fight for a worthless patch of ground in the name of honor.

Thus, insofar as *Hamlet* is a revenge tragedy, Laertes is the revenger figure, who, in Senecan fashion, is willing, unlike Hamlet, to reject "conscience" and "dare damnation" (4.5.133–34) to get his revenge for the death of his father, and cut Hamlet's throat in the church (4.7.126). He returns from France equipped with a deadly poison he can apply to a rapier (4.7.141), and proceeds to plot with Claudius a scenario that will insure the death of Hamlet. Laertes, of course, only finds out in 4.5 that his father has been killed, so the subplot of revenge is worked out swiftly, but in most respects Laertes from this point becomes a revenger like Vindice or Pyrrhus, and in his difference from Hamlet reveals something about the limitations of the revenge play. Revenge is a frequent motif in drama, but there are, in truth, few major revenge plays, since the basic plot offers limited possibilities of diversity. Revenge is always reactive, secondary, a response to some previous deed, and the most powerful tragedies develop from some primal act of violence.

Hamlet remains central in European and American culture as a work that continually challenges interpretation. Although commonly characterized as a revenge tragedy, a concern with the idea of revenge rarely figures in the way Hamlet has been characterized:

> The Romantics freed Hamlet the character from the play into an independent existence as a figure embodying nobility, or at least good intentions, but disabled from action by a sense of inadequacy, or a diseased consciousness capable of seeing the world as possessed by things rank and gross in nature, and hence a failure. Hamletism gained currency as a term to describe not only individuals, but the failings of intellectuals, political parties, or nations, and so *Hamlet* was restored to the public arena to characterize the condition of Germany, or Europe, or the world, or the decline of aristocracy in the face of democracy. As the idea of Hamletism prospered, so it came to affect the way the play was seen, and the most widely accepted critical readings of it have for a long time presented us with a version of Shakespeare's play reinfected, so to speak, with the virus of Hamletism, and seen in its totality as a vision of failure in modern men or even in Man himself. (Foakes 44)

Hamlet has often been extrapolated from the play as someone who reflects, hesitates, is inhibited from acting, or as one who is oppressed by a corrupt world in which action is useless. Such versions of the Prince ignore much that is in the play, but in focusing on action or inaction they are responding in some sense to a central issue in the play, which is not the matter of revenge, but rather the control or release of instinctual drives to violence. If the "How all occasions" lines are omitted, Hamlet's last major soliloquy is "To be or not to be," a question that has immediately to do not with suicide, but with action:

> Whether 'tis nobler in the mind to suffer
> The slings and arrows of outrageous fortune,

> Or to take arms against a sea of troubles,
> And by opposing end them.   (3.1.56–59)

To "take arms," like his father, would mean to kill, which was accepted as part of a heroic code, but is rejected by Christian commandments. Hamlet is trapped in the contradictions between the two codes, which make him a great exponent of the problem of violence. There is no solution; having passed up a chance to revenge himself on Claudius and worked himself into a passionate state on his way to confront his mother, he spontaneously stabs through the arras to kill Polonius. This act is a rite of passage, and makes it easy for him to send Rosencrantz and Guildenstern to their deaths, and to resign himself to his own. His initial act of violence changes his nature, so that he reconstructs himself as the agent of providence in punishing others. He needs to do so in order to live with what he has done. In exploring Hamlet's dilemma, the play probes deeply into the basic problem of human violence and the moral limits of action, and it is a misnomer to call it simply a revenge play.

NOTES

1. Neill, 251–61, finely analyzes the emotional and moral ambivalence of remembrance in the play in his treatment of Hamlet as a conventional revenger whose "dream of re-membering the violated past and destroying a tainted order is fulfilled only at the cost of repeating the violation and spreading the taint."

2. Frye, 113–21, shows how Fortune was opposed to prudence and wisdom in Shakespeare's age.

3. The first use of the word in this latter sense recorded in the *Oxford English Dictionary* dates from 1607, but Shakespeare surely had both meanings in mind here.

4. The Ghost refers to purgatory and says he was denied the last rites (1.5.77), but these Catholic associations conflict with those of the Senecan revenger, and with the suggestions of hell when the Ghost is heard like a pioneer or miner beneath the stage. Hamlet is understandably confused, but his first reaction is arguably Protestant, as limited to earth, heaven, and hell: "O all you host of heaven! O earth! What else? / And shall I couple hell?" (1.5.92–93). Hamlet has returned from Wittenberg, the most famous Protestant university, so that once he shakes off the overwhelming sense of his father's presence, he suspects the apparition may be a devil (2.2.595). The religious affiliations of the Ghost and of Hamlet have been much debated, as by Frye 14–24, by Jenkins 453–54, 457–59, by Prosser 118–42, and by McGee 13–54. I think Shakespeare chose to provide mixed signals about a Ghost that remains questionable still; the significant polarity in the play I believe is between Christian and classical, not between Catholic and Protestant attitudes and beliefs.

5. The Geneva Bible has a marginal gloss here: "But love and preserve thy brother's life."

6. The cry "Oh Vengeance!" (after 2.2.581) found only in the Folio text is thought by many to be an actor's addition, a rhetorical flourish that runs counter to the flow of the soliloquy; it is omitted from many editions, such as the Arden and the Riverside.

7. In his interesting study of the play Gurr also argued, 76–79, that the killing of Polonius is a turning point in the action.

8. The Geneva text has a marginal gloss here: "Paul sheweth that the end of God's Law is love, which cannot be without a good conscience. . . ."

9. In the Geneva text a marginal note adds: "For he is the minister of God to take vengeance on him that doth evil."

WORKS CITED

Alexander, R. N. *Poison, Play and Duel*. London: Routledge, 1971.

The Bible and Holy Scriptures, Geneva version (Geneva, 1560)

Bradley, A. C. *Shakespearean Tragedy*. London: Macmillan, 1904.

Casey, John. *Pagan Virtue: An Essay in Ethics*. Oxford: Clarendon Press, 1990.

Dodsworth, Martin. *Hamlet Closely Observed*. London: Athlone Press, 1985.

Edwards, Philip, ed. *Hamlet*. Cambridge: Cambridge University Press, 1985.

Foakes, R. A. *Hamlet versus Lear: Cultural Politics and Shakespeare's Art*. Cambridge: Cambridge University Press, 1993.

French, Marilyn. *Shakespeare's Division of Experience*. New York: Summit Books, 1981.

Frye, Roland Mushat. *The Renaissance Hamlet: Issues and Responses in 1600*. Princeton: Princeton University Press, 1984.

Gurr, Andrew. *Hamlet and the Distracted Globe*. Edinburgh: Sussex University Press, 1978.

Hibbard, G.R., ed. *Hamlet*. Oxford: Oxford University Press, 1985.

Jenkins, Harold, ed. *Hamlet*. New Arden Shakespeare. London: Methuen, 1982.

Kerrigan, John. *Revenge Tragedy*. Oxford: Oxford University Press, 1996.

McGee, Arthur. *The Elizabethan Hamlet*. New Haven: Yale University Press, 1987.

MacIntyre, Alasdair. *After Virtue: A Study in Moral Theory*. London: Duckworth; Notre Dame: Notre Dame University Press, 1981.

McMillin, Scott. "Acting and Violence in *The Revenger's Tragedy* and its Departures from *Hamlet*." *Studies in English Literature* 24 (1984), 275–91.

Mack, Maynard. "The World of *Hamlet*." *Yale Review*, New Series 47 (1951–52): 502–23.

Neill, Michael. *Issues of Death Mortality and Identity in English Renaissance Tragedy*. Oxford: Clarendon Press, 1999.

Nevo, Ruth. *Tragic Form in Shakespeare*. Princeton: Princeton University Press, 1972.

Oxford English Dictionary, 2nd. Edition (1989)

Prosser, Eleanor. *Hamlet and Revenge*. Stanford: Stanford University Press, 1967.

Thompson, Ann and Neil Taylor. *William Shakespeare: Hamlet*. Plymouth: Northcote House in Association with the British Council, 1996.

Wilson, John Dover. *What Happens in Hamlet*. Cambridge: Cambridge University Press, 1935.

The Dyer's Infected Hand: The Sonnets and the Text of *Hamlet*

PHILIP EDWARDS

Shakespeare's sonnets are bursting at the seams with thoughts about writing poems and preserving them for posterity. Can we transfer any of this to the writing of plays, and in particular *Hamlet*, and the insecure preservation of its text?[1]

Hamlet is a retrospective sort of play, building itself out of the past. It is a reworking of an older play. Within this reconstruction, there is an actor reciting a speech supposed to be taken from another old play, and this speech itself is retrospective, looking back at a story of revenge in the distant past, in ancient Troy. Hamlet himself, dedicated to "memory," is determined to keep alive in contemporary society the values and dictates of his father's times. Both in the writing of the play and in its subject matter, the idea of renewing the past is paramount.

The sonnets too make a point of interleaving past, present, and future. Published in 1609, they include poems known to exist in 1599 and apparently circulating a year or two earlier. When the speaker of the sonnets, whom I shall call the poet, imagines his poems being read in future years, he thinks of such readers handling "my papers (yellowed with their age)" and saying "This poet lies" (Sonnet 17). In 1609, Shakespeare may well have been turning over the pages of his own earlier poems, yellow with age, and ruefully commenting, "This poet lies." It now seems widely accepted that the order of the sonnets in the 1609 printing, formerly often regarded as jumbled and disconnected, has a convincing rightness about it that can hardly be accidental. A poet in his middle age is reassembling the poetry of his youth, and, no doubt with a good deal of rewriting, creates an astonishing story of love and disillusion, with a poet and a woman and a young man and a rival poet.

What is the present for the poet is the past for Shakespeare, and the future for the one is present for the other. The poet himself is deeply interested in the past, in what dead poets had to say about the circumstances in which he now finds himself. In "the chronicle of wasted time" he finds an "antique pen" creating praises which "are but prophecies / Of this our time, all you prefiguring" (Sonnet 106). This idea of successive re-creation is fundamental to Sonnet 59.

> If there be nothing new, but that which is
> Hath been before, how are our brains beguiled,
> Which, labouring for invention, bear amiss
> The second burthen of a former child!

He imagines himself finding "some antique book" dating from the earliest time when "mind at first in character was done." This is a remarkable phrase! The poet's predecessors go back to those who first put their thoughts into language. It is this insistence that each new poet is reinventing what the past has already said that gives such force to the disputed line in Sonnet 108, where "eternal love in love's fresh case" "makes antiquity for aye his page." This "page" is (as Helen Vendler argues) the page you write on, not a servant-boy (Vendler 461), and if "antiquity" partly refers to the age of the protagonists, it chiefly refers to the record of writers of the past.

It will be evident that the interleaving of past, present and future, which is fundamental to the sonnets, depends upon the preservation of thought in written form. It is this preservation that, the poet reiterates, will keep alive his picture of the young man when everything else has been subjected to the ruins of time (Sonnets 55, 65 and so on). The importance of the written form of poetry is the subject of Sonnet 23, a sonnet we shall return to.

> O let my books be then the eloquence
> And dumb presagers of my speaking breast . . . .

In Sonnet 77 the poet seems to be sending his young patron a blank notebook and encourages him to write down in it whatever "thy memory cannot contain." When in later times the patron looks at these thoughts, they will "take a new acquaintance of thy mind." Stephen Booth makes a good attempt at paraphrasing this rather awkward line; the idea is that these old thoughts will come upon him with the freshness and force of novelty (Booth 268).

It appears that the young man makes good use of the notebook, and sends it to his poet, who loses it, or at any rate, finds he hasn't it about him. He apologizes in Sonnet 122, saying that

> Thy gift, thy tables, are within my brain
> Full charactered with lasting memory . . . .

He does not therefore need the "poor retention" that writing provides for his friend's ideas; they are preserved in more vital form in his mind. The written record is indeed dismissed as a mere mechanical aid to memory: "Nor need I tallies thy dear love to score" (Sonnet 122). This depreciation of writing is an ingenious means of turning aside blame. It is a rare comic moment, and needn't be taken seriously. But (as commentators point out) it has great interest in its correspondence with Hamlet's two recording systems, the "book and volume" of his brain, from which he can delete unwanted entries, and the actual notebook, his "tables," in which he writes down new material (1.5.98–110).

Both *Hamlet* and the sonnets make in their own ways a strong point about the resurfacing of the past as an interrogation and a challenge, and about the preservation of the past, distilled in writing, which asks to be reinvented for current needs. In the sonnets the necessary next stage is foreseen, when these reinventions are taken up and surveyed in the future—for wonder or for scorn.

So the obvious question arises. In, say, 1614, when Shakespeare was fifty, was he satisfied with the shape in which he was handing on *Hamlet, Prince of Denmark* to later generations? If he was not satisfied, why was he indifferent to giving any guidance on the matter? There was in print a quarto of 1603, a much fuller quarto version of 1604–05, reprinted in 1611, and a manuscript version later to be used for the 1623 folio. There was wide variation between these versions, and there is total silence from Shakespeare on their relative authenticity. (Not that he was other than silent about his other works, but it is possible that any explanation we can give about *Hamlet* may help to explain the wider silence.)

The plea of the poet, which echoes throughout the sonnets, is: "O let me true in love but truly write!" (Sonnet 21). By and large, the magnificent poetry of the sonnets is there to demonstrate the hopelessness of the aspiration. "Truth proves thievish for a prize so dear"(Sonnet 48). I have never read a satisfactory comment on this line. Throughout the sonnet ("How careful was I when I took my way"), the poet is struggling with a recalcitrant conceit, comparing the retention of the young man's affection with locking up his treasures in a chest. In the third quatrain, he is torn between his knowledge of the straying youth and his sense that in his heart he still holds him fast.

> Thee have I not locked up in any chest,
> Save where thou art not, though I feel thou art,
> Within the gentle closure of my breast,
> From whence at pleasure thou mayst come and part.

But even this compromise is part of the self-delusion which fills so many sonnets:

> And even thence thou wilt be stol'n, I fear,
> For truth proves thievish for a prize so dear.

Truth steals his compromise from him. The exaggerated compliments and the sophistry of the ingenious conceits that fill so many of the sonnets beloved by anthologists are known to the poet to be specious, and designed by Shakespeare to be seen as specious. The poet's mission is to celebrate the "truth and beauty" of the young man; to rehearse "the perfect ceremony of love's rite" (Sonnet 23). But the early-expressed fear in Sonnet 17 that his poetry "is but as a tomb / Which hides your life" is never extinguished.

In the extraordinary charade of the Rival Poet, "the proud full sail of his great verse / Bound for the prize of all too precious you" (Sonnet 86) can hardly refer to anyone except the poet himself, who confers his own gifts on another while he himself plays the poet who, to remain true to truth, denies himself every advantage of the art he has been so zealously practicing. This strange new poet, having found that the young man "did exceed / The barren tender of a poet's debt" (Sonnet 83), falls back on the meaningless cliché that all a true admirer has to do is to "copy what in you is writ" (Sonnet 84) , using "true plain words" (Sonnet 82). Better still is silence. "I think good thoughts whilst other write good words" (Sonnet 85). The young man should respect him for his "dumb thoughts." In this role, our poet is playing Cordelia to his own Goneril.

Of course, what exercises the poet most is that having committed himself in Neo-Platonic enthusiasm to the young man as an embodiment of truth and beauty, he is faced not only with the problem of enshrining and perpetuating his qualities in verse, but also with his dawning consciousness that the young man is all too capable of falsehood, even to the extent of fornicating with the poet's own mistress. "Lascivious grace!" (Sonnet 40) His desperate uncertainty about the true nature of the young man, and about his own worth in dedicating himself to him, fuel some of the greatest of the sonnets, including Sonnet 53, which might well have been addressed to Hamlet.

> What is your substance, whereof are you made,
> That millions of strange shadows on you tend?

The concept of infection within a beautiful exterior is symbolized in "Eve's apple" in Sonnet 93. That which has, like the young man, become infected has the power of passing on infection, and, through being able to "grace impiety" (Sonnet 67), extends the range of deception. I am haunted by Sonnet 101, in which the poet, disowning his own knowledge, decides to go on writing poems in praise of his patron.

> O truant muse, what shall be thy amends
> For thy neglect of truth in beauty dyed?
> Both truth and beauty on my love depends;
> So dost thou too, and therein dignified.

Katherine Duncan-Jones says that "truth in beauty dyed" means "truth which is an integral part of the beauty it inhabits" (Duncan-Jones 312). I don't agree. I think it means just the opposite. What has seemed to be truth is in fact a substitute dyed to make it look like the real thing. Beauty thaty is so attractive to us is (in this case) a stain capable of disfiguring and disguising truth. What we adore in consenting to the union of truth and beauty is (in this case) a sham. All things foul would wear the brows of grace (*Macbeth*, 4.3.23). That beauty necessarily denotes truth is a mistake generated by affection. This is what I understand to be the poet's implication in the third line. Worse is to come. His poetry depends on his affection, and attains its dignity by being complicit with him in the task of glorifying that which he knows to be false. The truest poetry, we remember Touchstone saying, is the most feigning (*As You Like It*, 3.3.20). Many commentators have pointed out the irony in the couplet:

> Then do thy office, muse; I teach thee how
> To make him seem long hence as he shows now.

The admiring flattery of poetry will preserve and perpetuate the young man's "seeming," his "show" of virtue.

That a dye interferes with and may alter the nature of a thing should be clear from 111.

> O for my sake do you with fortune chide,
> The guilty goddess of my harmful deeds,
> That did not better for my life provide
> Than public means which public manners breeds.
> Thence comes it that my name receives a brand,
> And almost thence my nature is subdued
> To what it works in, like the dyer's hand.
> Pity me then, and wish I were renewed,
> Whilst like a willing patient I will drink
> Potions of eisel 'gainst my strong infection;
> No bitterness that I will bitter think,
> Nor double penance to correct correction.
> > Pity me then, dear friend, and I assure ye
> > Even that your pity is enough to cure me.

The image of "brand" is followed by that of "dye" and then by that of "infection" to denote the poet's feeling of debasement caused by his social situation. John Kerrigan cites Geoffrey Hill in noting that the Latin for "infect" is *inficere*, the primary meaning of which is "to stain or dye" (Kerrigan, 1986, p. 326.).

Perhaps the word "stain" is the best link between dyeing and infecting, since it applies to both, and is strongly used in the sonnets to indicate the incipient or temporary corruption of the good, with reference both to the poet and to the object of his devotion. "Suns of the world may stain when heaven's sun staineth" (Sonnet 33). In one of the "return" sonnets (Sonnet 109), the poet says he will himself "bring water for my stain," and that his patron should not think that his nature should "so preposterously be stained" that he would desert his patron for ever.

"O let me true in love but truly write !' (Sonnet 21). The great difficulty of celebrating the excellence of the young man in verse, and enshrining it for future generations to contemplate, becomes a much greater difficulty when the honesty of language (already under suspicion) is further challenged by the poet's realization that in spite of the magic of his charm his patron is far from being the paragon of virtue he thought him to be. The poet sees himself as corrupted (it is his own word; see Sonnet 35) in continuing to pay tribute to him. He acknowledges indeed that he is doubly corrupted. He serves two masters, his poetry and his patron, and the service of each demands from him conduct he despises.

The poet harps upon the lowliness of his social position, blaming fortune mostly, though the accident of birth is briefly touched on (Sonnet 91). He regards himself as an "outcast" (Sonnet 29), and in groveling self-abasement accepts that it damages his patron to admit their relationship (as in Sonnets 88 and 89). In Sonnet 111, he perceives the brand, the stain, the infection, working to alter his nature and leading him into harmful deeds, as the responsibility of fortune "that did not better for my life provide / Than public means which public manners breeds." Although syntactically manners may breed means or means breed manners, the force of this surely is that he is made to seek a living by trading in the public throng, and that this environment engenders a conduct and lifestyle which (in his starry-eyed way) he thinks would be unacceptable in the high society inhabited by his patron.

He is learning, however, or has learned, or is about to learn (I shall comment shortly on the time-scheme of the "events") that the charm of his patron's "external grace" (Sonnet 53) is like "Eve's apple" (Sonnet 93), so that, as I say, he is further staining his own conduct in continuing to write poems in his patron's praise.

There is a way out of this problem. It appears that the poet slackens in his devotion, attention and service — and then returns, in contrition and humility, asking like a prodigal son to be readmitted to favor, expressing his affection in the highest possible terms (as in Sonnets 108, 110, 116). I am not alone in thinking that the poet's eye has moved into higher regions of the Neo-Platonic scale, and that the love he is talking about has little to do with his all too human patron. If I am right, the poet is no longer worried about the moral problem of praising an unworthy aristocrat. He accepts the hypocrisy and deception as a necessary part of the poet's life (cf. *Timon of Athens*), reassuring himself that what is mendacious in a literal sense is true in an allegorical sense.

It is a question whether this descent from high-mindedness into expediency as regards the morality of the poet's activity in aristocratic society is accompanied by a similar acceptance of expediency in the public life deplored in Sonnet 111. I imagine most people feel that the poet is closely shadowing Shakespeare's own feelings in this sonnet, and that when he says that his nature is almost subdued "to what it works in" he is talking about writing for the theater. How could Shakespeare consider writing for the public theater as in any way alien to his genius? It is the essence of his plays that they were written for peformance. But it would be a brave person who could say that performance at the Globe was the exclusive and ultimate destination of all that Shakespeare wrote. It is one thing for a writer to exult in the creation of an art that demands performance and another thing to be satisfied with the performance of that art on some Wednesday afternoon at the Globe, with all the frayed edges that talent, weather, and the clock can inflict. Shakespeare's prodigious contribution to scripted drama does not limit his aspiration to the exigencies of any given performance. As a leading partner in a theatrical company he is of course devoted to the practicalities of success, but as a poet his art constantly transcended those necessary practicalities, which subdued his nature. The theater audience takes the place of the patron in the sonnets. In the sonnets, the need to flatter and please the young aristocrat distorts the truth of what the poet writes. In the plays, the immediate exigencies of the theater may have a corresponding effect.

The sonnets depict the prolonged anxiety of a poet, first that his language should match his conception, and then that his conception should match his experience. I imagine that this anxiety reflected Shakespeare's own anxiety to get things right in his dramatic writing as well as in his non-dramatic writing.

A constant in the poet's meditations is the idea of the moment of perfection.

> When I consider everything that grows
> Holds in perfection but a little moment . . . .   (Sonnet 15)

The poet has the notion that his art might be able to arrest the qualities of his patron at their moment of youthful perfection and preserve them while the subject himself inevitably declines and decays. His art itself has a perfect moment, between inadequacy and exaggeration, when that crystallization of beauty is possible. This concept of the perfect moment of art meeting the perfect moment of beauty dissolves as the poet's wrestling with words is complicated by the consciousness of his ignorance: "What is your substance, whereof are you made?" (Sonnet 53). The puppet has to learn what his master has painfully learned of the unattainable inscription of the unattainable knowledge.

Textual critics in the past followed the poet in their belief in the perfect moment, and sought to reconstruct from the shards of the printed relics of Shakespeare's plays the single text that set the seal on his efforts. We have learned that the greater the play, the less likely it is that there ever was a moment when he felt that his labors were complete, and that he could open the window and shout to the waiting actors, "Consummatum est!" There never was such a moment either with, shall we say, Wordsworth's *Prelude* or Yeats's *Countess Cathleen*.

But the acceptance of the mobile text is attended with as many problems as the acceptance of the single ideal text. The mobile text of *Hamlet*, as represented by the three different printed texts, Q1, Q2, and F, reflects changes due to quite different forces. There are changes in the text of *Hamlet*, as in that of *Lear,* that suggest Shakespeare's own hesitations and second thoughts. There are other changes that suggest his accommodation to ends different from the ends of his fiction. And there are still other changes that suggest total incomprehension of his art, made presumably by people responsible for preparing texts for the stage. Who is to judge in discriminating between these three kinds of change? Why, we are, or we shirk our responsibility as literary critics. Nevertheless, the results of these subjective decisions contradict each other in ludicrous fashion. At one extreme is John Jones, in his 1995 *Shakespeare at Work,* who seems to believe that every variant in the Folio *Hamlet* is Shakespeare's personal intervention or at least his eager assent to a suggestion from the players. And I suppose that I stand at the other extreme (Edwards 30–32). So someone has to discriminate between the judges. I have no doubt at all that Shakespeare was there on the stage in the forenoon with his sleeves rolled up trying to argue Burbage out of jumping into Ophelia's grave. But I have no doubt either that as a creator of scripted drama at this revolutionary period he had, in creating Hamlet, ideas in mind that went beyond Burbage.

One of the most impressive qualities of the sonnets is the antagonism, in mood, in tone, in language, in idea, of one poem to another. These oppositions show themselves in brutal interruptions and contradictions when a theme running through preceding sonnets is abandoned, an argument interrupted, a style transformed. I mean such sonnets as Sonnet 20, "A woman's face with nature's own hand painted"; or Sonnet 40, "Take all my loves, my love, yea take them all"; or Sonnet 67, "Ah, wherefore with infection should he live"; or Sonnet 117, "Accuse me thus, that I have scanted all"; or Sonnet 129, "Th' expense of spirit in a waste of shame," or Sonnet 146, "Poor soul, the centre of my sinful earth." All of these great sonnets are sudden, dramatic revaluations, as the poet circles and recircles the same complex relationship, surveying and resurveying it, measuring and remeasuring it. They do not advance the story, nor do they change the story. They just deepen it.

The texts of *Hamlet* reveal a measuring and a remeasuring of the old revenge story, just as the text of the sonnets measures and remeasures the old betrayal story. It is in this activity of constantly changing the perspective while the object remains the same that I find the closest link between the sonnets and *Hamlet*. The shock of each of the major soliloquies resembles the shock of the oppositional sonnets above. Each one is for us in the audience a major revaluation and reinterpretation of the situation we have been watching, a major surprise. It is not possible within the narrative of a play to contain the contradictions that are allowable within the sonnets, so in one text a major soliloquy is omitted; and in another text another major soliloquy is slotted into a quite different point in the action. The sonnets as a whole, however ordered, do not make up a single coherent interpretation and presentation of a mobile relationship. Nor does *Hamlet*, not even in the fullest text that can be assembled.

The sonnets, while all the time suggesting a narrative sequence of events, can happily deny the requirements of a beginning, a middle, and an end, and indeed can deliberately confuse a time-scheme in order to suggest the multiple possibilities existing at any time within the threefold relationship of Poet, Patron, and Woman. The staging of a revenge story such as *Hamlet* is much less hospitable to the indefiniteness that characterizes the sonnets. Yet, as I see it, in the play as in the sequence of poems, the hero is trying to find himself, and the search for a commitment is as arduous for the author as for his creature. The control and constriction requisite for the stage is then a limitation that is for the artist as much a distortion as his social position is. The great value for us in having three distinct printed versions of *Hamlet* is that they convey much better than any single version could the richness of often conflicting possibilities within the hero's situation.

We need to return to Sonnet 23.

> As an unperfect actor on the stage,
> Who with his fear is put beside his part,
> Or some fierce thing replete with too much rage,
> Whose strength's abundance weakens his own heart;
> So I for fear of trust forget to say
> The perfect ceremony of love's rite,
> And in mine own love's strength seem to decay,
> O'ercharged with burthen of mine own love's might.
> O let my books be then the eloquence
> And dumb presagers of my speaking breast,
> Who plead for love and look for recompense
> More than that tongue that more hath more expressed.
> > O learn to read what silent love hath writ.
> > To hear with eyes belongs to love's fine wit.

This sonnet might be read as an allegory on the difference between the written play-text as it leaves the dramatist's hands and the performed play; between the writing and the saying of a play. The notion that his writings are the "dumb presagers" of his speaking breast is extraordinary. John Clare said that: "Language has not the power to speak what love indites. / The Soul lies buried in the ink that writes." On the contrary, says Shakespeare's poet. The words I write seem to know in advance what the heart would wish to say. As W. R. Rodgers put it: ". . . the arriving winds of words . . . speak for me—their most astonished host" (Clare 216, Rodgers 8).

In the person of "an unperfect actor," the stage makes a hash of what the dramatist has written. To take this actor as a synecdoche for all actors seems terribly unfair. It is really a synecdoche for stage-presentation and all that it requires—including very good actors. The important point is in lines 11 and 12. Writing looks for "recompense" "more than that tongue that more hath more expressed." If I transfer this from writing of his love to his patron to writing for the stage, I take it that "recompense" is understanding, recognition of meaning, and that the spoken performance, which seems to express more than writing does, in fact offers less. "O learn to read!" the sonnet ends; learn "to hear with eyes." The written *Hamlet* is hardened into the concision and definiteness required for a spoken play. It then may expand again in the voices of those men and women whose inspired interpretation of their parts gives new life to the words on the page— fierce things displaying their "strength's abundance"! You would think that glory was recompense enough.

The reduction of the magnificent unactable amplitude of the written versions of such plays as *Hamlet* and *Lear* to stage-size must have been a task that took an enormous amount of time, Shakespeare's time as well as that of others, and presumably those others were as baffled as we are as to why he couldn't shape his work for the temporal limits of stage performance in the first place (as he later did in *The Tempest*).

> Desiring this man's art, and that man's scope,
> With what I most enjoy contented least. (Sonnet 29)

Commentators are divided on the significance of "enjoy." Does it mean simply "possess," or does it mean "take pleasure in"? I think "possess" dominates and almost drives out the pleasure. Almost! The poet writes "in these thoughts myself *almost* despising" (Sonnet 29). So he does take *some* pride in doing what he does best! And at least part of that is the collaborative honing down of the generosity of his "foul papers" into the succinctness of the stage version, of which the Folio *Macbeth* may be an example.

Who would want *Macbeth* any longer? Well, I for one. In Sonnet 11, the poet, urging his newfound patron to marry and beget an heir, and so perpetuate his unsurpassed quality, writes thus.

> As fast as thou shalt wane, so fast thou grow'st
> In one of thine, from that which thou departest.

The last clause is an enigma. In the context of what follows—"that fresh blood which youngly thou bestow'st"—the meaning would seem to be that the replica of the young man will grow from the seed that he has implanted and left behind. Here again, I can see this as allegory. The work that Shakespeare has written wanes, as the play grows from that which he has written. It is very fine, but it is not the totality that he created.

The printed texts of *Hamlet* are neither the "totality" nor the reduced play as staged. The totality is a mass of papers that Shakespeare's company would not recognize as playable; the acted play is a script that might not be saluted by Shakespeare as more than a truncation. It is temerarious to suggest that what

Shakespeare felt about his work was that it had become infected—since the unin-
fected body is purely an idea, there was no available alternative to the production
of a stage version. But the whole concept of the dyer's hand argues a rift between
aspiration and achievement, when achievement is something forced on you by
circumstance, staining your nature.

The lesson I take away from the printed texts of *Hamlet* is that if the art of
poetry is the imaginative reconstitution of the basic conflicts of life in the vocabulary of contemporary experience, then the greater the artist, the less satisfied he
or she is with any single formulation. But there is a double dissatisfaction, and
both are present in the sonnets as well. There is the dissatisfaction of the artist in
the truth of what he writes, and dissatisfaction in disseminating his work in the
form requisite to earn a living.

Given that Shakespeare did not take on the task of reconstituting in a single
text his efforts vis-à-vis the Prince of Denmark, I think the idea of reassembly on
our part is an impertinence. What rescue-operation is now possible? The
reassembly of an aspiration? We should be grateful to have (to use Ralegh's
words) "the broken monuments of his great desires." We can edit the extant texts,
making clear what each contains, what its origins are and how it differs from its
fellows, and leave it at that.

NOTE

1. This essay continues the argument of "The Performance of Shakespeare's
Sonnets," published in *The Arts of Performance in Elizabethan and Early Stuart Drama*,
ed. M.Biggs, P. Edwards, I-S. Ewbank, and E.M.Waith. (Edinburgh: Edinburgh
University Press, 1991).

WORKS CITED

Booth, Stephen, ed. *Shakespeare's sonnets*. New Haven and London: Yale University
    Press, 1977.
Clare, John. *The Poems of John Clare's Madness*, ed. Geoffrey Grigson. London:
    Routledge and Kegan Paul, 1949.
Duncan-Jones, Katherine, ed. *Shakespeare's Sonnets* (The Arden Shakespeare: Third
    Series). London: Thomas Nelson, 1997.
Edwards, Philip, ed. *Hamlet Prince of Denmark* (The New Cambridge Shakespeare).
    Cambridge: Cambridge University Press, 1985.
Jones, John. *Shakespeare at Work*. Oxford: Clarendon Press, 1995.
Kerrigan, John, ed. *The Sonnets and "A Lover's Complaint"* (The New Penguin
    Shakespeare). Harmondsworth: Penguin Books, 1986.
Rodgers, W. R. *Awake! and Other Poems*. London: Secker and Warburg, 1941.
Vendler, Helen, *The Art of Shakespeare's Sonnets*. Cambridge, Mass. and London:
    Harvard University Press, 1997.

Part II
Subsequent *Hamlet*s

"The Cause of This Defect": *Hamlet*'s Editors

PAUL WERSTINE

This essay explores an analogy between the character Hamlet and the text of *Hamlet*. By the time he makes his first entrance, Hamlet is already, according to those around him, a changed man, in both appearance and behavior. The changes in him provoke in Gertrude and, especially, in Claudius an obsession to know the cause. Mastery of the kingdom of Denmark seems to depend on this knowledge. Consequently, a large part of the play consists of interrogation and surveillance of Hamlet by Gertrude and Claudius either directly or, more often, through informants and agents like Polonius and Rosencrantz and Guildenstern.[1] Like Hamlet, *Hamlet* has evidently changed before we first get a chance to see it in print in the Quarto of 1603 (Q1), whose text, along with suffering other alterations, seems to have gone to the barber to be shortened along with Polonius's beard. And *Hamlet* has changed yet again by its second printing in the 1604–05 Quarto (Q2); this book offers a much longer version but, littered as it is with obvious errors, not a version that can be confidently identified as what *Hamlet* must first have been. Yet other changes separate the 1623 Folio text (F) from both of its predecessors. Many twentieth-century textual critics and editors have been as concerned to account for these changes in *Hamlet* as Claudius and his agents are to explain Hamlet's transformation. Since, for these scholars, editorial mastery of the play has appeared to depend on their knowledge of the origin of differences among the texts, they have striven to persuade their readers that they have achieved such knowledge. In heady rhetoric, some have even represented themselves invigilating Shakespeare in the act of writing and revising. But the analogy between Hamlet and the *Hamlet* text ought not to be pursued so far as simply to reduce these scholars to figures of a Claudius relentlessly inquisitive about changes in Hamlet's disposition. In their satisfaction at having located the causes of the defects in *Hamlet*'s early printed texts, these scholars set themselves apart both from Claudius, who never seems satisfied that he knows what has happened to Hamlet, and from most readers of the play, who continue to wonder at *Hamlet* and are never simply content with scholarly interpretation but are always finding in it meanings that are new to them. As this essay will argue, editors too may need to be more skeptical about their claims to know the origins of differences among the *Hamlet* texts.

There are other ways in which an analogy between Hamlet and the texts of *Hamlet* is necessarily less than exact. While we can never know how *Hamlet* looked in manuscript before it got into print, we do have one perspective on what Hamlet was like before he first appears in the play. Ophelia gives us a portrait of the prince before he was transformed by mourning, by the visitation of the ghost, and by what he felt to be the necessity to put on an antic disposition:

> O, what a noble mind is here o'erthrown!
> The courtier's, soldier's, scholar's, eye, tongue,
>   sword,
> Th' expectancy and rose of the fair state,
> The glass of fashion, and the mold of form,
> Th' observed of all observers, quite, quite down!
> And I, of ladies most deject and wretched,
> That sucked the honey of his musicked vows,
> Now see that noble and most sovereign reason,
> Like sweet bells jangled, out of time and harsh;
> That unmatched form and stature of blown youth
> Blasted with ecstasy. O, woe is me
> T' have seen what I have seen, see what I see!
>   (3.1.163–75)

Although, as will later be noticed, the level of Ophelia's idealization of Hamlet has been rivaled in the reception of *Hamlet* by some of its notable readers, her speech is unrivaled in the play as an expression of profound desolation at Hamlet's evident decline. And her lines are equally rare in the absence from them of any speculation about the cause of Hamlet's descent into apparent madness and in their loving concentration instead only on what has thus been lost.

Claudius shares Ophelia's absorption with Hamlet, but, unlike Ophelia, the King never privately acknowledges personal affection for his stepson. Rather, Claudius makes it clear that he tolerates Hamlet for as long as he does only for Gertrude's sake:

>   The Queen his mother
> Lives almost by his looks, and for myself
> (My virtue or my plague, be it either which),
> She is so conjunctive to my life and soul
> That, as the star moves not but in his sphere,
> I could not but by her.
>   (4.7.13–18)

When, from the perspective of the just-married Claudius and Gertrude, Hamlet misbehaves by continuing to mourn his dead father instead of joining them in celebrating their new beginning, Claudius does not waste time on sympathy but pointedly inquires as to the cause of this defect in Hamlet: "How is it that the clouds still hang on you?" (1.2.68). In response to the persistence of the new royal couple, Hamlet attempts to locate his motive in the depths of an inwardness that cannot be plumbed by interrogation:

> 'Tis not alone my inky cloak, good mother,
> Nor customary suits of solemn black,
> Nor windy suspiration of forced breath,
> No, nor the fruitful river in the eye,
> Nor the dejected havior of the visage,
> Together with all forms, moods, shapes of grief,
> That can denote me truly. These indeed "seem,"
> For they are actions that a man might play,
> But I have that within which passes show,
> These but the trappings and the suits of woe.
>
> (1.2.80–89)

Claudius, however, is undeterred by Hamlet's bid to evade scrutiny—Hamlet's citing of cloaks and suits and trappings—and tears aside the "inky cloak" to expose the unseen spiritual and intellectual state that he constructs behind it,

> to persever
> In obstinate condolement is a course
> Of impious stubbornness. 'Tis unmanly grief.
> It shows a will most incorrect to heaven,
> A heart unfortified, a mind impatient,
> An understanding simple and unschooled.
>
> (1.2.96–101)

Confident though Claudius seems to be in having detected that which "within [Hamlet] . . . passes show," the King does not rest secure in this initial speculation. Rather, he enlists into the royal service Rosencrantz and Guildenstern, "both . . . brought up with [Hamlet] / And sith so neighbored to his youth and havior" (2.2.10–12), instructing them to "glean, / Whether aught to us unknown afflicts him thus, / That, opened, lies within our remedy" (16–18). This entreaty is a frank confession of uncertainty about what may lie unknown behind Hamlet's "inky cloak," a confession that reiterates Claudius's expression of utter puzzlement earlier in the same speech:

> What it should be,
> More than his father's death, that thus hath put him
> So much from th' understanding of himself
> I cannot dream of.
>
> (7–10)

A few lines later Polonius turns up at court with the claim, which he guarantees in extravagant terms, that he has "found the very cause of Hamlet's lunacy" (51–52). In reporting Polonius's assertion to Gertrude, Claudius is careful to say "*He tells me* . . . he hath found the head and source of all your son's distemper" (57–58, italics mine). When Gertrude preempts Polonius's hypothesis with one of her own, "I doubt it is no other but the main— / His father's death and our o'erhasty marriage" (59–60)—a hypothesis that the audience at the play would readily have validated had it just heard Hamlet's first soliloquy, but not one that it would likely accept after the rest of the events of the first Act—Claudius suspends judgement: "Well, we shall sift [Polonius]" (61). Polonius attests in very strong terms to the truth of his belief that Hamlet is mad for love of Ophelia:

> Hath there been such a time (I would fain know
>   that)
> That I have positively said "'Tis so,"
> When it proved otherwise?

and

> Take this from this [perhaps indicating his head and shoulders], if this
>   be otherwise.
>
> (163–65, 167)

Yet Claudius is not swayed into credulity. Instead he seeks other opinion by asking Gertrude, "Do you think 'tis this?" and only upon finding her willing to grant at least a measure of probability to Polonius's claim is he willing, not to accept it, but to inquire "How may we try it further?" (161, 172).

While he awaits the opportunity to test Polonius's hypothesis, he does not postpone other investigation. The third act begins with Claudius and Gertrude's meticulous questioning of Rosencrantz and Guildenstern about their success in getting from Hamlet "why he puts on this confusion" (3.1.2). It is to be noted that the royal couple say nothing of Polonius's belief to their other agents. Each investigation is to proceed independently. Once he further tests Polonius's theory of Hamlet's love-madness by observing, in the company of the old man, Hamlet's abusive treatment of Ophelia, Claudius is decisive in abandoning the theory without regard to the initially persuasive evidence of the love letter from Hamlet to Ophelia that Polonius had read him. It does not matter to Claudius that he has no theory of Hamlet's behavior with which to contest the theory of love-madness; Claudius will not embrace Polonius's evidently incorrect solution only for the sake of having some explanation of Hamlet's change and therefore the delusion of mastery over Hamlet. Nor is he reduced to paralysis without a theory of the problem:

> Love? His affections do not that way tend;
> Nor what he spake, though it lacked form a little,
> Was not like madness. There's something in his soul
> O'er which his melancholy sits on brood,
> And I do doubt the hatch and the disclose
> Will be some danger; which for to prevent,
> I have in quick determination
> Thus set it down: he shall with speed to England
> For the demand of our neglected tribute.
> Haply the seas, and countries different,
> With variable objects, shall expel
> This something-settled matter in his heart,
> Whereon his brains still beating puts him thus
> From fashion of himself.
>
> (3.1.176–89)

Polonius, however, lacks the intellectual rigor of his King and refuses to give up his theory after the King has declared it exploded. Instead he argues that it ought to be preserved as a supplementary hypothesis to whatever later will be revealed to be the truth about Hamlet:

> But yet do I believe
> The origin and commencement of his grief
> Sprung from neglected love.
>
> (190–92)

In the play-within-the-play scene, Polonius is still angling to construct evidence to present the King in favor of his exploded hypothesis:

> *Queen:* Come hither, my dear Hamlet, sit by me.
> *Hamlet:* No, good mother. Here's metal more
> attractive. [Hamlet takes a place near Ophelia.]
> *Polonius:* [to the King] Oh, ho! Do you mark that?
> (3.2.115–18)

After the play-within-the-play is over, Polonius is off to Gertrude's rooms, sure that if he can keep Hamlet under observation he will come to know the secret(s) behind Hamlet's "inky cloak" and "antic disposition." He tells the King, "I'll call upon you ere you go to bed / And tell you what I know" (3.3.37–38). Once

Polonius blunders to his death behind the arras of Gertrude's chamber, Claudius recognizes that

> It had been so with us [i.e., me], had we been there.
> His liberty is full of threats to all —
> To you yourself, to us, to everyone.
>   (4.1.14–16)

Fearing the immediacy of Hamlet's threat to his life, Claudius loses interest in the reasons for Hamlet's behavior, and the play turns away from the epistemological considerations on which I have focused and turns toward the naked aggression of power politics.

But before this turn in the play's direction, its representation of the desire of Claudius, Gertrude, and Polonius to know the cause of Hamlet's transformation throws up some intriguing analogies to efforts by textual critics and editors to satisfy their desire to know the causes for the changes that the play endured on its way into print the three different times it was published in the first quarter of the seventeenth century. For most of the twentieth century, scholars wished fervently to know where they could locate Shakespeare behind the printed versions, which are so different from each other that they can hardly be imagined all to have issued only from the same mind and hand. To fulfill this wish, these scholars liked to fancy themselves in the Polonian role of the unseen observers, not of Hamlet, but of Shakespeare, dead for three centuries, but reborn to be invigilated in scholarly fantasy as he worked on his plays. A. W. Pollard imagined himself in the act of reading an early printed Shakespeare text as ushered "straight into the room in which [the play—Pollard used *Richard II*] was written and . . . [looking] over Shakespeare's shoulder as he penned it." And Shakespeare might be imagined to wear more than one inky cloak; with reference to another early printed text, Pollard wrote, "we can look over Shakespeare's shoulder, not only when he is in the first heat of inspiration, but also when he is revising" (Pollard xxi, xxvi).

Through such rhetoric as this, Pollard was initially responsible for promoting the idea, dear to many Shakespeare enthusiasts of the twentieth century, that some early printings of Shakespeare's plays must have been based directly on Shakespeare's own manuscripts. No matter how popular this idea became, however, it could never quite be fitted to the first printing of *Hamlet* in 1603 (Q1). There is space here to give only a taste of the quality of this text, namely its version of Ophelia's speech idealizing Hamlet, the modern edited text of which I have quoted above:

> *Ofe*. Great God of heuen, what a quicke change is this?
> The Courtier, Scholler, Souldier, all in him,
> All dasht and splinterd thence, O woe as me,
> To a seeme what I haue seene, see what I see.

For the dozen lines of the edited text that is based on Q2 and F, Q1 gives us a four-line speech, which, like the fuller text, begins with and ends with exclamations.[2] However, apart from being an exclamation, Q1's opening line bears little resemblance to its counterpart in the edited text, and Q1's closing exclamation contains three verbal errors in a line and a half ("as" for "is," "a" for "haue," and "seeme" for "seene"). In between, Q1's text has flattened the complex construction "The courtier's, soldier's, scholar's, eye, tongue, sword" (i.e., the courtier's eye, the scholar's tongue, the soldier's sword) into a list of just three nouns, "The Courtier, Scholler, Souldier," filling out the iambic pentameter with the equally prosaic "all in him."

Editors have been severe in their characterization of the quality of Q1's text; J. Dover Wilson called it a "strange thing 'of shreds and patches.'" (Wilson *Manuscript* 1:20) And, like Claudius inquiring of Hamlet the cause of his defect, they have wanted to know what was behind Q1—how such a text as this could possibly have come to be. At the beginning of the twentieth century, the prevailing theory of Q1's origin was its compilation from notes, perhaps in shorthand, taken down from performance by someone in the audience and later filled out by a hack poet so as to become the text printed in Q1 (Ward and Waller 5:263). Such a theory could roughly account for the correspondences noted above between Ophelia's Q1 speech and Q2/F's: these lines were based on the notes taken down, more or less accurately from performance. And the same theory could also explain the differences between Q1 and Q2/F; these were the work of the hack poet.

In the twentieth century, this two-pronged explanation has been displaced by what has come to be called the memorial-reconstruction theory. Continued editorial adherence to this latter theory eerily reproduces Polonius's commitment of the love-madness theory of Hamlet's transformation. Just as Polonius's hypothesis is supported by the love letter from Hamlet to Ophelia, so memorial reconstruction of *Hamlet* Q1 seems to be indicated by some patterns evident early in its text. Even before the end of the nineteenth century, scholars had been able to identify in the first two acts some sudden fluctuations in Q1's verbal correspondence to Q2/F that occurred in connection with the entrances or exits of particular characters.[3] For example, as long as Claudius's Danish ambassadors to Norway, Cornelius and Voltemand, are onstage in 1.2, Q1 (although missing the first two dozen lines or so of Q2's version of this scene and then marring the next few as well) maintains a high level of verbal correspondence to Q2. Yet once the ambassadors exit, Q1 quickly flies apart from Q2. Here are the Q1 lines that immediately precede and follow the ambassadors' exit in 1.2:

> and Wee heere dispatch
> Yong good *Cornelia*, and you Voltemar
> For bearers of these greetings to olde
> Norway, giuing to you no further personall power
> To businesse with the King,

Then those related articles do shew:
Farewell, and let your haste commend your dutie.
Gent. In this and all things will wee shew our dutie. [*They exit.*] [note
that exit is marked only in F]
King. Wee doubt nothing, hartily farewel:
And now *Leartes*, what's the news with you?
You said you had a sure what i'st *Leartes*?
Lea. My gratious Lord, your fauorable licence,
Now that the funerall rites are all performed,
I may haue leaue to go againe to *France*.

Here is the counterpart to this passage from Q2:

and we heere dispatch
You good *Cornelius*, and you *Valtemand*,
For bearers of this greeting to old *Norway*,
Giuing to you no further personall power
To busines with the King, more then the scope
Of these delated articles allowe:
Farwell, and let your hast commend your dutie.
Cor.Vo. In that, and all things will we showe our dutie. [*They exit.*]
*King.*We doubt it nothing, hartely farwell.
And now *Laertes* whats the newes with you?
You told vs of some sute, what ist *Laertes*?
You cannot speake of reason to the Dane
And lose your voyce; what wold'st thou begge *Laertes*?
That shall not be my offer, not thy asking,
The head is not more natiue to the hart
The hand more instrumentall to the mouth
Then is the throne of Denmarke to thy father,
What would'st thou haue *Laertes*?
Laer. My dread Lord,
Your leaue and fauour to returne to Fraunce.

Other evidence of the association of accurate reproduction of Q2 in Q1 with the
appearance onstage of actors in particular roles is to be found in 2.2, again with
Cornelius and Voltemand, as well as in 1.1, 1.2, and 1.4, in connection with the
entrances and, at the end of 1.1, the exit of Marcellus. On the basis of such evidence, H. D. Gray argued in 1915 that *Hamlet* Q1 must have been reconstructed
by the actor who played Marcellus from his memory of a performance of the full
Q2/F version of the play. According to Gray, this actor was "as dull as he was
venal" (Gray 177). Since Marcellus is nowhere to be seen after the first act, J.
Dover Wilson tried, in the style of Polonius, to save this problematic theory of
the reconstruction of the whole play by supplementing it with other speculation:
the Marcellus-actor must have doubled in several other minor parts, including
Voltemand's as well as one of the traveling players, one of the gravediggers, the

priest who is to bury Ophelia, and so on ("The Copy for 'Hamlet'" and "The 'Hamlet' Transcript"). This would explain why the Q1 text is *sometimes* so much closer to Q2/F when *some* of these parts were to be personated onstage than when they were not, as well as why Q1 *sometimes* departs so much from Q2 once the actor playing one of these parts has left the stage.

Until very recently, twentieth-century editors of *Hamlet* have embraced this theory as *the* explanation of the genesis of Q1 with an enthusiasm and conviction that match Polonius's as he arrives in the court of Claudius and Gertrude in 2.2 to announce that he has "found the very cause of Hamlet's lunacy." According to Stanley Wells and Gary Taylor, for example, the case for memorial reconstruction was proved in its initial presentation: "Gray first identified the reporter as the actor who played Marcellus; he probably doubled Voltemand and Lucianus" (Wells and Taylor 398). In the same vein, neither Philip Edwards nor Harold Jenkins sees any need to sift the theory further. Edwards writes: "It is generally thought, in view of the superiority of the text whenever he is on stage, that the actor playing Marcellus, perhaps doubling Lucianus in the play-within-the-play, was responsible for the piracy [i.e., Q1]" (Edwards 24); Jenkins's assertion of the rightness of the theory is even stronger: "once it is perceived, from the nature of their corruptions, that certain texts have been put together from memory, and hence by actors," we can know that "the principal agent in the creation of this text was an actor who had played the part of Marcellus. . . . And this must be the chief, if not necessarily the sole, reason for the progressive deterioration from the relative fidelity of the first act, with which the part of Marcellus ends, to the freely paraphrased and often highly condensed last two. But Marcellus presumably doubled other roles: . . . Lucianus . . . Voltemand . . ." (Jenkins 20).[4]

Not all Shakespeare scholars have been as credulous as the editors just quoted in accepting Gray and Wilson's theory of the genesis of *Hamlet* Q1. Some have put to the theory Claudius's question to Polonius, "How may we try it further?" [5] However, only recently have scholars appreciated that further trial of the theory leads to the conclusion that Q1 does "not that way tend." If Q1 was indeed memorially reconstructed by an actor playing Marcellus, Voltemand, Lucianus, and some other bit parts, then the quality of its reproduction of the Q2/F should vary only and always with movement of this actor on and off the stage. It doesn't—not even in the first act, where Q1, on the whole, is closer to the other texts than anywhere else. When Marcellus leaves the stage near the end of 1.2, or when he leaves again at the end of 1.4, Q1's text ought, according to the theory, begin to depart markedly from Q2/F, just as when Marcellus comes on partway through 1.5, Q1's text ought, according to the theory, to approximate Q2/F much more closely than it did before his entrance. Nothing of the sort happens; instead, Q1's correspondence to Q2/F is unaffected by these comings and goings of Marcellus. Thus the theory is invalidated. And, according to the theory, Q1's text should never suddenly swing into close correspondence with Q2/F's unless the Marcellus-actor has just entered. But in the middle of Polonius's advice to

Laertes in 1.3, with the Marcellus-actor nowhere to be found in any of his line of parts, quite suddenly Q1 snaps into nearly word-perfect reproduction of Q2/F, even though, up until this point, Q1had been going very much on its own way, leaving out Q2/F lines and often supplying those of its own. Here is the passage in Q1:

> there my blessing with thee
> And these few precepts in thy memory.
> "Be thou familiar, but by no means vulgare;
> "Those friends thou hast, and their adoptions tried,
> "Graple them to thee with a hoope of steele,
> "But do not dull the palme with entertaine,
> "Of euery new vnfleg'd courage,
> "Beware of entrance into a quarrell, but being in,
> "Beare it that the opposed may beware of thee.
> "Costly thy apparrell, as thy purse can buy.
> "But not exprest in fashion.

Here is the counterpart from Q2:

> Looke thou character, giue thy thoughts no tongue,
> Nor any vnproportion'd thought his act,
> Be thou familiar, but by no meanes vulgar,
> Those friends thou hast, and their adoption tried,
> Grapple them vnto thy soule with hoopes of steele,
> But doe not dull thy palme with entertainment
> Of each new hatcht vnfledgd courage, beware
> Of entrance to a quarrell, but being in,
> Bear't that th' opposed may beware of thee,
> Giue euery man thy eare, but fewe thy voyce,
> Take each mans censure, but reserue thy iudgement.

These passages fall into verbal alignment with each other at their third lines and fall out again after their third last lines, and Marcellus has neither come nor gone. Again the theory of memorial reconstruction is falsified by the evidence of the texts.[6]

    The falsification of the memorial-reconstruction hypothesis need not drive us to accept some other theory of the origin of Q1, such as the old shorthand-hack-poet theory or the even older early-Shakespearean-draft theory. After all, in the play, Claudius hardly feels compelled to adopt a rival theory of the cause of Hamlet's defect when, in the King's judgment, Polonius's love-madness theory fails to hold up under testing. Although it is impossible to accept the memorial reconstruction hypothesis, it is difficult not to sympathize with the early memo-rial-reconstructionists that Q1somehow originated in a "miching mallecho," i.e., a skulking misdeed. After all, our culture has idealized *Hamlet* as, in Tennyson's words, "the greatest creation in literature . . . ," or in Salvadore de Madariaga's, "one of the few great masterpieces of the European spirit" (quoted in Foakes 1–2). Anyone who ever reads Q1 is led to do so because of an interest in the play that she has already come to know in the Q2/F text, which is the object of the idealizations I have quoted and against which Q1 can appear only as a poor thing. Although some recent critics have urged us to transcend this particular historical situation and see Q1 as it was seen in 1603 (Clayton), such transcendence, whether desirable or not, seems quite impossible. Even advocates of the Q1 text such as Peter Guinness, who played the lead role in a production of it, can manage to praise it only in language that emphasizes its clumsiness and incompleteness: "all those stumbling thoughts, those half-thoughts, those unfinished sentences, those uncompleted ideas" (quoted in Clayton 124). Yet someone in 1603, who had access to a text of the play that we now revere, thought the text of Q1, even in comparison to the other and, for us, infinitely better text he knew, nonetheless worthy the labor of inscription; someone printed it, and enough people bought it to create the expectation of a market for a second edition only a year or so later.

And scholars have been every bit as anxious to discover what lies behind the "inky cloak" that is this second edition (Q2, 1604–05) as they have with Q1. While it appears that the printer of Q2 almost certainly consulted Q1 at least as typesetting was getting under way, for the title-pages and the beginning of the texts of both editions are too much alike in their formats for coincidence, nevertheless Q2 is usually considered by editors and textual critics primarily in relation to the F text of 1623. Once again, this time with Q2 and F, J. Dover Wilson showed the way for twentieth-century editors to persuade themselves that they knew the origins of *Hamlet*'s texts. Wilson was profoundly influenced by Pollard's promotion of the idea that some early printed texts of Shakespeare must have been set into type from the dramatist's own manuscripts. Just as much as Pollard, Wilson wanted to imagine that as he read these printed texts he entered into the presence of Shakespeare himself. In 1921, he wrote that "we feel confident that often nothing but a compositor stands between us and the original manuscript; we can at times even creep into the compositor's skin and catch glimpses of the manuscript through his eyes. The door of Shakespeare's workshop stands ajar" (Quiller-Couch and Wilson). Returning to this topic in 1956, he talked of how he had hoped "to push [the door] open and walk in" (Wilson "New Way" 69). Thus he began his investigation into the origins of Q2 and F with the presumption that one or the other of them cloaked in ink Shakespeare's "original manuscript." From the beginning of his research, he favored Q2: "if it can be shown that the text of 1623 [F] was printed from a manuscript which was not in Shakespeare's autograph, we thereby tend to increase the presumption in favour of direct descent for Q2" (*Manuscript* 1:20). Claudius's principle of carrying out one investigation without prejudicing another was not favored by Wilson.

Using this binary logic, Wilson set about to distance the F text as far from Shakespeare as he could. He found F to be a particularly voluminous "inky cloak," concealing within it no fewer than two different scribes, whom he called Scribe P and Scribe C. Wilson imagined that his Scribe P—"P" for prompter—had transcribed from Shakespeare's own manuscript a copy to be used in the theater to guide production of the play. Wilson anachronistically used the nineteenth-century term *prompt-book* to designate this, the first of two manuscripts that he inferred to have stood between Shakespeare and F. He called the second scribe of his creation Scribe C—"C" perhaps for careless corrupter. To this scribe's allegedly careless transcription of Scribe P's work Wilson attributed all of the errors found in F's printed text that he was unwilling to believe could have stood in the play's so-called prompt-book. Wilson's success in distancing the F text from Shakespeare by the removes of two successive transcriptions of the dramatist's own papers depends on his success in dividing between his two hypothetical scribes the features that distinguish F's text from Q2's.

Wilson creates Scribe P by identifying two principal categories of variation between F and Q2 as arising from what he regards as distinctively theatrical concerns, the unique province, he assumes, of the prompter within a theatrical company. These categories are (1) cuts from the dialogue and (2) reductions in the number of parts needing to be cast. The F text lacks over two hundred lines that are present in Q2. Cuts are scattered across the play from the first scene to the last, although they are not found in every scene and there are particularly high concentrations of them in some scenes. To indicate only the major cuts: F leaves out the speeches of Barnardo and Horatio that immediately precede the Ghost's second appearance (1.1.120–37); most of Hamlet's speech about the "vicious mole of nature" that immediately precedes the Ghost's first appearance to him (1.4.19–41); the first nine lines of Hamlet's concluding speech in 3.4, in which, speaking to his mother, he threatens retaliation against Rosencrantz and Guildenstern (225–33); all but the first nine lines of 4.4, including Hamlet's famous soliloquy "How all occasions do inform against me" (4.4.10–69); a good deal of the exchange between Claudius and Laertes in 4.7, especially lines 76–92 and 130–40; much of the exchange between Hamlet and Osric in 5.2, especially lines 119–48 and151–56; and, finally, the appearance of the Lord sent to Hamlet by Gertrude to advise him to "use some gentle entertainment to Laertes" (5.2.211–22).

But what, from the beginning, called into question Wilson's identification of F's cuts as the book-keeper's made in the course of preparing the "prompt-book" for *Hamlet* is the fact that F cuts some lines of which there are vestiges in Q1. For example, in 1.2 of Q2, Polonius informs Claudius that he has already given his paternal consent for Laertes's return to France in the following terms:

> *King*. Haue you your fathers leaue, what saies *Polonius*?
> *Polo*. Hath my Lord wroung from me my slowe leaue

> By laboursome petition, and at last
> Vpon his will I seald my hard consent,
>   I doe beseech you giue him leaue to goe.
>
>   (1.2.59–63)

In F the exchange is cut down to two verse-lines:

> *King*. Haue you your Fathers leaue. What sayes Pollonius?
> *Pol*. He hath my Lord: I do beseech you giue him leaue to go.

Yet what has been cut from F turns up after a fashion in Q1 (in which Polonius goes by the name "Corambis"):

> *King*. Haue you your fathers leaue, *Leartes*?
> *Cor*. He hath, my lord, wrung from me a forced graunt,
> And I beseech you grant your Highnesse leaue.

As has already been observed, Wilson and his followers are committed to the view that Q1 has been memorially reconstructed by an actor from performance. Thus, for them, there can be no lines in Q1 that were not delivered on stage and that were not therefore in the "prompt-book." If Q1 and F are both witnesses to a "prompt-book" and if Q1 and F differ from each other, then there may have been more than one prompt-book. However, Wilson cannot admit this possibility. If there could have been more than one prompt-book, then Wilson's demonstration that behind F lay a prompt-book would not preclude there being another prompt-book behind Q2. But Wilson's attempt to show that F derives from a transcription of a prompt-book is an effort to eliminate the possibility that a prompt-book lies behind Q2, which then, for him, may be said to be based on Shakespeare's own manuscript. Thus Wilson has to conclude that some cuts from F, like the one detailed just above, cannot have been made by the book-keeper, but must have occurred by accident. The explanatory power of Wilson's argument that F is based in some way on the "prompt-book" is thus compromised from the beginning.

Besides cuts to dialogue, Wilson also attributes to the hand of his Scribe P another feature that distinguishes F from Q2. F eliminates roles found in Q2. A number of these are supernumeraries. For example, 4.2 begins in Q2 with the stage direction "*Enter Hamlet, Rosencraus, and others*," even though the scene can be played with only one other actor besides Hamlet and "Rosencraus," namely Guildenstern. In F, only the three absolutely necessary parts are specified in the opening stage directions. Again, 4.3 opens in Q2 with the stage direction "*Enter King, and two or three*." F cuts Q2's "two or three"—an unfortunate cut because it turns the first speech in the scene, which is a public speech of self-justification by Claudius, into a soliloquy. Sometimes F takes away a Q2 speaking part. In 4.5, for instance, F cuts the role of the Gentleman, and redistributes the scene's dialogue between the remaining speakers, the Queen and Horatio; the Gentleman's lines go to Horatio, and Horatio's lines go to the Queen. These are only a few of the alterations in Q2 roles made in F.

There are still other ways in which F differs from Q2 that Wilson was unwilling to lay to a book-keeper's responsibility. As Wilson correctly observed, there are errors in F's dialogue that are not typical of the work of F's typesetters as we can observe it in the thirty-five other plays besides *Hamlet* that make up the 1623 Shakespeare First Folio. The F text of *Hamlet* is marred by a significantly greater number of careless repetitions than is usual. Where Q2 reads "My newes shall be the fruite to that great feast," F has "My Newes shall be the Newes to that great Feast" (2.2.55). Later, where Q2 prints "That spirit vpon whose weale depends and rests / The liues of many," F again blunders into "That Spirit, vpon whose spirit depends . . ." (3.3.15–16). Yet again for Q2's lines "Come, come, you answere with an idle tongue" and "Goe, goe, you question with a wicked tongue," F repeats "idle tongue" for "wicked tongue" (3.4.14–15). Beyond such simple repetitions, F also provides a large number of ridiculous variants from Q2. There is space for only a pair of examples. Hamlet's Q2 reference to "the proude mans contumely [i.e., contemptuousness]" becomes in F "the poore mans Contumely" (3.1.79), and Hamlet's joking greeting to one of the players, "Why thy face is valanc [i.e., bearded] since I saw thee last, com'st thou to beard me in Denmark?" is spoiled in F by the substitution of "valiant" for "valanct" (2.2.447–8). Wilson cannot believe that the standards of transcription among book-keepers in the theatrical industry of Shakespeare's time was so low as to tolerate such carelessness, and so he postulates that his Scribe P's "prompt-book" was transcribed by his Scribe C to become the printer's copy for F (Wilson *Manuscript* 1:22–87).

Having established to his satisfaction that F was based on such a scribal transcript and not therefore on Shakespeare's own manuscript, Wilson presumed that Shakespeare's manuscript lies instead immediately behind Q2. A major difficulty in the way of such a presumption is Q2's failure to print about eighty-five apparently authentic lines that are found in F. Among the major cuts from Q2 are two sizable passages from the conversation between Hamlet and Rosencrantz and Guildenstern in 2.2—the passage in which Hamlet compares Denmark to a prison (258–89) and the one in which he learns of the rise of the children's acting companies (360–85); and an important exchange between Hamlet and Horatio in 5.2, in which Hamlet both resolves that he is justified in killing Claudius and in which he decides for himself to court Laertes's favors (77–91). As has been noted, such cuts as these are, for Wilson, one of the two distinctive characteristics of "prompt-book" origin of an early printed text. In order to avoid the conclusion that Q2 is based on a "prompt-book," Wilson has to charge Q2's omissions, large and small, to the carelessness of the man he identifies as the lone compositor who set Q2 into type in James Roberts's printing house in 1604, even though there is no evidence that Roberts's compositors, or any others, habitually committed such massive and grave errors as to omit the three long passages just listed, as well as several shorter ones.

In order to explain the other distinctive feature of Q2, however, Wilson has to characterize Roberts's typesetter as anything but the careless man responsible for the omissions. This other feature of Q2 is a rash of patently absurd readings, a feature too, as has already been noted, of F's text. According to Wilson the F errors originated with Scribe C. Yet, by Wilson's account, the errors in Q2 were not even in the printer's copy for that book, but instead were introduced by the compositor because the handwriting of his printer's copy was, at the stage of his career he had reached by 1604, particularly challenging for him: "a learner or a young journeyman . . . who cannot work quickly because he has not mastered his craft," he was a scrupulously careful "plodder reproducing his copy letter by letter" (Wilson *Manuscript* 1:100). As a result of this alleged method of typesetting, he produced utter nonsense if he misread one letter for another. So at 1.2.80 he has Hamlet address Gertrude as "coold mother," rather than "good Mother," as in F (1.2.80); and he has Polonius contrast "madness" with "reason and sanctity," rather than with "Reason and sanitie," F's reading (2.2.228–29). Among a host of further possible examples of Wilson's compositor's allegedly careful but incompetent plodding, we might note that he puts "blacke verse" for "blanke Verse," turns "innocculate" into the nonsense word "euocutat," and makes Hamlet's memorable F line "this is hyre and Sallery, not Reuenge" into "this is base and silly, not reuendge" (2.2.349, 3.1.128, and 3.3.84). Wilson is driven toward such a contradictory representation of his Q2 compositor because, in accounting for corruption in Q2's text, Wilson cannot afford to admit into his narrative any other agent but the compositor if Q2 is to have been set directly from an authorial manuscript (Wilson *Manuscript* 88–121). Wilson's story of Q2 was dealt a severe blow in 1955, when John Russell Brown demonstrated that not one but two different compositors worked on Q2 and that their work was divided so that each of them set into type a heap of obvious errors and each was responsible for parts of the text from which F lines were omitted. Now, in order to conserve Wilson's conclusion that copy for Q2 was Shakespeare's own manuscript, one had to believe that two different workmen were each grossly negligent in leaving out lines and, at the same time, hopelessly incompetent at making out words in their copy.

In spite of the incoherence of Wilson's identification of the printer's copy for Q2 and F, his analysis has been widely accepted. It has constituted the foundation not only for Harold Jenkins's conservative edition of the play (Jenkins 37–64), but also for innovative editions by Philip Edwards (Edwards 31), by Stanley Wells and Gary Taylor (Wells and Taylor 401), and by George Hibbard (89–130) that, in their various ways, assume Shakespeare's revision of the Q2 version to become the F version. All of these editors are in agreement that Q2 derives immediately from Shakespeare's own manuscript and that F is based on successive transcriptions of that manuscript.[7] Their hypothesis of Shakespearean revision has the advantage of resolving some of the contradictions in Wilson's narrative, especially in his characterization of the Q2 typesetter(s). If Shakespeare revised the play, then after Q2 was printed he could have added to its text those passages that are unique to F. In that case, it would no longer be necessary to hold the Q2 compositors responsible for omitting them. Although revision cannot be ruled out as an hypothesis, it nevertheless raises at least as large a problem as it resolves. No one has been successful in discovering a purpose for such a revision. The differences between the Q2 and F texts are so many and various, involving not only passages and lines but also hundreds of individual words and phrases, that they defy attempts to impose on them an intelligible pattern that can absorb any significant number of them. Nonetheless, alone among the revisionists, Hibbard pushed the revision hypothesis to the extreme of attributing transcription of F's printer's copy, like Q2's, to Shakespeare himself. Shakespeare himself would then have been responsible for the ridiculous repetitions and errors as well as the many cuts that pock that text. In this improbable account, all other agents who are documented to have participated in the transmission of texts into print—actors, book-keepers, scribes, censors—disappear behind the author.

It seems past time that Claudius's question to Polonius be put to Wilson's influential account of the genesis of the Q2 and F texts: "How may we try it further?" The test is a comparison of Wilson's assumptions against the evidence of extant dramatic manuscripts from the period. Wilson assumed that at some remove behind the F text must lie a book-keeper's inscription of a "promptbook" because he believed that only a book-keeper would cut roles and dialogue. There do exist dramatic manuscripts annotated by book-keepers in which both dialogue and roles are cut. Yet there also exist other dramatic manuscripts that are marked up with marginal brackets to indicate cuts and that contain no other indications of theatrical use, such as the marginal book-keepers' annotations typical of theatrical manuscripts. An extreme case of a non-theatrical manuscript marked up with cuts to both roles and text is to be found in the splendid transcription of *The Country Captain,* a play by William Cavendish, earl of Newcastle. Originally designed as a presentation copy, this manuscript is inscribed in the beautiful semi-calligraphic hand of the anonymous scribe who also made a similarly lavish copy of James Shirley's play *The Court Secret.* While there is nothing in this manuscript to suggest any association with a playhouse or a book-keeper, nonetheless the scribe has cut roles from some of the stage directions, stroking through the designations of the roles and then emphasizing his deletions with cross-hatching over the initial strokes. Thus, for example, he cut the "and his man" from the stage direction at line 189, "Enter Mounsir Device and his man," and he did the same to a "page" at line 648 when he changed "Enter Engine and his page" to "Enter Device." The manuscript also contains marginal brackets indicating dialogue cuts; these the Malone Society editors attribute to Newcastle himself on the grounds of the similarity in ink between the brackets and corrections made by Newcastle to dialogue. While it is impossible to be sure about this attribution, nonetheless there is nothing to suggest a book-keeper's hand in this manuscript—or in some others, like *The Parliament of Love*, that have been cut. Thus Wilson's presumption that cuts in the F text of *Hamlet* necessarily indicate the agency of a book-keeper in its provenance cannot stand. There is no need to allow for two successive transcriptions of the text behind F; there is the possibility that there may have been only one.

Since 1934, when Wilson published his investigation of *Hamlet*, the handwriting of another extant dramatic manuscript, John Fletcher's *Bonduca*, has been identified as that of Edward Knight, book-keeper of Shakespeare's acting company the King's Men from 1624, if not earlier.[8] This identification allows us to examine a transcription of a play by a book-keeper and thereby to test Wilson's assumption that such a figure would be faithful to a dramatist's text when copying it. The assumption fails. For example, Knight introduces into his transcript of *Bonduca* a species of repetition that, when found in the F text of *Hamlet*, became one of the motives for Wilson's creation of Scribe C, as distinct from his book-keeper, Scribe P. We can detect Knight's repetitions and his other errors by comparing his text to the one printed in the 1647 Beaumont and Fletcher First Folio. At 1.2.65, for example, in the Folio line "Your lays, and outleaps *Junius*, haunts, and dodges," Knight carelessly alters "out-leaps" to "out leys," picking up his substitution from "lays" earlier in the line. Again, at 4.2.76–78, where the Folio reads "For by the vertue of your charging-staff, / And a strange fighting face I put vpon't, / I haue outbrau'd hunger," Knight repeats the form of the first line in the second line, changing it to begin "and by a stronge." Other readings introduced by Knight are every bit as ridiculous as the worst to be found in both Q2 and F *Hamlet*. At 2.1.28, for the Folio's "fierce Britain Swains," Knight substitutes "Swanns." When in the Folio Bonduca's daughters threaten to kill some Romans they have captured, the threat takes this form: "Do ye see these arrows? / Wee'll send 'em to your wanton livers, goats" (3.5.46–47). Knight writes "to waite on your louers" for "to your wanton liuers." In light of the actual standards of transcription achieved by a book-keeper in the role of a scribe in the seventeenth century, it is every bit as likely that the printers of both Q2 and F were separated from Shakespeare's own papers by scribes as it is that the two different compositors of Q2 each introduced into it a host of errors.

Wilson's claims to have come to know what is behind the inky cloaks of *Hamlet*'s early printings do not deserve the long acceptance that they have enjoyed among editors. Recently, both textual critics and editors have come to realize that they neither can know nor need to know what kind of manuscripts served as printer's copy for the earliest printings of Shakespeare's plays. These recent editors too may thus reproduce in another way the story that is *Hamlet*. After all, as that story turned out, it really did not matter to Polonius or to

Claudius if they figured out the cause of Hamlet's transformation; all that mattered was not getting stabbed.

NOTES

1. This particular "take" on *Hamlet* is indebted to Neill. All references to *Hamlet* not drawn directly from the early printed texts are to Mowat and Werstine's edition.

2. Early modern texts often use the question mark where modern printers would use the exclamation mark.

3. Bracy notes that in 1880–81, W. H. Widgery suggested that Q1 *Hamlet* was a memorial reconstruction by the actor playing Voltemand and the Player King, supplemented by shorthand notes taken down by reporters in the audience, and R. Grant White that Q1 was a memorial reconstruction by the actor playing Voltemand (35–36).

4. George Hibbard, in his Oxford Shakespeare *Hamlet,* also subscribed to the theory of memorial reconstruction (67–89).

5. Among those who have noted difficulties with the theory are E. K. Chambers (Chambers 1: 416), Alfred Hart (Hart 348–49) and J. M. Nosworthy.

6. For a much more detailed falsification of the theory, see Laurie Maguire; also see my "A Century of 'Bad' Shakespeare Quartos."

7. Edwards departs from Wilson only in one minor respect, by converting Wilson's "prompt-book" into a book-keeper's transcription intermediate between Shakespeare's manuscript and a prompt-book.

8. Knight's hand was first identified by J. Gerritsen in 1952. Knight's name heads the King's Men's livery list of December 27, 1624. He may have belonged to the company since as far back as 1620, since the last comparable list before the livery list dates from December 20, 1619 (Bentley 1:14–16). Knight, although a book-keeper, is not apparently transcribing *Bonduca* for use in the theater, but for a private patron.

WORKS CITED

Bentley, G. E. *The Jacobean and Caroline Stage* . 7 vols. Oxford: Clarendon Press, 1941–68.

Bonduca, ed. Cyrus Hoy. *The Dramatic Works in the Beaumont and Fletcher Canon.* Gen. ed. Fredson Bowers. Cambridge: Cambridge University Press, 1979. 4:151–259.

Bracy, William. *The Merry Wives of Windsor: The History and Transmission of Shakespeare's Text.* Columbia, Missouri: Curators of the University of Missouri, 1952.

Brown, John Russell. "The Compositors of *Hamlet* Q2 and *The Merchant of Venice.*" *Studies in Bibliography* 7 (1955): 17–40.

Chambers, E. K. *William Shakespeare: A Study of Facts and Problems.* 2 vols. Oxford: Clarendon Press, 1930.

Clayton, Thomas, ed. *The Hamlet First Published (Q1, 1603): Origins, Form, Intertextualities.* Newark: University of Delaware Press, 1992.

The Country Captain by William Cavendish, Earl of Newcastle. Ed. Anthony Johnson and H. R. Woudhuysen. Malone Society Reprints. London: Malone Society, 1999.

Edwards, Philip, ed. *Hamlet, Prince of Denmark.* New Cambridge Shakespeare. Cambridge: Cambridge University Press, 1985.

Foakes, R. A. *Hamlet versus Lear: Cultural Politics and Shakespeare's Art*. Cambridge: Cambridge University Press, 1993.

Gerritsen, J., ed. *The Honest Man's Fortune: A Critical Edition of MS Dyce 9 (1625)*.Groningen: Wolters, 1952.

Gray, H. D. "The First Quarto 'Hamlet'." *Modern Language Review* 10 (1915): 171–80.

Hart, Alfred. *Stolne and Surreptitious Copies: A Comparative Study of Shakespeare's Bad Quartos*. Melbourne: Melbourne University Press, 1942.

Hibbard, G.R., ed. *Hamlet*. The Oxford Shakespeare. Oxford: Oxford University press, 1987.

Jenkins, Harold, ed. *Hamlet*. The Arden Shakespeare. London: Methuen, 1982.

Maguire, Laurie. *Shakespearean Suspect Texts: The 'Bad' Quartos and Their Contexts*. Cambridge: Cambridge University Press, 1996.

Mowat, Barbara A. and Paul Werstine, eds. *Hamlet*. New Folger Library Shakespeare. New York: Washington Square Press, 1992.

Neill, Michael. "*Hamlet*: A Modern Perspective." Ed. Mowat and Werstine. 307–26.

Nosworthy, J. M. "*Hamlet* and the player who could not keep counsel." *Shakespeare Survey* 3 (1950): 74–82.

The Parliament of Love. Ed. K. M. Lea. Malone Society Reprints. London: Malone Society, 1928.

Pollard, A. W. *Shakespeare's Fight with the Pirates and the Problems of the Transmission of his Text*. 2ⁿᵈ ed. rev. Cambridge: Cambridge University Press, 1920.

Quiller-Couch, Sir Arthur and John Dover Wilson, eds. *The Tempest*. Cambridge: Cambridge University Press, 1921.

Ward, A. W. and A. R. Waller, eds. *Cambridge History of English Literature*. Cambridge: Cambridge University Press, 1918.

Wells, Stanley and Gary Taylor. *William Shakespeare: A Textual Companion*. Oxford: Clarendon Press, 1987.

Werstine, Paul. "A Century of 'Bad' Shakespeare Quartos." *Shakespeare Quarterly* 50 (1999): 310–33.

Wilson, John Dover. "The Copy for 'Hamlet,' 1603," and "The 'Hamlet' Transcript, 1593." *The Library* 3rd ser. 9 (1918): 153–85, 217–47.

———. The Manuscript of Shakespeare's *Hamlet* and the Problems of its Transmission. 2 vols. Cambridge: Cambridge University Press, 1934.

———. "The New Way with Shakespeare's Texts: An Introduction for Lay Readers III. In Sight of Shakespeare's Manuscripts." *Shakespeare Survey* 9 (1956): 69–80.

Figure 1. John Massey Wright, Hamlet, *Act 5*. From the RSC Collection with the permission of the Governors of the Royal Shakespeare Theatre.

"Was Hamlet a Man or a Woman?": The Prince in the Graveyard, 1800–1920

CATHERINE BELSEY

(I)

Inevitably, Hamlet wears black, and for most of the nineteenth century a plumed hat. John Massey Wright's watercolor shows him taller than Horatio and marginally broader, but it is the relationship between Hamlet and the skull of Yorick that dominates the pictorial space (fig. 1). Facing the death's head the Gravedigger holds out to him, the hero reaches toward it with one hand to touch what we may see as his similitude, and with the other recoils from contact with decay, decomposition, and his own destiny. In this mid-nineteenth-century picture, the Gravedigger's evident familiarity with the emblem of mortality he offers the Prince is oddly reassuring, while the setting is not entirely hostile. Hamlet's individual encounter with death is framed by growing things, as well as substantial monuments and a church, or perhaps a ruined abbey, so ancient and so enduring that they almost pass for nature. This contrast, and the small but decisive distance between Hamlet and Horatio, stress the hero's isolation and his exceptional sensitivity. Moved by the skull in a way that the others are not, at once appalled by death and drawn to it, he seems alienated from the everyday, but in touch with the great questions of human existence.

Hamlet has always been something of a puzzle. Why doesn't the hero just do it? The conventional editorial practice of producing a single text by conflating three different early modern versions resulted in a play that, leaving out nothing that Shakespeare could possibly be thought to have written at any time during its life in the repertory of the company, was in consequence inclined to be both repetitive and confusing. The problem was too many soliloquies, too much self-castigation, but too little decisive action, in a play that went on too long. Although usually cut in performance, often drastically, *Hamlet* has been extraordinarily popular on the stage and, more recently, on film. Something in the hero's predicament strikes a chord, and not just with professional Shakespeareans—

actors, directors or scholars—but with intellectuals in other fields, among them writers and artists (Foakes).[1]

In the nineteenth century, the great age of the novel, it was widely assumed that the solution to the puzzle of the play was to be found in the hero's character, his psychological specificity, the attributes that distinguished him both from the figures who surrounded him in the play and from the protagonists of Shakespeare's other tragedies. The explanation of *Hamlet* lay in Hamlet. But what exact component of his subjectivity was the source of the hero's inertia? Irresolution? A morbid preoccupation with death? Or something deeper?

Visitors to Stratford-upon-Avon will have seen Ronald Gower's bronze monument to Shakespeare, unveiled in 1888. Hamlet is one of four figures at the base of a plinth bearing Shakespeare himself, with a sheaf of foul papers in his hand, his gaze fixed on the infinite. Gower's Hamlet, hunched in thought, rests his slightly unkempt head on one hand; in the other, almost absent-mindedly, he holds a skull (fig. 2). A miniature replica, currently in the RSC Museum, indi-

cates that a sword, now missing, once hung idle at his side. One wrinkled cuff betrays his abstraction, preoccupied as he is by questions that transcend mere appearances. By this time, Shakespeare belonged to the whole of Europe, and nineteenth-century actors who made their reputations playing the Prince of Denmark were also identified by the skull in their hands. Josef Kainz still holds up the remains of Yorick in Vienna; the Italian actor, Ernesto Rossi, is immortalized holding a death's head in the role of Hamlet in 1902.[2] The tradition goes back two centuries at least to John Philip Kemble, who was painted as Hamlet with a skull by Sir Thomas Lawrence in 1801.

In one sense the image was faithful, of course, to the text. With characteristic inventiveness, Shakespeare's play took from contemporary portraiture the conventional image of a

Figure 2. Ronald Gower, *Hamlet* from the *Monument to Shakespeare*, 1888. Stratford-upon-Avon.

young man with a memento mori, and set it in motion in the graveyard scene, where it indicates both the urgency and the probable consequences for the hero of Hamlet's avenging mission. The episode, which has virtually no value in advancing the plot, thus condenses emblematically the contradictory imperatives to act and to defer action that simultaneously impel and inhibit the good son required to kill his uncle and his king. This new emblem's implications were evidently not lost on Shakespeare's own period. Within a very few years, *The Revenger's Tragedy* picked it up in the opening scene, where Vindice holds the skull of the lady he vows to avenge. The "shell of death" constitutes both a reminder of the mutability of her once-bright beauty and a motive for vengeance, but "death's vizard" also points ironically to the consequent fate of the hero himself, since revenge repeats the crime and incurs the same punishment: "Who e'er knew/ Murder unpaid?" Vindice ironically asks (1.1.15, 49, 42–43).

What is missing, however, from so many of the nineteenth-century images, and cut, indeed, from the majority of productions in the period (Hapgood 7) is the energy of Hamlet's wit as he plays with the traditional commonplaces of mutability, and his delight in remembering the jester he now mimics so sardonically in this incongruous setting. The central figure of the paintings is generally motionless; often he shrinks visibly from a task he clearly finds all but overwhelming. Oil paint offers more scope for intensity than watercolor. In Eugène Delacroix's work of 1839, there is much less to console the spectator than in Wright's comfortable background (fig. 3). An altogether more delicate Hamlet is palpably out of place among the muscular Gravediggers in this bleak and rocky landscape, and Horatio's evident maturity throws into relief the youth and vulnerability of the protagonist. All four figures stare intently at the skull in the center of the canvas, which stands out against the lurid sky "like a kind of alternative sun" (Sérullaz and Bonnefoy 24). The diagonal slope of the mountain behind him echoes the line of the Prince's fascinated gaze, but in this instance he draws back from contact with mortality, his hand occupied in pulling his cloak about him, as if to protect a fragile interiority. The key now to Hamlet's delay is not an ethical hesitation between regicide and stoic endurance, but a paralyzing constitutional weakness, which springs from an excess of sensibility. Delacroix admired Goethe as well as Shakespeare, and his image of Hamlet in the graveyard might evoke Wilhelm Meister's widely influential analysis of the play:

> To me it is clear that Shakspeare meant . . . to represent a great action laid upon a soul unfit for the performance of it. . . . A lovely, pure, noble and most moral nature, without the strength of nerve which forms a hero, sinks beneath a burden which it cannot bear and must not cast away. (Farley-Hills 24–25)[3]

Delacroix visited Sir Thomas Lawrence to pay his respects in London in 1825, and saw Charles Kemble's *Hamlet* in Paris two years later. In Lawrence's portrait, John Philip Kemble's lofty melancholy and his soulful expression also stress in their own way the troubling character of Hamlet's avenging mission to a figure whose natural disposition is contemplative rather than active. The artistic tradition confirms stage history and critical comment. Lawence's image of Kemble's Hamlet was available to a range of spectators: like so many pictures of

Figure 3. Eugène Delacroix, *Hamlet and Horatio in the Graveyard*, 1839.
Louvre Museum. Photo © RMN.

Figure 4. Sir Thomas Lawrence, *John Philip Kemble as Hamlet*. Engraving after the portrait. By permission of the Folger Shakespeare Library.

the period, the portrait was repeatedly copied by engravers and put into wide circulation both among and beyond a theater-going and play-reading public. By this means it became part of the consciousness of the period (fig. 4).

Though there were other visual images of *Hamlet* in the nineteenth century—the confrontation with the Ghost was popular as, of course, was the death of Ophelia—it is above all the scene in the graveyard that comes by a kind of visual synecdoche to stand for the play as a whole. The story of *Hamlet* thus takes on a life of its own as the representation of a reluctant encounter between a prince and a skull, and Shakespeare's genius is seen as the ability to explore the depths of a complex and tormented soul. Hamlet becomes a Romantic, and the graveyard setting, more or less Gothic according to taste, the appropriate location for an elemental experience of human finitude.

Sensitive but ineffectual, the Romantic Hamlet also pushes, however, toward the edge of absurdity. John Philip Kemble's solemn, somewhat mannered performance, for instance, elicited ridicule as well as admiration. Among the innovations designed to surpass his predecessors, and especially Garrick, hitherto the arch-exponent of Hamlet's character, Kemble chose for the first time a semblance of period dress (Mills 56). A contemporary cartoon, also set in the graveyard, shows him haughty and aloof. One of the Gravediggers, taking a break from his labors, caustically addresses the skull: "Mr Yorick pray tell us what figure is that/ Like a Ninepin dress'd up in a Blanket & hat[?]." The skull replies, "Master Delver Our Hamlet I'm told it resembles/ Such a Dress I neer saw but the Portrait is   —." Meanwhile, Kemble himself admonishes them from above: "Ye Num sculls be silent how dare ye presume/ To find fault with my Dress tis your Danish Costume."[4] The assumption is that the scene and the characters are sufficiently familiar to need no exposition or explanation. Is it only Kemble's appearance that is the butt of the comedy here, or is the Prince's own lofty indifference to the ordinary also a target?

In either case, Kemble himself came to define Hamlet for a new generation, and his own (possibly apocryphal) betrayal of the sensitive hero was in due course to furnish further material for comedy. On one occasion, apparently, the blend of gloom and anxiety that Kemble brought to the part seems to have deserted him (fig. 5), at least according to an anecdote recounted in Dickens's edition of the *Memoirs of Joseph Grimaldi*, published with illustrations by George Cruikshank in 1838. While Kemble was starring as Hamlet in a provincial theater in the north of England, the Gravedigger was played by a well-known comedian called Davis, who specialized in comic faces. These grimaces had become habitual with him, as had the consequent laughter of the audience. Outraged by the distraction this created from his tragic observations, Kemble stepped out of his role, stamped his foot in rage and swore at the actor, whereupon Davis threw his hands in the air in mock horror, and thereafter lay down flat in the grave and refused to come out, leaving Kemble to complete the scene without a Gravedigger ("Boz" 179–82). Whether or not the story is true, its appearance in

Figure 5. George Cruikshank, *A Startling Effect*, 1838. Illustration. By permission of the Folger Shakespeare Library.

the book, accompanied by Cruikshank's drawing, suggests that readers were expected to be sufficiently familiar with the normal image of the scene to recognize that the joke depends on the radical reversal of the conventional relationship between the shrinking Prince and the coarse but relaxed laborer, at ease with the thought of death.

Just over twenty years later, Dickens would once again make comedy depend on his readers' recognition of the gap between an inept production of the play and more orthodox renderings. Mr. Wopsle's failure to enlist his audience reached its high point, *Great Expectations* records,

> in the churchyard, which had the appearance of a primeval forest, with a kind of small ecclesiastical wash-house on one side, and a turnpike-gate on the other. Mr Wopsle, in a comprehensive black cloak, being descried entering at the turnpike, the gravedigger was admonished in a friendly way, "Look out! Here's the undertaker a coming to see how you're getting on with your work!" I believe it is well known in a constitutional country that Mr Wopsle could not possibly have returned the skull, after moralising over it, without dusting his fingers on a white napkin taken from his breast; but even that innocent and indispensable action did not pass without the comment, "Wai-ter!" (Dickens 255)

The napkin was not Dickens's invention. William Charles Macready habitually employed a cambric handkerchief in his role as Hamlet. According to James Murdoch, having tossed the offensive skull over his own head, he then took out the handkerchief, "unfolded it, carefully wiped his hands, and continued" (Mills 103). He included this gesture in 1844 when he played the part in Paris, where it strongly impressed Théophile Gautier, and reappeared in a painting by Pascal Dagnon-Bouveret, as an indication of the hero's fine fastidiousness.

This French Hamlet surrounded by flowers is an altogether more dapper figure than usual, and displays a characteristically Gallic sangfroid in all other respects. But here it is surely the exception that proves the rule. When D. H. Lawrence saw a small-town production of *Amleto* in Italy just before the First World War, he noted that the actor "took the skull in a corner of his black cloak. As an Italian, he would not willingly touch it. It was unclean." "But he looked," Lawrence continues, "a fool" (Lawrence 150).[5]

(II)

Whether they were found to be tragic or ludicrous, however, Hamlet's difference, his delicacy and sensibility, were seen as consistent with his failure to take the requisite action. Almost without exception, nineteenth-century critics took it for granted that the deferment until act 5 of the death of Claudius was to be explained by a deficiency in Hamlet's character. August Wilhelm Schlegel judged him more harshly than Goethe, stressing his weakness of will and want of resolution (Farley-Hills 49–52), and Coleridge followed Schlegel: "He is a man living in meditation, called upon to act by every motive human and divine, but the great object of his life is defeated by continually resolving to do, yet doing nothing but resolve." According to William Hazlitt, "when he is most bound to act, he remains puzzled, undecided and sceptical, dallies with his purposes, till the occasion is lost, and finds out some pretence to relapse into indolence and thoughtfulness again" (Farley-Hills 59, 116). The Ghost's command is treated as unequivocally binding, a sacred duty imposed by a father on his son, while Hamlet's self-castigation is taken as the voice of the play.

The explanation of the consistent assumption that there must be something wrong with a Hamlet who does not unhesitatingly kill Claudius is to be sought, I believe, deep in nineteenth-century culture. We might link it with the filial obedience thought due to the stern father of Victorian convention; with the popularity of ghost stories showing revenants in possession of a truth withheld from mortal knowledge, and the widespread belief in spiritualism in the latter part of the century; and with the emergence of psychology and psychopathology as medical disciplines, as well as the readiness with which the Victorians confined their non-conforming relatives, especially their wives, to mental asylums. But above all, the conventional nineteenth-century interpretation of *Hamlet* takes for granted that wrongs are best righted by violence, and that to kill your enemies is both proper and manly.

Tennyson saw his poem *Maud*, first published in 1855, as, he says, "a little *Hamlet*, the history of a morbid, poetic soul, under the blighting influence of a recklessly speculative age" (Tennyson 162). The solitary hero's predisposition to melancholy, reinforced by the financial ruin and death of his father, gives way to madness when the heir of the man who has become wealthy at his father's expense divides him finally from the woman he loves. He is restored, however, and becomes one with his kind, when he fights for his country, embracing the purpose of God in the Crimean War. Violence was still to a high degree heroic in the revolutions of 1848, as well as in the ruthless imperialist repression practiced in the name of European civilization.

Hamlet's reluctance to kill was therefore perceived by many as a form of pathology, "the perversion," as August Doering put it in 1865, "of an undeceived idealism into an embittered and passionate pessimism" (Furness 320), or worse, A. C. Bradley's paralyzing melancholia, perhaps madness. Charles Kemble believed Hamlet to be mad, and his performance in Paris in 1827 influenced successive

Figure 6. *Henry Irving as Hamlet.* By permission of the Folger Shakespeare Library.

French stage productions (Taranow 141). Some idealized Shakespeare's Prince as a secular version of the holy fool: George Sand believed his madness was part of the universal protest at the human condition; Sainte-Beuve saw him "as the most sublime victim of that sacred malady—knowing everything, divining everything, surprised at nothing, great in intelligence, weak in character, wise in madness"(Bailey 73–74). Others, however, condemned his condition as sick: Hippolyte Taine saw it as "nervous disease" and "moral poisoning" (Taine 336, 339). Henry Irving characteristically gave the role its full intensity, playing the Prince as distraught to the point of insanity (Mills 159–60, Dawson 60–66) (fig. 6). Reviewing his performance in 1874, Clement Scott noted "the black disordered hair," symptomatic—in a reference back to Taine's account—of "moral poison" and "the distraction of the unhinged mind, swinging and banging about like a door" (Scott 61, 62, 67).[6] D. H. Lawrence, following his own anti-ascetic, anti-democratic agenda, had no patience with Shakespeare's protagonist:

Figure 7. Viktor Müller, *Hamlet and Horatio at the Grave of Ophelia*, 1868. Städelsches Kunstinstitut, Frankfurt am Main.

> I had always felt an aversion from Hamlet: a creeping, unclean thing he seems,
> on the stage. . . . His nasty poking and sniffing at his mother, his setting traps
> for the King, his conceited perversion with Ophelia make him always intolera-
> ble. The character is repulsive in its conception, based on self-dislike and a spir-
> it of disintegration. (Lawrence 143–44)

As Bradley and Ernest Jones were to discover in due course, it was tempting to seek out medical or psychoanalytic explanations of Hamlet's symptoms,
not excluding eating disorders. My own favorite, published in the American
Popular Science Monthly in 1880, attributes the hero's chronic inertia to obesity,
"fatty degeneration," an excess of adipose tissue, which is well-known to inhibit sensation and impair activity. The author, E. Vale Blake, is outraged that

"Painters, as well as actors, have done much to foist a false [emaciated] Hamlet upon the public imagination" (Blake 63),[7] though in fact, there had been considerable debate about the hero's physique, on the basis of Gertrude's comment in the duel scene that he was "fat and scant of breath." Goethe's Wilhelm Meister assumed that he was plump (Farley-Hills 38). The Italian actor, Tommaso Salvini, himself a substantial figure, saw him as "adipose, lymphatic, and asthmatic" (Winter 413). When Sarah Bernhardt came out for a thin Hamlet, two French critics fought a duel on the issue (Taranow 34). Blake's alternative case is fully textually documented: Hamlet acknowledges from the beginning the excess weight of his "too too [solid] flesh." (1.2.129) In promising to remember the Ghost, "While memory holds a seat In this distracted globe," (1.5.96–97) Hamlet again draws attention to his own corpulence, as does Ophelia's reference to the sigh that shatters his "bulk" (2.1.95). In practice, he cannot help behaving exactly like the "fat weed" (1.5.32) that the Ghost condemns, not least because he knows he has reason to fear cardiac arrest: "thou would'st not think how ill all's here about my heart" (5.2.208–9). Hamlet's fine intellect, so the argument goes, and his undoubted insight are "imprisoned in walls of adipose" (Blake 70).

Blake is right to recognize, however, that the painters commonly show Hamlet as thin to the point of anorexia, and with a tendency to green-sickness. His problem, sometimes unnamed, but implicit in the recurring nineteenth-century adjectives ("gentle," "delicate," "weak"), was widely seen as a lack of proper masculinity. In an 1868 painting, Viktor Müller sets the Prince on a desolate cliff above a Northern winter sea (fig. 7)[8]. Here Hamlet's attention is distracted from the skull by Ophelia's funeral procession in the distance. He is a slight, girlish, impressible figure, pale and youthful beside the altogether more vigorous Horatio, whose masculinity is emphasized by his hunting costume. Real men, we are to understand, track down their quarry—and kill. Delacroix, who depicted Hamlet again and again in paintings and lithographs, consistently used a woman as the model for the Prince (Wilson-Smith 83).[9]

The assumption that there was something feminine in Hamlet was pervasive. Paradoxically, Hartley Coleridge—eldest son of Samuel Coleridge, who also commented extensively on *Hamlet*—evidently acknowledges as much when he contests the dominant view, firmly denying that "in all his musings, all the many-coloured mazes of his thoughts, is there anything of female softness." His own opinion—that Hamlet's "anguish is stern and masculine"—is put forward as "a new theory" (Farley-Hills 191). Like Romeo, Hamlet was regularly played by women in the period. This elicited differing reactions in the critics, but the majority conceded the femininity of the character, even when they disliked the female impersonations. Although he deplored Sarah Bernhardt's performance as what the critics called "Hamlette" in 1899, A. B. Walkley recognized the case for the effeminate Hamlet when he insisted that his resemblance to a woman was spiritual, not physical; in consequence, he affirmed, "a woman can no more present the partly feminine Hamlet than a man can present the partly masculine Lady

Macbeth" (Tanarow 86). As did Hartley Coleridge before him, the American William Winter also acknowledged the prevailing view when he observed sourly, "It was a bad day for 'the glass of fashion' when some misguided essayists began to call him 'feminine' and the ladies heard of it" (Winter 431). Winter's compatriot, Edwin Booth, however, wrote, "I doubt if ever a robust masculine treatment of the character will be accepted so generally as the more womanly and refined interpretation" (Hapgood 36).

Booth's own performance was praised for the "feminine qualities in his style" (Foakes 24). Meanwhile, Clement Scott, who admired Bernhardt's version unreservedly, remembers that when the Anglo-French actor Charles Fechter played the part in London in 1861, notoriously wearing a blond wig to look Danish,[10] he displayed the Prince's melancholy "with almost effeminate suggestion" (Scott 86). G. H. Lewes was more decisive: in Fechter's performance, "The refinement, the feminine delicacy, the vacillation of Hamlet are admirably represented" (Lewes 136). How else, after all, but in terms of femininity was it possible to characterize Hamlet's inertia? D. H. Lawrence was not alone in believing that "[a]n ordinary instinctive man, in Hamlet's position, would either have set about murdering his uncle, by reflex action, or else would have gone right away" (Lawrence 144).

(III)

Hamlet's delay was attributed to an inadequacy in his character, and this deficiency was named as feminine. More widespread identification of Hamlet's femininity was inhibited, however, by the general respect for his profound philosophical insight; intellect was, on the whole, a property of men. Here, then, the puzzle only became more perplexing: Hamlet might be effeminate, but effeminacy was evidently not the whole story. It was the conjunction of exceptional intelligence with a dreamy wistfulness that especially endeared him to poets and artists. Like them, Hamlet faced the ultimate questions in all their unresolved complexity. The paintings show little trace of the specific verbal exchanges of 5.1. Instead, the pictures seem to capture an ethos that the period attributes to the play as a whole, and this ethos is in turn abstracted from the text itself. According to the German critic, Julian Schmidt, in 1873, what defines the play is not simply the events themselves, but "a certain expressive coloring" in excess of the plot:

> {I}t is night, but no friendly moonlit night, no trace of green, no color that hints at life. It is a cold, gray, weird night, overcast and darkly shaded. No wonder that Ghosts appear; the place is made for them. No wonder that we linger so long in the churchyard; the whole earth is a churchyard. The skulls which the Clown throws out are the only realities that survive of the living world, and as to those who still live,—what is true? what is real? (Furness 349).

If there is a textual moment that authorizes the nineteenth-century interpretation of the play, it is not the specific exchanges in the graveyard, but "To be or not to be," delivered two acts earlier, which effectively takes their place in the popular appropriation of the play. According to most of the critical readings, this soliloquy has no very specific meaning or theme: on the contrary, it is variously seen as synonymous with the riddle of the Sphinx,[11] a contemplation of the infinite,[12] and an investigation of the enigmatic nature of evil or, indeed, of life.[13] But for this very reason, it informs the episode in the graveyard and, indeed, pervades the whole play, so that according to Jones Very in 1839,

> "*To be or not to be*" is written over [*Hamlet*'s] every scene, from the entrance of the ghost to the rude inscription over the gateway of the church-yard; and, whenever we shall have built up in ourselves the true conception of this the greatest of the poets, "To be or not to be" will be found to be chiseled in golden letters on the very key-stone of that arch which tells us of his memory. (Very 63–4)

Reviewing Macready's performance in Paris in 1844, Théophile Gautier argued that the Prince's horrified response to the Ghost was real, but was not his central concern. Instead, the more general question that confronts the "pale dreamer" is the one posed in the great soliloquy: the question of life itself (Bailey 71). This speech defines Hamlet's character, and thus informs everything he says, including his observations in the graveyard, infusing into them a splendor and a melancholy that exceed their content. According to an unnamed author in the *Quarterly Review* in 1847:

> The commonest ideas that pass through his mind are invested with a wonderful freshness and originality. His meditations in the churchyard are on the trite notion that all ambition leads but to the grave. But what condensation, what variety, what picturesqueness, what intense, unmitigated gloom! It is the finest sermon that was ever preached against the vanities of life. (Anon. 333–34)

The Hamlet the period castigates for his failure to act is thus at the same time greatly admired for his confrontation of the great existential issues, and for the depth and intensity of his emotion. Isolated, reflective, a dreamer, irresolute, unmanly, Hamlet is also, paradoxically, a model for the writers who condemn him. A French caricature of 1825 shows "the Romantic" sitting on a rock before an ivy-clad Gothic ruin. His hair disheveled, he ignores the poetry he has brought with him, whether his own or others'. The abstraction of his fine features indicates that his mind is given over entirely to ultimate issues, while bats flutter about his oblivious head.[14] Samuel Taylor Coleridge, even as he condemns Hamlet's inability to act, at the same time attributes this to imagination, the creative faculty of the poet. His withdrawal into the world of his own perceptions is not inconsistent, Coleridge claims, with genius (Farley-Hills 57), and in *Table Talk* he adds modestly, "I have a smack of Hamlet myself, if I may say so" (Coleridge 61).

Figure 8. Eugène Delacroix, *Portrait de l'artiste dit Portrait de Delacroix en Hamlet*. Louvre Museum. Photo © RMN.

One of Delacroix's self-portraits, often dated 1824, shows the artist in an inky cloak and a doublet and hose of solemn black, against an undefined Gothic background (fig. 8). The inscription "Ravenswood" penciled on the stretcher of the canvas has puzzled art historians. Is Delacroix here impersonating the hero of Walter Scott's *Bride of Lammermoor* (1819), or is Ravenswood the nickname of the recipient? If the stance of the subject evokes Velasquez, the gaze, mournful and reflective, like the costume, nearer to the fashions of 1600 than 1800, suggests Hamlet, the figure Delacroix went on to portray so repeatedly in his paintings and lithographs. Certainly, the costume is not unlike Kemble's in Lawrence's portrait, though the resemblance is by no means exact.

It may not be necessary to choose. Scott's Ravenswood is also an ambivalent revenger, linked irresistibly to the man he holds responsible for his father's death. Toward the end of his own tragic story, Ravenswood too encounters a gravedigger in a churchyard and learns unpalatable truths. The epigraph to this chapter of Scott's novel is a quotation from *Hamlet* 5.1, the scene in the graveyard.[15] Perhaps Delacroix identified with what he saw as Hamlet's difference as an intellectual, and his consequent isolation. In 1824, he wrote in his journal:

> Ignorant, common people are very happy. Everything in nature is plainly laid out for them. They understand whatever there is, because there it is. And, for that matter, are they not more reasonable than all the dreamers, who go so far that they suspect even their own thoughts? Suppose their friend dies? According to their conception of death, they do not add to the grief of tears that cruel anxiety of not being able to explain so natural a happening. . . . Wise men and thinkers seem much less advanced than ignorant people, since what would serve them as proof is not even proved for them. I am a man. What is this I? What is a *man*? (Delacroix 62).

Shocked by the death of Géricault a week earlier, the twenty-five-year-old Delacroix confronts the question of mortality. He almost certainly overestimates the equanimity of ordinary people, but his envious contempt for their acquiescence in suffering is the mirror image of Coleridge's ambivalence toward Hamlet's intellectualism.

Baudelaire, who certainly saw himself as a latter-day Hamlet, covered the walls of his apartment with Delacroix's lithographs of the play (Lamont 81–87). In 1886, Jules Laforgue gave his own features to the Decadent hero of his story, "Hamlet, or the Consequences of Filial Piety," but Laforgue's Hamlet does not kill anyone—only a canary. Although we know that by 5.1 Polonius, Rosencrantz, and Guildenstern are already dead, it is as if the Hamlet that these nineteenth-century intellectuals perceive in the graveyard has as yet no blood on his hands. It is as if, in other words, the youthful Prince represents an innocence they too long for, a repudiation of the masculine world of violence that they also paradoxically condemn him for evading. The delicate, fastidious, sensitive, idealistic hero is thus for the nineteenth century both a reproach and a legitimation. The image of Hamlet that the epoch creates at once rejects and vindicates an alternative to the public obligations of manhood, a heroism of interiority, which cannot quite be acknowledged, but must not be lost to sight.

If the writers and artists of the period were Hamlet, Hamlet himself was also the writer who created him. "You recognise in {Hamlet}," Taine affirms in 1866,

> a poet's soul, made not to act, but to dream, which is lost in contemplating the phantoms of its creation, which sees the imaginary world too clearly to play a part in the real world; an artist whom evil chance has made a prince, whom worse chance has made an avenger of crime, and who, destined by nature for genius, is condemned by fortune to madness and unhappiness. (Taine 340)

Here the requirement to act is seen as a misfortune; public obligation is attributed to "evil chance." And Taine adds, "Hamlet is Shakespeare, and, at the close of this gallery of portraits, which have all some features of his own, Shakespeare has painted himself in the most striking of them all" (Taine 340).

(IV)

Ambivalence toward violence runs through much of the writing of this period. In Germany, the play became the site of a political struggle over the social role of the intellectual. Reacting against the Romantic idealization of otherworldliness, the Young Germany movement of the 1830s and 1840s notoriously identified the Prince with a whole nation, and after Ferdinand Freiligrath's poem of 1844, "Germany is Hamlet," any number of writers and scholars would reiterate the view that Germany, which had failed to unite, and failed to effect a revolution, shared the intellectualizing weaknesses of Shakespeare's hero.[16] But it is possible to detect in some of this self-castigation a simultaneous echo of the widespread self-congratulation on the depth of feeling and the intellectual subtlety that transcends the reductiveness of mere political intervention. In the account of Friedrich Theodor Vischer in 1861:

> Justice to Hamlet demands that it should be clearly seen how easy it is to say that the right is the higher union of the thinking and active powers, and how hard it is to accomplish this union. One must take care what he is about in demanding the higher unities. A man without depth may easily seize the right moment, and act right off; when the depth reaches a certain degree, then the good fortune of this lightmindedness ceases. Men with brains have in their weaknesses a strength which should well save them from ridicule; we pity them, but in their misfortunes there is a tragic greatness, which mingles reverence with our pity. In Hamlet there has justly been found the type of the German character; the Frenchman, the modern Englishman, laugh at us for our irresoluteness. The former is more lightminded, more versatile in his organization, and the latter narrower and harder; and both, while they ridicule us, have a dim suspicion that there is something in us for which they have no plummet. (Furness 311–12)

Meanwhile, in Tennyson's *Maud*, the poem that represents his "little Hamlet," if violence finally redeems the hero, it is also violence that tragically separates him for ever from his beloved, when, responding like a man to her brother's aggression, he kills him in a duel, in accordance with what he calls "the Christless code, / That must have life for a blow" (Tennyson II 26–7). If in Tennyson's ambivalent poem, true masculinity is the cure, it is also in its own way another kind of poison.

Perhaps the most striking instance of ambivalence occurs in Thomas Mann's *Tonio Kröger*, published in 1903. Mann's story juxtaposes the alienation of the artist with what its hero calls the "seductive banality" of ordinary life (Mann

161). As a writer, Tonio Kröger is always an outsider, unable to live fully because books get in the way. Life and art appear to him eternal opposites, fixed in an antithesis that recapitulates, of course, one of the conflicts that dominates so much English Victorian verse.[17] No wonder Hamlet in the graveyard seemed to a whole century the appropriate emblem of the poet: paralyzed, cut off from the world, both Shakespeare's hero and the artist are living beings imprisoned in the terrain of death.[18] Tonio Kröger, whose upright father dies, and whose flighty mother rapidly marries again, names Hamlet, "that typical literary artist," as his predecessor, and compares his Russian friend Lisaveta Ivanovna to Horatio (Mann 159–60).

In Mann's novel, however, the parallels are ultimately ironic. When a lieutenant ventures to recite a poem he has composed, Kröger is appalled, not so much by the poem itself as by the effrontery of the idea that a soldier, a real man, could also be a poet, that it might be possible to fight as well as write, "to pluck even a single leaf from the laurel-tree of art and not pay for it with one's life." In response, Lisaveta–Horatio, who, as a painter, simply does the work she enjoys without guilt or self-denial, reproaches Kröger as a self-indulgent "bourgeois manqué" (Mann 163–4). The text lends some support to her view: on his way to Denmark, where he will see his own ghosts from Elsinore, he travels first-class, on the grounds that one who has given his life to art is entitled to physical comfort. When a merchant on the boat, who indulges in romantic speculation, as well as a lobster omelette, paraphrases Hamlet's "What a piece of work is a man!," Kröger fails to recognize it and dismisses the speaker as having "no literature in his system" (Mann 176). A business man, after all, engages in action; he intervenes in the world; what can he know of art and its paralyzing solitude?

These ironies spell the beginning of the end of Hamlet as an excuse for the aesthete's combined self-indulgence and self-reproach, and at the same time of Hamlet's poetic subjectivity as the explanation of the tragedy. But Jules Laforgue's parody, "Hamlet, or the Consequences of Filial Piety," had already anticipated Mann's more nuanced ambiguities by nearly twenty years. In Laforgue's literary self-portrait, Hamlet turns out to be Yorick's half-brother. He longs to act, to be a hero, but preferably the hero of a play; he wants "to be," but only on condition that this means being a famous playwright. His sporadic resolutions to concern himself with the world of events, or even to escape his lonely ivory tower, are repeatedly dissipated in "words, words, words." His own lengthy meditation on mortality fails to involve this narcissistic dandy. On the contrary, death seems remote, deferred, even though he enjoys imagining the respect his dead body will elicit. In the graveyard he "takes his future skull in both hands, and tries to shiver all along his bones" (Laforgue 31). Laforgue's Hamlet decides that he does not care about his throne; and having induced the actors to frighten the King and Queen with his own play, he feels he has now punished the royal couple enough. In the course of eloping with the actress who greatly admires his play, Hamlet stops for a last look at the graveyard. There he is killed without a fight by Laertes, and returns to nature his "hamletic soul" (Laforgue 45).

This, we are to understand, is no great loss: "One Hamlet less: the race won't die out in consequence, let it be known" (Laforgue 45, 47). But which race is the object of this laconic reference? The human race, which can well manage without Hamlet? Or the rest of the race of wistful artist–Hamlets who had become so prolific and so pervasive in Laforgue's own culture? In the story the artist, not particularly special, after all, is "at only one remove from his half brother, the clown" (Hannoosh 88).

(V)

Parody is deliberately anachronistic. Laforgue's depends on the gap between ancient heroism and modern self-indulgence; Mann's protagonist is not a prince but a bourgeois. In a different but not unrelated way, all interpretation from a period other than the text's own is anachronistic to a degree, and reproduces the preoccupations of its time. The nineteenth century and part of the twentieth abstracted the Prince from the surrounding text in order to explore its own anxieties about violence and masculinity. Shakespeare's play had finally become, as an effect of this process, a case history, fascinating in the study, but probably less interesting in the theater. It is hard to believe that Bradley's melancholic Hamlet or Ernest Jones's oedipal one would be as good in performance as they are on the page.

If, on the other hand, Hamlet's nineteenth-century problem was an anxiety about the obligations of masculinity, and if in Thomas Mann's text it is a woman who displays impatience with male agonizing, it was decisive, dynamic, resourceful women in the role who began the rescue of *Hamlet* for the stage, by calling in question the image of Hamlet the ineffectual dreamer. Sarah Bernhardt's performances in Paris, London, and Stratford in 1899, and in New York the following year, delivered a resounding challenge to the existing interpretations. Bernhardt's Hamlet was alert, witty, vigorous, and decisive, and audiences in general loved him. Her production reinstated much that had been excised to protect Hamlet's delicate sensibility. The prayer scene was usually cut as too shocking, too incompatible with Hamlet the sensitive dreamer; so too were the exchanges with Claudius on the disposal of Polonius. Bernhardt reintroduced both, and claimed that she was reviving the Hamlet of the Elizabethan revenge tradition. Indeed, it seemed that she was contesting the nineteenth-century reading in its entirety. The London *Morning Post* of June 13, 1899 commented, "Madame Sarah Bernhardt has undoubtedly rendered a great service to the interpretation of Shakespeare's play, for she has restored to Hamlet the strong character which Goethe took away from him and which hardly any later critic . . . has allowed him" (Taranow 58). Four days later, Bernhardt herself wrote in French to the *Daily Telegraph* in defense of her reading:

> What people are determined to see in Hamlet is a feminized, hesitating,
> bemused creature. What I see, however, is a person who is manly and resolute,
> but nonetheless thoughtful. . . . Hamlet, characteristically, thinks before he acts,
> a trait indicative of great strength and great spiritual power. (Taranow 68)

Although her performance was intense, and intensely moving, there was no trace here of the languid, thought-sick pessimist. Opinion varied on whether her "Hélas, pauvre Yorick" was in a lower key than usual, or more sublime. There was no handkerchief (Taranow 175). Indeed, a publicity photograph for the production shows her more than equal to a confrontation with mortality (fig. 9).

Figure 9. Sarah Bernhardt as Hamlet, 1899. *Illustrated London News* Picture Library.

But if Bernhardt challenged the ineffectual Hamlet, her impersonation also represented the reinscription of the femininity implicit in so many readings since Goethe. Because her own visual image on the stage took for granted what she saw as the feminine component of Hamlet's character (Edmonds 61),[19] Bernhardt had no need to emphasize it further. So pervasive, indeed, was the slight, girlish image the painters in particular had created, that in her own view, fit male actors were too muscular, too substantial physically, to play Hamlet adequately (Bernhardt 141–42).[20] Ironically, William Winter, who had no sympathy with Bernhardt's own performance, showed how much he shared of this general view when he said of the American Edwin Forrest: "Being a resolute, formidable, athletic man, of combative disposition and truculent aspect, he was as little like Hamlet as it would be possible for any person to be. . . . The moment he was seen in that character all possibility of any illusion of poetry, pathos, tenderness,

Figure 10. Asta Nielsen as Hamlet, 1920. By permission of Allan O. Hagedorff.

and grace was forestalled." Winter felt much the same about "the massive frame" and "leonine demeanor" of Salvini. The Italian actor, Winter maintained, "presented a stalwart, puissant, dominant, capable man, who would have disposed of uncle Claudius, without the least hesitation or difficulty, in the twinkling of an eye," and was thus "the literal opposite of everything that *Hamlet* is or means" (Winter 334–5, 411).[21]

Bernhardt's version of the play did not challenge the fundamental values of the culture: violence was still the the proper way to deal with Claudius. Nor did she change the story: on the contrary, the production was quite unconventionally faithful to Shakespeare's text. But when Asta Nielsen starred as Princess Hamlet in a German film made in 1920, she radically rewrote the plot. In *Hamlet: The Drama of Revenge*, Nielsen's cross-dressed protagonist is a woman brought up as a man; as a result, she possesses all of the masculine skills, including fencing, but she has "a woman's heart" and consequently she simply lacks the killer instinct. Princess Hamlet does not waste time reproaching herself for lack of virility, but sets about the detective work of checking the Ghost's story by staging the play and interviewing the Gravedigger. The graveyard scene is cut in its entirety. This version of the character is not remotely ineffectual: Nielsen's Princess has strong feelings and, in love with Horatio, she contemplates suicide in the "To be or not to be" speech; but she is resourceful, inventive, capable, and self-controlled. The problem she faces is Claudius, not her own psyche (fig. 10).

The Nielsen film was based on what was by then a forgotten reading of the play. E. P. Vining's *The Mystery of Hamlet*, published in 1881, compared the three early modern texts of the play to find an increasingly feminine protagonist. Vining addressed directly the question that had remained in the margins of so many nineteenth-century accounts. If Hamlet lacked the readiness to act that was properly manly, why was he still admired? The answer, however improbable, was precisely his femininity:

> There is not only a masculine type of human perfection, but also a feminine type; and when it became evident that Hamlet was born lacking in many of the elements of virility, there grew up in him, as compensation, many of the perfections of character more properly the crown of the better half of the human race. . . . The depths of human nature which Shakespeare touched in him have been felt by all, but it has scarcely been recognized that the charms of Hamlet's mind are essentially feminine in their nature. (Thompson 218)

It had been recognized, but not unequivocally as a virtue. In Vining's account, Hamlet's femininity has become his strength, the element he has in common with all human beings. Understandably, Vining's book was not very well received in its own day (Taranow 86–87): the male anxiety of the time was unlikely to be allayed by the idea that the feminine was synonymous with human nature.

When the Nielsen film was distributed in America in 1921, the trade paper *Wid's Daily* recommended marketing it under the "teaser," "Was Hamlet a man or a woman?" (Thompson 216). The publication of *Ulysses* in 1922 showed that the same option had also occurred to Joyce's Leopold Bloom, prompted by a poster for Mrs. Bandman Palmer's appearance as Hamlet in Dublin in 1904. "Perhaps he was a woman. Why Ophelia committed suicide?" Bloom muses (Joyce 1993, 73).[22] In one sense, the question summarized more than a hundred years of deliberation. Ultimately, the nineteenth century found in *Hamlet* everything it wanted to find: ambivalence toward violence as a way of resolving problems; prosecution and defense of art as a reserved occupation; both recrimination and sympathy for reluctant masculinity; and, of course, a novelistic explanation of the play at the level of character. But the character of Hamlet had been made to bear contradictions the culture itself was unable to resolve. Unlike Vining's protagonist, Shakespeare's remained a mystery.

By 1920 the waste of life in the First World War had given Nielsen's promotion of other values a certain timeliness. After a further World War and any number of more local conflicts, most of us are now less sanguine still about violence, about masculinity to the degree that this is defined as unthinking aggression, and also about unquestioning obedience to the father. We are no longer persuaded that masculinity and femininity are polar opposites, or that intellectual speculation belongs to men. Moreover, in the light of a century of sociology, cultural theory, and psychoanalysis, we have come to believe that subjectivity, whether masculine or feminine, is neither an origin nor an explanation, but a component of an altogether more complicated story. Our *Hamlet* is about more than Hamlet, and what is hard for us to resolve is his ethical and political dilemma.

The two women who did most to modify the meaning of *Hamlet* for the subsequent century were both sophisticated actors and established stars when they offered their radical interpretations of the play. Weren't they, in addition, considerably ahead of their time?

NOTES

1. See especially Foakes 12–44, to which I am indebted throughout.

2. The statue is now in the Royal Shakespeare Company Museum at Stratford-upon-Avon.

3. German criticism helped to bring about in France a change from the Enlightenment contempt for the play as barbaric. A. W. Schlegel lectured in Paris, and his *Cours de la littérature dramatique* was published in 1814. A new and more faithful French translation of *Hamlet* appeared in 1821 (Bailey 43–51).

4. Aquatint, n.d., by James Sayers, 1748–1823. This is now in the Folger Shakespeare Library.

5. I owe this reference to Stefania Michelucci.

6. In Taine's version, "his mind, as a door whose hinges are twisted, swings and bangs to every wind with a mad precipitance" (Taine 338).

7. I owe this essay to Alan Dessen.

8. I am grateful to Monika Reichert for this photograph.

9. Ann Thompson, who pointed this out to me, also draws attention to the fact that when the French publishers used a detail of the Delacroix painting (fig. 2) as the cover of a bilingual edition of *Hamlet*, they excluded the figure of the Prince himself, presumably on the grounds that he was not sufficiently masculine to represent the twentieth-century version of the hero (*Hamlet*, trans. François Maguin. Paris: Flammarion, 1995).

10. Wilhelm Meister had urged that, as a Dane, Hamlet must be fair-haired (Farley-Hills 1996, 38).

11. By the German critic G. F. Stedefeld in 1871 (Furness 344).

12. By François-Victor Hugo in 1873 (Furness 390).

13. By Philarète Chasles (Chasles 94).

14. Lithograph, Bibliothèque Nationale, Paris. Reproduced in Vaughan 1994, fig. 1.

15. Chapter 24 (Scott 254). Lines 65–69 (Shakespeare, 1982).

16. See Pfister 1986, Zimmerman 1994.

17. When Tennyson's Lady of Shalott, confined in her island chamber, looks away from her mirror toward life, what she sees is Lancelot, who is a soldier. The experience destroys the tapestry that is her work of art, and kills her. As late as 1923, in *Meditations in Time of Civil War*, Yeats describes the envy elicited in the poet by soldiers, "an affable Irregular" and a "brown Lieutenant": meanwhile, by contrast, "I . . . turn towards my chamber, caught/In the cold snows of a dream" (Yeats 230).

18. "Paralysis; barrenness; ice; and intellect! and art!" (Mann 189).

19. I am grateful to Jane Thomas for this essay.

20. Charles Lamb asked rhetorically of Garrick's "eye" and "commanding voice," "what have they to do with Hamlet?"; Hazlitt did not like to see Shakespeare acted, "and least of all, *Hamlet*" (Farley-Hills 103, 119).

21. Edwin Booth, by contrast, possessed "the slender, nervous physique" appropriate to the character (Winter 340).

22. John Eglinton also mentions Vining's theory (Joyce 190). I am grateful to John Astington for these references and to Laurent Milesi for discussion of their implications.

WORKS CITED

Anon. "Recent Editions of Shakespeare." *Quarterly Review* 79 (1847): 310–35.

Bailey, Helen Phelps. *"Hamlet" in France from Voltaire to Laforgue*. Geneva: Librairie Droz, 1964.

Bernhardt, Sarah. *The Art of the Theatre*, trans. H. J. Stenning. London: Bles, 1924.

Blake, E. Vale. "The Impediment of Adipose.—A Celebrated Case." *The Popular Science Monthly* 17 (May-October 1880): 60–71.

"Boz" (ed). *Memoirs of Joseph Grimaldi*. 2 vols, vol 1. London: Richard Bentley, 1838.

Bradley, A.C. *Shakespearean Tragedy: Lectures on Hamlet, Othello, King Lear, Macbeth*. London: Macmillan & Co., Ltd., 1904.

Chasles, Philarète. *Etudes contemporaines: théâtre, musique et voyages*. Paris: Amyot, 1867.

Coleridge, S. T. *Table Talk. Collected Works*, 14, ed. Carl Woodring. 2 vols, vol 2. Princeton, NJ: Princeton University Press, 1990.

Dawson, Anthony B. *"Hamlet," Shakespeare in Performance*. Manchester: Manchester University Press, 1995.

Delacroix, Eugène. *The Journal*, trans. Walter Pach. New York: Hacker, 1982.

Dickens, Charles. *Great Expectations* (1860–61), ed. Charlotte Mitchell. London: Penguin, 1996.

Edmonds, Jill. "Princess Hamlet." *The New Woman and Her Sisters: Feminism and Theatre 1850–1914*, eds. Viv Gardner and Susan Rutherford. Hemel Hempstead: Harvester Wheatsheaf, 1992, pp. 59–76.

Farley-Hills, David, ed. *Critical Responses to "Hamlet" 1600–1900*, 3 vols, vol. 2, 1790–1838. New York: AMS Press, 1996.

Foakes, R. A. *Hamlet versus Lear: Cultural Politics and Shakespeare's Art*. Cambridge: Cambridge University Press, 1993.

Furness, H. H., ed. *"Hamlet," A New Variorum Edition of Shakespeare*. Philadelphia, Penn.: Lippincott, 1877. 2 vols, vol. 2.

"Hamlet": The Drama of Revenge. Dir. Svend Gade and Heinz Schall. Germany, 1920.

Hannoosh, Michele. *Parody and Decadence: Laforgue's "Moralités légendaires."* Columbus, Ohio: Ohio State University Press, 1989.

Hapgood, Robert, ed. *Hamlet Prince of Denmark*, Shakespeare in Production. Cambridge: Cambridge University Press, 1999.

Joyce, James. *Ulysses*, ed. Jeri Johnson. Oxford: Oxford University Press, 1993.

Laforgue, Jules. "Hamlet, ou les suites de la piété filiale." *Moralités légendaires*, ed. Daniel Grojnowski. Geneva: Librarie Droz, 1980, pp. 2–47.

Lamont, Rosette. "The Hamlet Myth." *Yale French Studies* 33 (1964): 80–91.

Lawrence, D. H. *Twilight in Italy and Other Essays*. London: Penguin, 1997.

Lewes, George Henry. *On Actors and the Art of Acting*. London: Smith, Elder, 1875.

Mann, Thomas. *Tonio Kröger. Death in Venice and Other Stories by Thomas Mann*, trans David Luke. New York: Bantam Books, 1988, pp. 133–92.

Mills, John A. *Hamlet on Stage: The Great Tradition*. Westport, Conn.: Greenwood, 1985.

Pfister, Manfred. "Germany is Hamlet: The History of a Political Interpretation." *New Comparison* 2 (1986): 106–26.

Scott, Clement. *Some Notable Hamlets of the Present Time*. London: Greening, 1900.

Scott, Walter. *The Bride of Lammermoor*, ed. Fiona Robertson. Oxford: Oxford University Press, 1991.

Sérullaz, Arlette and Yves Bonnefoy. *Delacroix & Hamlet*. Paris: RMN, 1993.

Shakespeare, William. *Hamlet*, ed. Harold Jenkins. London: Methuen, 1982.

Taine, H. A. *History of English Literature*, trans. H. van Laun. Edinburgh: Edmonston and Douglas, 1871.

Taranow, Gerda. *The Bernhardt Hamlet: Culture and Context*. New York: Peter Lang, 1996.

Tennyson, Alfred. *Tennyson's Maud: A Definitive Edition*, ed. Susan Shatto. London: Athlone Press, 1986.

Thompson, Ann. "Asta Nielsen and the Mystery of *Hamlet*." *Shakespeare, the Movie*, ed. Lynda E. Boose and Richard Burt. London: Routledge, 1997, pp. 215–24.

Tourneur, Cyril. *The Revenger's Tragedy*, ed. R. A. Foakes. London: Methuen, 1975.

Vaughan, William. *Romanticism and Art*. London: Thames and Hudson, 1994.

Very, Jones. "Hamlet," *Poems and Essays*. Boston: Houghton Mifflin, 1886, pp. 53–66.

Wilson-Smith, Timothy. *Delacroix: A Life*. London: Constable, 1992.

Winter, William. *Shakespeare on the Stage*. New York: Moffat, Yard, 1911.

Yeats, W. B. *Collected Poems*. London: Macmillan, 1958.

Zimmerman, Heiner O. "Is Hamlet Germany?: On the Political Reception of *Hamlet*." *New Essays on* Hamlet, ed. Mark Thornton Burnett and John Manning. New York: AMS Press, 293–318.

Part III
Hamlet after Theory

Ways of Seeing *Hamlet*

JERRY BROTTON

"Words, words, words" (2.2.192).[1] Hamlet's "words" have, over the last two decades, led to critical preoccupation with the relations among language, representation, and the formation of subjectivity. Drawing on the lessons of post-structuralist theory, a range of critics produced invaluable work that focused on the ways in which Hamlet became the ultimate representative of early modern subjectivity (Weimann), a figure who stood for a peculiarly modern manifestation of identity that continues to speak to us existentially in our late modern (or what some might still call postmodern) era. As this perception of Hamlet hardened into orthodoxy, critical positions also polarized about the relatively progressive nature of Hamlet's "representativeness." A more humanistic response celebrated the progressive Renaissance humanism the Prince appeared to represent, and his implicit critique and rejection of the absolutist world within which he finds himself embroiled.[2] Alternatively, an anti-humanist perspective has questioned the ways in which the celebration of the discourse of the Prince is conducted at the cost of the women in the play, who come to bear the brunt of critical and aesthetic expectations (Armstrong). This position is most elegantly captured by Jacqueline Rose, who has noted that in a critical tradition of reading the play that runs from Freud through T.S. Eliot to André Green, "[f]ailing in a woman, whether aesthetic or moral, is always easier to point to than a failure of integration within language and subjectivity itself" (Rose 118). Building on this approach, Patricia Parker has more recently elaborated upon the ways in which the play's language conflates surveillance in both a political and sexual sense to focus vicariously on the problematic "matter" of women's bodies. Commenting on this connection, Parker argues that:

> As with the possibility of the queen's adultery (or Desdemona's in *Othello*),
> what is at issue is fascination with unseen events, the obsession everywhere in
> *Hamlet* with spying and being spied upon linked with the secrets of women that

can be exposed to show, a fascination that makes women, marginalized as *char-acters* within the play, paradoxically central to it. (Parker 256)

Parker develops our understanding of the ways in which the play's obsessive linguistic focus on the materiality of the woman's body discloses an anxiety about the apprehension of material objects, a situation that reaches its emotional peak in 3.4:

> In the closet scene itself, the link between a female matter and revealing secrets from a closet is suggested first in the harping, just before, on "matter" and "mother" (*mater*)—in Hamlet's "but to the matter: my mother." (Parker 254)

The frail "matter" of the voyeuristic desire to reveal, but also avoid, the site of the woman's body is conflated with the wider political atmosphere of spying and political dissimulation that "informs" the play's emergence (Parker 252–58). Building on the psychoanalytic insights of critics like Rose, Parker develops an approach to the play based upon the ways in which its sensuous materiality affects the ways in which we understand its dramatization of subjectivity. I am in broad agreement with Parker's understanding of the "matter" that remains "unseen" in the play, and wish to offer a more situated reading of the material objects that constitute the dramatic action so central to Parker's argument—Act 3, scene 4, the so-called "closet scene."

This essay proposes a stronger reading of subjectivity and its encounter with "matter" than that produced by Parker (a reading that is complementary to and implicit within Parker's own argument). I want to explore the ways in which, contrary to so much criticism of the play, identity is shaped and defined but also limited and constrained by encounters and negotiations with material objects and artifacts whose personal significance and wider cultural meaning have been lost to us over time. This approach is theoretically indebted to the work of cultural anthropologists who have drawn the attention of Renaissance scholars to what Arjun Appadurai has called "the social life of things" (Appadurai 1986), the ways in which the reciprocal relationship between subject and object both endows the object with value, while at the same time defining the shape of personal subjectivity. The importance of this approach is that it offers us new ways of thinking through the formation of early modern subjectivity, once it becomes possible to reconsider subject–object relations prior to Marx's theorization of the commodity. As Appadurai argues:

> Even if our own approach to things is conditioned necessarily by the view that things have no meanings apart from those that human transactions, attributions, and motivations endow them with, the anthropological problem is that this formal truth does not illuminate the concrete, historical circulation of things. For that we have to follow the things themselves, for their meanings are inscribed in their forms, their uses, their trajectories. It is only through the analysis of

these trajectories that we can interpret the human transactions and calculations that enliven things. Thus, even from a theoretical point of view human actors encode things with significance, from a methodological point of view it is the things-in-motion that illuminate their human and social context. (Appadurai 5)

Appadurai's insight into the complex relationship between subject and object have been developed in the more recent collection of essays entitled *Subject and Object in Renaissance Culture*, edited by Margreta de Grazia, Maureen Quilligan, and Peter Stallybrass, in which the editors "urge an exploration of the intricacies of subject/object relations, so as to undo the narrative we have been ourselves over and over again: the rise of subjectivity, the complexity of subjectivity, the instability of subjectivity" (de Grazia et al. 11). The text that is most commonly invoked to confirm this narrative of the rise, complexity, and instability of subjectivity is, of course, *Hamlet*. By introducing the question of the ways in which subjectivity in the play is developed and dramatized at certain key moments through negotiations with material objects, we begin to see that if "the subject (or author or painter) is no longer assumed to be prior to and independent of objects, criticism can attend to a dialectic in which subjects and objects reciprocally take and make each other over." (de Grazia et al. 8) This approach is perhaps best summarized through recourse to the metaphorical conceit of the mirror in *Hamlet*, and its subsequent significance for psychoanalytically informed readers of the play. When Hamlet informs the troupe of Players that "the purpose of playing, whose end, both at the first and now, was and is to hold as 'twere to hold the mirror up to nature" (3.2.20–22), or tells his mother in 3.4 that "You go not till I set you up a glass / Where you may see the inmost part of you" (3.4.18–19), recourse is invariably made to the Lacanian notion of the splitting of the subject in the fractured process of identification known as the mirror stage. This essay is as concerned to focus on the material signification of the mirror, and the ways in which its presence constrains identity, as the process of identification that simply sees the mirror as a vanishing mediator, or reflector, of subjectivity.

How do objects and artifacts alter our perception of *Hamlet*? Clearly they are not structural to the plot, as is the case of the handkerchief in *Othello*, or central to the play's climax, as in the case of the rings in *The Merchant of Venice*. However, I want to offer a close reading of one particularly climactic scene in the play, where there is a complacent tendency to overlook the importance of its cultural objects, which are, as it were, hidden in plain view, amid the intense psychological violence that we too readily assume the play is offering us. I want to suggest that by reading for the presence of the object, we can often reascribe our understanding of motivation in the reading of character, and in particular the ways in which blame is ascribed throughout the play. I choose to focus on Act 3, scene 4, the so-called "closet scene" between Hamlet and Gertrude, as it remains one of the most dramatically powerful scenes in the entire play, as well as the basis for Freudian and Lacanian readings of the play.

The first problem in reading (as well as performing) this scene is its location. In 3.2, at the culmination of the performance of *The Mousetrap*, Rosencrantz informs Hamlet that Gertrude "desires to speak with you in her closet ere you go to bed" (2.2.322–23), and Polonius confirms the site of the meeting between mother and son when he tells Claudius that Hamlet is "going to his mother's closet" (3.3.27). However, what do we mean when we refer to "Gertrude's closet"? For contemporary film and theater directors, the closet is synonymous with Gertrude's bedroom. Laurence Olivier's 1948 film of *Hamlet* established a cinematic tradition of reading "closet" as "bedroom," a sleight of hand that was particularly useful in sexualizing the encounter between Hamlet and his surprisingly youthful mother (played by Eileen Herlie),[3] further strengthening the crudely Freudian oedipal reading of the play that Olivier was eager to develop after his encounters with Freud's disciple, Ernest Jones, in the 1930s (Jones, Donaldson). If his audience was left in any doubt as to the sexual significance of Gertrude's bedroom, Olivier topped and tailed his film with tracking shots of the cinematically charged spaces that constituted the emotional topography of Elsinore. The camera lingers over Gertrude's bedroom, dominated by an enormous canopied bed, with its gendered connotations of death and ensnarement.[4] This approach to the play provided a suitably modern, post-Freudian ambience, a perspective uncritically reproduced by later filmmakers, including Kenneth Branagh and Franco Zeffirelli.[5] Similarly, theatrical productions of the play have also reproduced this intimate and erotically charged space when performing the closet scene. The problem with this approach to the closet scene is that it privileges a modern theoretical perception of the scene (predominantly driven by Freudian–Lacanian analysis), over and against the historically specific sense of what Gertrude's closet actually signified within the context of the play's original production.

One clue to the significance of Gertrude's closet comes with Polonius's counsel to Gertrude before he hides behind the arras. Polonius advises the Queen to speak frankly to her son the Prince:

> Tell him his pranks have been too broad to bear with
> And that your Grace hath screen'd and stood between
> Much heat and him. (3.4.2–4)

Their discussion is to be a frank and serious one concerning public matters of state, and the ways in which Hamlet's volatile "pranks," culminating in the politically irresponsible performance of *The Mousetrap*, are becoming a threat to political stability. This is hardly the stuff to be discussing while seated on the edge of your mother's bed. However, this more discursive sense of the exchanges that take place in Gertrude's closet is more in keeping with sixteenth-century perceptions of the closet. As several scholars have pointed out recently, the closet emerged within the architectural space of the Elizabethan domestic interior as a space of intense and dynamic social interaction, partitioned off from the rest of the household, a secret place where public affairs were conducted. Writing in 1592, Angel Day claimed that the closet was "the most secret place in the house appropriate unto our owne private studies, and wherein wee repose and deliber- ate by deepe consideration of all our waightiest affaires." It was "a place where our dealings of importance are shut up, a roome proper and peculier onely to our selves" (Stewart 83). Commenting on the architectural and social function of the closet, Alan Stewart has pointed out that "both the lord and the lady of the six- teenth-century house would possess a personalized closet, possibly leading off a main social room, but more likely built inside their respective bedchambers" (Stewart 82). This seems to be the kind of marital arrangement dramatized in *Hamlet*, where Claudius retires to his bed while Polonius rushes off to counsel his wife, Gertrude. Stewart also observes the highly pragmatic nature of the woman's closet and its functions, noting that a typical lady's closet from the later sixteenth century contains "a table, a cupboard, several chests, caskets and ham- pers, a desk, working baskets, boxes, glasses, pots, bottles, jugs, conserve jars, sweetmeat barrels, an hourglass, a grater, knives . . . and a grand total of five books" (Stewart 82). Not very sexy. However, Stewart also suggests that the apprehension as to what secretaries and their masters (or mistresses) are actual- ly doing behind the closed door of the closet is often translated into a sexual anx- iety, a development that is graphically demonstrated in *The Changeling* when Beatrice–Joanna cries out from within her closet, an ambiguous climactic moment which pivots on a momentary ambiguity as to whether she is dying at the hands of De Flores, or crying out with sexual delight.[6]

So the closet is in fact a far more pragmatic and transactive space where social rather than sexual intercourse takes place. However, the assumption of sexual scandal is never far away from a space that is paradoxically both desired and feared as a space of intimate personal transactions, as Lisa Jardine has point- ed out in her astute reading of the "excess" that defines the closet scene in *Hamlet*. Noting the scandalous presence of four men in her private closet, Jardine argues that:

> When the intimacies of the early modern closet are interpreted from a public
> perspective, the intimate transaction is perceived as erotically charged . . . the
> physical spaces of intimacy in the early modern play readily lend themselves to
> a psychoanalytical interpretation—or rather a reinterpretation from the perspec-
> tive of a world which no longer honours spatial thresholds between differing
> registers of publicness and privacy. (Jardine 1996: 153)

The historical and material significance of the space of the closet disclosed here offers a much more complex understanding of Gertrude's motivations within this scene. It also provides a clearer understanding of how the Freudian, oedipal read-

ing of the play emerges partially as the result of historical inattention to the specificity of the material contexts within which the dramatic action occurs, a mispri-
sion that, as Rose points out, invariably leads to the play's faults being laid at the
door of Gertrude. However, in pursuing the material contexts of the closet scene,
a subtly different reading of motivation begins to emerge.

Recent work in art history has offered new perspectives on the ways in
which elite women attempted to exert control over their intimate domestic
spaces. While retaining an awareness of how such spaces remain the site of sexual anxiety, feminist art historians have remained alive to the ways in which elite
women strove to fashion a more proactive sense of their public identity, displayed within semi-private chambers and closets. For instance, in their discussion of the portrait collection of the Habsburg regent of the Netherlands,
Archduchess Margaret of Austria (1480–1530), housed in the Palais de Savoie in
Mechelen (Malines), Dagmar Eichberger and Lisa Beaven point out that
Margaret was an enthusiastic and astute collector, whose collection "ranged in
scope from jewellery, paintings, sculpture, liturgical objects, and precious gold
and silver plate to corals, gems, and ethnographic objects from the New World.
Like her Burgundian ancestors she also had a large collection of tapestry sets"
(Eichberger and Beaven 225). The creation of such a collection by a woman of
Margaret's stature is not in itself unusual, but what interests Eichberger and
Beaven are the ways in which the location of the various items in the collection
establish their purpose and function in fashioning Margaret's public *personae*, as
well as the wider dynastic alliances and aspirations of the House of Habsburg.
Throughout the spatial logic of palaces like the Palais de Savoie, "a clear distinction was made between sections reserved predominantly for official functions such as receptions or formal banquets, and other parts which had more intimate character and were reserved for the ruler or his spouse" (Eichberger and
Beaven 228). In Margaret's case, public rooms such as her Première Chambre
were lined with portraits of her Habsburg relations and their dynastic alliances,
providing highly public support and justification for her own political authority
and position in the Netherlands. However, in other rooms within the palace
Margaret also created a more personal, but no less strategic definition of her
dynastic position. In both her library and *petit cabinet* (one of her most private
apartments, identified as her private study) Margaret displayed paintings and
sculptures of herself and her late husband Philibert of Savoy. The untimely death
of her husband and newly acquired status as widow placed extra pressures upon
Margaret, which she skillfully negotiated through her careful display of appropriate art objects of herself and her dead husband:

> Margaret of Austria obviously intended to project herself as a woman who was
> spiritually and emotionally attached to her former husband . . . whenever she
> presented foreign dignitaries with a portrait of herself, she preferred to stress her
> status as a devout widow. . . . The seriousness of Margaret's intention to honour
> the memory of Philibert of Savoy is further demonstrated by the large number

of portraits of him in the library and in other parts of the palace. (Eichberger and Beaven 240)[7]

Here the display of the art object (the portrait of the dead husband) functions as a commemorative gesture, shielding the politically vulnerable widow from potential charges of public as well as private transgression. Margaret treads a careful line between her public celebration of Habsburg power and authority (and her own subservience within this narrative), and a semi-private representation of herself as dutiful widow.

By now, hopefully, the example of Margaret of Austria's astute manipulation of semi-private space and art objects offers a different perspective on the nature of Gertrude's closet, and the ways in which its artistic artifacts are themselves central to the intense psychological drama played out between mother and son. Hamlet's outbursts against his mother consistently focus on the idea of a visual revelation of her "guilt." His first impulse is to sit her down where "You go not till I set you up a glass / Where you may see the inmost part of you" (3.4.18–19). Hamlet then claims that Heaven's "tristful visage" balefully looks down upon Gertrude's second marriage, before Hamlet's dramatic invocation of the portraits of Gertrude's husbands:

> Look here upon this picture, and on this,
> The counterfeit presentment of two brothers.
> See what a grace was seated on this brow,
> Hyperion's curls, the front of Jove himself,
> An eye like Mars to threaten and command,
> A station like the herald Mercury
> New-lighted on a heaven-kissing hill,
> A combination and a form indeed
> Where every god did seem to set his seal
> To give the world assurance of a man.
> This was your husband. Look you now what follows.
> Here is your husband, like a mildew'd ear
> Blasting his wholesome brother.   (3.4.53–65)

In this dramatically compelling moment of *ekphrasis* Hamlet invokes two "pictures" of his father and uncle, apparently of similar appearance and dimensions, as the Prince is so careful to juxtapose the images as companion portraits deliberately. Their superficially similar appearance as art objects only underlines the radical difference in appearance of the two brothers. However, as the picture of Claudius is presumably an official portrait, Hamlet ironically alludes to its "counterfeit" appearance, which gives him enough rhetorical latitude to gloss the image with an account of the degenerate appearance of his uncle.

Editors of the play have endlessly disputed the status and significance of these "pictures." In his Arden edition of the play, Harold Jenkins sums up the predominant belief that Hamlet brings two small portable portraits of Old Hamlet and Claudius, reminiscent of the "picture in little" (2.2.362) of his uncle that Hamlet mentions earlier in the play.[8] Jenkins dismisses what seems an extremely valid objection that Hamlet is unlikely to possess the type of picture that he has already condemned for both its subject matter and sycophancy "demands too much of psychological consistency," while "[v]erisimilitude could equally object to the Queen's having portraits of two husbands in her chamber" (Shakespeare, ed. Jenkins 519). However, the example of Margaret of Austria would suggest that the figure of the dead husband could easily be seen hanging in the semi-private rooms of a woman like Gertrude, even if such a portrait were perhaps uneasily juxtaposed with the figure of her present husband. In dismissing such a possibility, Jenkins also refuses any possibility of reading for Gertrude's proactive attempt to signal her commemoration of one husband, and loyal obedience to another, however uneasy this scenario may have been. In the process Hamlet is seen as the dynamic active agent in the exchange, Gertrude as a passive, guilty figure. On the contrary, I would argue for providing Gertrude with a degree of agency in the artistic artifacts that line her walls. It seems unlikely that Hamlet drags two paintings onstage at this point, or (as Jenkins suggests as an alternative) that he wears one miniature painting (of his father) while grasping the other miniature (of Claudius) attached to Gertrude's neck, thus losing the dramatic force of Hamlet's deeply partisan piece of art criticism.[9] All of these possibilities deny Gertrude any space for commemoration, however silent and discreet it may be, hanging on the walls of her closet. However, to reread Gertrude's strategic deployment of these "pictures" offers a very different perception of Hamlet's outburst in this scene. Hamlet's rage at his mother has invariably been interpreted as a wider symptom of the lack of mourning in the play, emanating from Lacan's point that "in all the instances of mourning in Hamlet, one element is always present: the rites have been cut short and performed in secret" (Lacan 40). Or perhaps such rites are performed in plain view, displayed on the walls of Gertrude's closet, a silent but visually compelling reminder of her dilemma. Hamlet's "fault" at this point is to misrecognize these signs of commemoration. The subsequent critical tradition has accepted the assumption that in the display of material and artistic artifacts, Hamlet has to be the active agent, in the process denuding Gertrude of agency and reaffirming her "blame" for the play's tragic conflict. In drawing attention to the ways in which elite women utilized art objects (and in this particular case commemorative portraits) within semi-autonomous private domestic space, this approach to the materiality of the closet scene offers one way of reascribing social agency to Gertrude.

The pictures in Gertrude's closet have attracted a certain level of critical attention, most of which I have argued unreflectively denies Gertrude any latitude for ethical responsibility, and colludes in the assumption that Hamlet's behavior in the scene is justifiable. However, there is one other particularly prominent artistic artifact that exist in Gertrude's closet, an object hidden in plain view and yet almost completely neglected by editors and critics of the play, and that is the "arras," or tapestry. Polonius is at pains to point out to Claudius as they hatch their plan to spy on Hamlet and Gertrude that "Behind the arras I'll convey myself / To hear the process" (3.3.28–29); the 1603 first quarto has Polonius informing Gertrude that "I'le shrowde my selfe behind the Arras" (Holderness and Loughrey 78). Gertrude later informs Polonius that in a "lawless fit" Hamlet has stabbed Polonius "Behind the arras" (4.1.8–9). Critics have often dismissed the reference to the arras and Polonius's fatal eavesdropping as an almost tragic-comic moment for the old counselor, caught hiding behind the early modern equivalent to window curtains. However, as with the complacent assumptions made about the portraits that appear in Gertrude's closet, this response to the arras elides its artistic and social status within the period of the play's production.

Tapestry was referred to as "arras" in sixteenth-century England due to the commerce between England and the town of Arras in Flanders that saw English wool sold as the raw material for the beautifully woven decorative and narrative tapestries that often found their way back into the great halls and courts of the English nobility. Candace Adelson has succinctly explained the significance of tapestry throughout the courts of Europe in the following terms:

> In an age when tapestries were an integral part of European decoration, they were a luxury item only the wealthy could afford. In terms of workmanship, tapestries, along with finely chased armour, were the most costly form of movable art that could be bought. . . . Tapestry was considered a more luxurious, movable form of monumental painting, and appraisals in inventories of the time indicate that tapestries were much more highly valued than paintings. . . . They were also the most practical of furnishings for the mobile courts of feudal and early modern Europe. As lords and rulers inspected their dominions, they could carry tapestries with them from castle to castle, where they not only impressed subjects with their master's grandeur but also provided warmth and aesthetic pleasure. (Adelson 16)

Adelson's argument is an important corrective to those who see the tapestry as simply domestic insulation, an approach that sums up responses to the arras in *Hamlet*. However, as Lisa Jardine and I argue in *Global Interests: Renaissance Art between East and West*, throughout the sixteenth century the imperial courts of mainland Europe sought to invest their commissioning of huge, monumental narrative tapestry cycles with increasingly strident messages of political power and authority (Jardine and Brotton 63–131). While the Spanish, French, and Portuguese courts commissioned lavish cycles of tapestries from the great weaving workshops of Brussels, the English courts lacked the purchasing power to order tailor-made tapestries, settling instead for ready-made tapestries.[10] This had several particularly significant consequences for English perceptions of tapestry. The materiality and iconography of tapestries were both intimately associated not only with the Low Countries (in terms of their production), but also with

Catholic imperial power (in terms of the political and imperial messages woven into the tapestries). In the summer of 1554, the magnificent series of twelve Habsburg-commissioned tapestries entitled *The Conquest of Tunis*, commemorating Emperor Charles V's victory over the Ottomans at Tunis in 1535, was displayed for the first time at the marriage of Charles's son Philip to Mary Tudor. To an English audience enthusiastically embracing Protestantism, the images of the Habsburg Empire brutally despatching that other "infidel" that haunted Europe, the Islamic Ottoman Empire, were clearly meant to threaten and intimidate (Jardine and Brotton 82–113).

If the subject matter of such tapestries was meant to intimidate and coerce its (English) audience, then their alien status also provoked anxiety. In November 1565, a patent was bestowed upon thirty so-called "Dutchmen" residing in Norwich, described as "aliens born, not denizens," allowing them to practice "the trades of making bayes, arras, sayes, tapestrye, stamens, carsay and other such outlandyshe commodities as have not been used to be made in England" (*Calendar* 210). It was these "outlandyshe commodities," tapestries, or "arras" that hung in Gertrude's closet, that in terms of both their subject matter and origin would have been "strange" and troubling for an English audience. Two particularly striking examples of Elizabeth I's own encounter with arras vividly illustrate the anxieties associated with tapestry. In May 1555, Elizabeth met her sister Mary to protest at her virtual house arrest since Mary's recent marriage to Philip. Recounting the meeting in his *Acts and Monuments*, John Foxe claimed that, in a moment reminiscent of Polonius's own covert piece of surveillance, "It is thought that King Philip was there behind a cloth, and not seen" (Foxe 621). This association between the arras, secrecy, spying, and surveillance runs right throughout Elizabeth's reign. In 1601, John Harington noted that the Queen, in an almost comic parody of Hamlet, "walks much in her privy chamber, and stamps with her feet at ill news, and thrusts her rusty sword into the arras in great rage" (Schmidgall 95).[11] Even if these stories are apocryphal, they reflect a trace of the anxiety associated with both what the tapestry literally and figuratively *represents*, and also what lurks behind its glittering, seductive surface, a trace that we can also detect in *Hamlet*.

If this exploration of the contemporary significance of tapestry seems somewhat tangential to its appearance in the closet scene, it is worth noting other climactic moments in Shakespeare's work where tapestry is invoked. In Act 2, scene 4 of *Cymbeline*, for example, Iachimo provides proof for Posthumous that he has gained access to his wife Imogen's bedchamber by describing her chamber as "hang'd / With tapestry of silk and silver, the story / Proud Cleopatra, when she met her Roman" (2.4.68–76). Similarly, in *The Rape of Lucrece*, following Lucrece's rape at the hands of Tarquin, she invokes a tapestry (or "counterfeit arras")[12] of the fall of Troy:

> At last she calls to mind where hangs a piece
> Of skilful painting made for Priam's Troy,
> Before the which is drawn the power of Greece,
> For Helen's rape the city to destroy. (Shakespeare, ed. Evans 1366–69)

What is so striking about both of these textual moments of ekphrastic virtuosity is that they both make an explicit connection between imperial authority and sexual violence. The stories of Antony and Cleopatra and the fall of Troy both mediate scenes of (in the first example) figurative and then (in the second example) actual sexual violence. Stephanie Jed has already brilliantly traced the ways in which the figure of rape, and in particular the story of the rape of Lucrece, mediates Italian humanist justifications of political "liberty" and republicanism (Jed 1989). I would argue that something similar happens in these moments in Shakespeare, where the apparent threat of external imperial power (in this case the specter of the Spanish, Habsburg empire) is perceived through the emotionally intense representation of the sexually vulnerable, or damaged, woman. Sexual assault becomes the modality through which imperial aggression is understood. Gertrude stands in a similar relation to the dramatic action of *Hamlet*, a figure slandered for her sexual behavior, relentlessly pushed into a private, interior world, yet mediating the dynastic and political tensions that structure the wider world of the play.

In pursuing such an approach, it is worth noting the ways in which the Russian director Grigori Kozintsev uses tapestry in his own film of the play, first released in 1964. In his reading of Kozintsev's use of tapestries, Jack Jorgens has argued that:

> By contrasting the dead generations with the living, they help develop the theme of "mortality," but are by no means limited to this theme. The tapestries furnish warmth and provide cosmetics for the brutal fortress and are thus part of the "seeming" which disgusts Hamlet. They are both the scenic backdrop for and a comment upon the "acts" of the Danish courtiers. Figures in the hangings are artificial, lifeless, distorted, two-dimensional like Claudius' followers. (Jorgens 226)

Jorgens analyzes the ways in which Kozintsev has appreciated the oppressive quality of tapestry, its coercive political overtones, and its connotations of spying and surveillance. In his reading of Kozintsev's visualization of the closet scene, Jorgens notes:

> Gertrude looks but does not see, like the tapestry figures. The development of her character is made clear by a shot in her bedroom as Hamlet enters – as she stands near the hangings, her dark silhouette makes it seem that she has been cut loose and lifted out of their two-dimensional world. And indeed this is what Hamlet has come to do—to make her self-conscious, to jar her loose and force her into a three-dimensional existence . . . Hamlet's victory over the tapestries

is short-lived, for they help to destroy him by veiling reality. When Hamlet stabs recklessly through the royal figures on the arras, he is attempting to cut himself loose from time and fate. But as with Macbeth, struggling against fate only enmeshes him even further. (Jorgens 227)

This is an astute reading of Kozintsev's use of tapestry, but it also recreates Gertrude as a hollow, duplicitous woman who is conflated with the lifeless, courtly figures that make up the tapestry hanging in her closet. In direct contrast, Hamlet is seen as the tragic hero cutting through the courtly artifice and deceptive "seeming" of Claudius's court, personified in the oppressive tapestries. Once again, Gertrude is denied any agency in controlling her private space and the artistic artifacts that define it; the figure of the tapestry, like the double portraits of the two kings, condemns her actions and justifies Hamlet's aggressive outburst. This is a telling example of the ways in which cinematic versions of *Hamlet*, from Olivier to Zeffirelli, tend to reproduce a deeply conservative representation of the play and of Gertrude's own culpability, suggesting that Gertrude carries "the play's burden of guilt so recognizably" (Jardine 157) and convincingly even today. However, as the example of Margaret of Austria has suggested, we have to be far more careful in our assumptions about elite women's proactive involvement in the deployment of artistic artifacts than the predominant critical and cinematic tradition would like us to believe.

With this in mind, I offer one final, contentious suggestion regarding the arras in Gertrude's closet. Having already noticed Shakespeare's persistent conflation of imperial power and sexual violence in his ekphrastic descriptions of tapestry, I would suggest that the tapestry that hangs in Gertrude's closet portrays the fall of Troy, and that it retains the trace of sexual violence and death that permeates the hanging in *The Rape of Lucrece*. This suggestion makes Hamlet's exchange with the players in 2.2 even more significant, in its evocation of "Aeneas' tale to Dido" (442–43) of the sack of Troy and Pyrrhus's murder of Priam. In describing Pyrrhus's pursuit of the aged Priam, the First Player declaims that:

> For lo, his sword,
> Which was declining on the milky head
> Of reverend Priam, seem'd I'th'air to stick;
> So, as a painted tyrant, Pyrrhus stood,
> And like a neutral to his will and matter,
> Did nothing.   (2.2.473–78)

Frozen in mid-air, the image of the *painted* Pyrrhus evokes a painting, or *tapestry*, as much as it draws on its literary origin, especially when compared with the earlier visual representation of Troy in *Lucrece* (indeed, representations of Troy in the form of tapestry were undoubtedly far more widely available and legible than literary accounts of the fall of the city). The moment is of course a wonderfully ambiguous encapsulation of not only Hamlet's personal dilemma but also his complex subjective identifications. It anticipates Hamlet's own reluctance to dispatch Claudius in 3.3, but at the same time such an identification with the "tyrant" Pyrrhus dispatching the "unnerved father" uncomfortably conflates Hamlet with Claudius himself, the tyrant who murderously dispatches his kin, and the play's controlling paternal authority, Hamlet senior. Hecuba's subsequent passionate grief and "clamour" for her murdered husband that "Would have made milch the burning eyes of heaven / And passion in the gods" (513–14), is favorably contrasted with Gertrude's lack of ostensible rituals of mourning. However, how would this moment echo in Hamlet's later exchange with his mother in front of tapestries of the fall of Troy in the closet scene? Here, Hamlet wields his sword with the murderous recklessness of Pyrrhus, killing Polonius and then chillingly placing Gertrude herself back within the tapestry by threatening to "wring your heart" "[i]f it be made of penetrable *stuff*" (35–36). Rather than drawing her out from the two-dimensional world of the tapestry (as Kozintsev seems to suggest), Hamlet is putting her back into the "stuff" that constitutes the woven tapestry. The potential for staging here is fascinating. Does Hamlet pierce the figure of Priam on the tapestry as he kills Polonius ("Is it the King?" 3.4.26), and is the woven image of the mourning Hecuba a powerful but silent testament and correlative to Gertrude's own mourning of the loss of her first husband? Both possibilities compromise Hamlet's motivation and offer a different way of understanding the dilemma within which Gertrude finds herself, and are the outcome of rereading the negotiations that silently take place on the early modern stage between subject and object.

This reading of the pictures and tapestry that appear in the closet scene is aimed at the theatrical possibilities of staging the scene, as much as it is concerned with offering a different intellectual and critical approach to 3.4. The objects I have discussed are, by their very nature, silent. However, in attempting to renew our sensitivity to the ways in which such objects did in effect "speak" to an early modern community, it might be possible also to reappraise the ways in which women silently appropriated artistic artifacts to shield themselves from the kind of accusations that Hamlet levels at his mother. How we want to act upon such insights in reading *Hamlet* in the twenty-first century is very much a question of our own ethical responsibilities as critics and directors.

NOTES

1. All references to the play refer to Harold Jenkins's Arden edition of the play (Shakespeare 1982).

2. For the most recent, if rather limited, encapsulation of this perspective, see Kiernan Ryan, *Shakespeare* (Hemel Hempstead: Prentice Hall, 1993).

3. For a discussion of the way films of the play from Olivier's version onward interpret closet as bedroom, and its ensuing Freudian implications, see Murray Biggs, "'He's going to his mother's closet': Hamlet and Gertrude on screen," *Shakespeare Survey*, 45

(1992), pp. 53–62. Biggs does not discuss the more specific sixteenth-century contexts of the closet.

4. There is an obvious connotation here between the bedroom as a sepulchral monument, a spider's web, and perhaps most graphically, a symbolic representation of female genitalia.

5. Modern stage productions also tend to reproduce this version of the closet, although the psychoanalytical investments in this approach make film a more appropriate medium to explore its own investments in this version of the scene. On this dimension of Shakespeare and film, see Julia Reinhard Lupton and Kenneth Reinhard, *After Oedipus: Shakespeare in Psychoanalysis* (Ithaca: Cornell University Press, 1993).

6. See Thomas Middleton, *The Changeling*, ed. N.W. Bawcutt (Cambridge, Mass.: Harvard University Press, 1958), 5.3.

7. Eichberger and Beaven note that "[a]fter the death of Philibert, Margaret was involved in an ongoing conflict with the Savoy family over her claims to the dowry" (p. 241), suggestive of the ways in which Margaret's skillful manipulation of her relationship to her dead husband was not simply altruistic.

8. Drawing on several other contemporary dramatic examples of the appearance of paintings on stage, Jenkins concludes that "the characters bring the pictures on and dispose them in the course of their roles, and Hamlet by all the analogies must be supposed to have done the same" (Shakespeare 1982: 517)..

9. Nevertheless, this is the option that Olivier chooses in his film of the play. While cinema can accommodate the use of close-up required to make the scale of the miniature painting effective, Olivier makes little of the presence of these art objects in the scene.

10. Henry VIII possessed over two thousand tapestries, but very few were actually designed specifically for the King, unlike his imperial rivals Francis I and Charles V, who commissioned extensive cycles of narrative tapestries displaying their own artistic and imperial grandeur. On Henry's collection see W.G. Thomson, *A History of Tapestry* (London: Hodder and Stoughton, 1906), pp. 239–61.

11. I am grateful to Michael Hatfield for drawing this reference to my attention.

12. As with the portraits in the closet scene, there has been much speculation as to the "skillful painting" in *The Rape of Lucrece*. Ironically, I would not suggest that it is a tapestry, but a so-called "counterfeit arras," a stained wall hanging made to imitate expensive Flemish tapestry. This is itself another manifestation of English anxieties regarding tapestry. On this debate see Clarke Hulse, "A piece of skilful painting in Shakespeare's *Lucrece*," *Shakespeare Studies*, 31 (1978).

WORKS CITED

Adelson, Candace. *European Tapestry in the Minneapolis Institute of Art*. New York: Abrams, 1994.

Appadurai, Arjun. "Introduction: Commodities and the Politics of Value." *The Social Life of Things: Commodities in Cultural Perspective*, ed. Arjun Appadurai. Cambridge: Cambridge University Press, 1986, pp. 3–63.

Armstrong, Philip. "Watching *Hamlet* Watching: Lacan, Shakespeare and the Mirror/stage." *Alternative Shakespeares Vol. 2*, ed. Terence Hawkes. London and New York: Routledge, 1996, pp. 216–37.

Biggs, Murray. "'He's Going to His Mother's Closet': Hamlet and Gertrude on Screen." *Shakespeare Survey*, 45 (1992): 53–62.

Calendar of Patent Rolls, Vol. III, 1563–66, London, 1890.

De Grazia, Margreta, Maureeen Quilligan, and Peter Stallybrass, eds. *Subject and Object in Renaissance Culture*. Cambridge: Cambridge University Press, 1996.

Donaldson, Peter. "Olivier, Hamlet, and Freud." *Shakespeare on Film*, ed. Robert Shaughnessy. London: Macmillan, 1998, pp. 103–125.

Eichberger, Dagmar and Lisa Beaven. "Family Members and Political Allies: the Portrait Collection of Margaret of Austria," *Art Bulletin*, 77 (1995): 225–48.

Foxe, John. *Acts and Monuments*. Ed. Josiah Pratt, London: Religious Tract Society, 1877.

Holderness, Graham and Bryan Loughrey, eds. *The Tragicall Historie of Hamlet Prince of Denmarke*. Hemel Hempstead: Harvester, 1992.

Hulse, Clark. "A piece of skilful painting in Shakespeare's *Lucrece*." *Shakespeare Survey*, 31 (1978): 13–22.

Jardine, Lisa. *Reading Shakespeare Historically*. London and New York: Routledge, 1996.

Jardine, Lisa and Jerry Brotton. *Global Interests: Renaissance Art between East and West*. London: Reaktion Books, 2000.

Jed, Stephanie. *Chaste Thinking: The Rape of Lucretia and the Birth of Humanism*. Bloomington: Indiana University Press, 1989.

Jones, Ernest. *Hamlet and Oedipus*. New York: Norton, 1976.

Jorgens, Jack. *Shakespeare on Film*. Bloomington: Indiana University Press, 1997.

Lacan, Jacques "Desire and the Interpretation of Desire in *Hamlet*." *Literature and Psychoanalysis: The Question of Reading: Otherwise*, ed. Shoshana Felman. Baltimore: John Hopkins University Press, 1982, pp. 11–52.

Middleton, Thomas. *The Changeling*, ed. N.W. Bawcutt. Revels Plays. Cambridge, Mass.: Harvard University Press, 1958.

Parker, Patricia. *Shakespeare from the Margins: Language, Culture, Context*. Chicago: University of Chicago Press, 1996.

Reinhard Lupton, Julia and Kenneth Reinhard. *After Oedipus: Shakespeare in Psychoanalysis*. Ithaca: Cornell University Press, 1993.

Rose, Jacqueline. "Sexuality in the Reading of *Hamlet* and *Measure for Measure*." *Alternative Shakespeares*, ed. John Drakakis. London and New York: Routledge, 1985, pp. 95–118.

Ryan, Kiernan. *Shakespeare*. Hemel Hempstead: Prentice Hall, 1993.

Schmidgall, Gary. *Shakespeare and the Poet's Life*. Lexington: University of Kentucky Press, 1990.

Shakespeare, William. *Hamlet*, ed. Harold Jenkins. Arden Edition. London and New York: Routledge, 1982.

Shakespeare, William. *The Narrative Poems*, ed. Maurice Evans. London: Penguin, 1989.

Stewart, Alan. "The Early Modern Closet Discovered." *Representations*, 50 (1995): 76–101.

Thomson, W.G. *A History of Tapestry*. London: Hodder and Stoughton, 1906.

Weimann, Robert. "Mimesis in *Hamlet*." *Shakespeare and the Question of Theory*, ed. Patricia Parker and Geoffrey Hartman. London: Methuen, 1985, pp. 275–91.

The Old Bill

TERENCE HAWKES

1. LAW AND ORDER

We can begin in Berlin. It seems distinctly odd that, in the late summer of 1945, at the end of the most destructive war in human history, the victorious allied armies occupying the German capital should take it upon themselves to act as Masters of the Revels. Yet in addition to the countless tasks inseparable from the administration of a huge city now reduced to rubble, each of them solemnly embarked on the business of censoring plays.

In the American sector, the Office of Military Government of the United States (OMGUS) duly appointed a number of so-called Theater Officers. It also circulated two lists: a "black" list of proscribed plays, and a "white" one of works whose public performance was deemed to be of benefit to a defeated, traumatized populace in need of radical political reeducation. The black list featured two major pieces by Shakespeare: *Julius Caesar* and *Coriolanus*. Performances of these were roundly banned, in light of their supposed "glorifications of dictatorship." The white list contained *Macbeth* and *Hamlet*, the former held brusquely to affirm that "Crime Does Not Pay," the latter's inclusion more curiously justified on the basis of its alleged treatment of "corruption and justice."[1]

More than fifty years later, on October 19, 1999, in London, the state visit to Britain of President Jiang Zemin of China was marked by a series of scuffles between some of the spectators and the police. Protesters against China's record on human rights shouted slogans and tried to unfurl appropriate banners. Their efforts were vigorously suppressed, apparently in sympathy with the Chinese president's frequently expressed sensitivities in the matter. His view that, in a civilized society, dissident voices should be kept firmly in check was evidently fully supported by the British government. That afternoon it was arranged that he should visit the new Globe Theatre in Southwark. Plainly, the issue wasn't whether the president liked Shakespeare's plays or not. His visit raised the much more complex question of cultural meanings in modern Britain and the social and political use to which both plays and Bard may be put in generating them. The incidents in this case point to the operation of a well-defined binary structure: dissidence and disruption on the one hand (located in the protesters) and appeasement and pacification on the other (located in Southwark).

It seems not unreasonable to suggest that these events in the middle and toward the end of the twentieth century hint at—even coyly propose—a certain meaningful role for Shakespeare in the general scheme of things British and American. Effectively, they construct him as an agency of law and order.[2]

2. ON WATCH

Of course the notion of William Shakespeare as "The Old Bill," a Bard deployed as an instrument of "policing," is scarcely a new development.[3] *Hamlet* in particular seems to have been associated with that sort of activity almost from the first. Two of its earliest recorded performances took place, remarkably enough, on board a ship off the coast of Sierra Leone. The journal of William Keeling, captain of the East India Company's vessel the *Dragon*, bound with the *Hector* and the *Consent* for the East Indies, gives the details:

> 1607, Sept. 5. I sent the interpreter, according to his desier, abord the Hector whear he brooke fast, and after came abord mee, wher we gaue the tragedie of Hamlett.

The performance's "policing" purpose becomes clear in a later entry:

> 1608, Mar. 31. I envited Captain Hawkins to a ffishe dinner, and had Hamlet acted abord me: which I permitt to keepe my people from idleness and unlawful games, or sleepe.[4]

In truth, the notion of the Bard as a kind of policeman lies at a deep and sensitive level in the English-speaking psyche. The "legitimate" theater's long, Shakespeare-fueled climb to its present summit of respectability has always required the conspicuous shedding of various degrees of inherited "lawlessness," followed by the acquisition, among audiences at least, of the lineaments of probity and solid citizenship. Roads and streets named after the playwright have, since the nineteenth century, been a feature of British suburbia. In Chicago, the 14th police district has long been known as "Shakespeare."

Congruent tendencies among veteran Shakespearean scholars are not unknown. W.W. Greg, hero of the "new bibliography," virtual founder of modern Shakespearean textual scholarship, and author of the magisterial, law-and-order enforcing *The Editorial Problem in Shakespeare* (1942), bonded eagerly with the constabulary, even recording that, during the first World War, he drove a police car "for Scotland Yard." Later in life, the same rectitudinous zeal impelled him to "enrol as a special constable and to drive a car once more for

Scotland Yard during the general strike of May 1926."[5] Unsurprisingly, Greg also enjoyed detective novels. His favorite was Michael Innes's classic, *Hamlet, Revenge!* (1937), in which a murder mystery is solved by a detective in the context of a modern performance of the play (Wilson, F. P. 331). The novel notably draws attention to, and to a small extent focuses on, some of the moments when the play *Hamlet*, rather than any of its characters, seems to take on a "controlling" role in respect of its audience, reaching out into it in order to marshal, restrain, prevent, or "police" its responses.

3. FELL SERGEANT

As Innes need not point out, one of the most effective examples occurs right at the beginning of the play. A man comes out onto the stage, dressed as a soldier and carrying the large military spear, the partisan. He takes up a position, evidently as a sentry. A second man enters, similarly dressed, also carrying a partisan. He approaches the first man, in the role of a relieving sentry. Suddenly, he freezes, manifests extreme fear, and brings his spear from the "rest" or "trail" position into an offensive one. The effect is startling. It immediately involves the audience in an atmosphere of grotesque unease which, they can see, already generates breaches of military discipline onstage, forcing these soldiers into error. Indeed, discipline so completely deserts the second man (it is Barnardo) that he blurts out the play's first line, not as a soldier, but merely as a very frightened onlooker: "Who's there?" (1.1.1). In consequence, the play's second line, uttered by the first man (Francisco) manifests all the exasperation of the professional who, having kept his nerve, seeks to correct his colleague on matters of military procedure; "Nay, answer me. Stand and unfold yourself" (1.1.2). Barnardo, the challenger challenged, then nervously confirms the restoration of order by uttering the password "Long live the King" (1.1.3).

The irony is intense. The King, we suspect, will not live long. We know that his predecessor did not. Worse, a hint of the presence of that predecessor's ghost is the factor that ignites the sentry's nervousness, and provokes his indiscipline. But it is in that simple movement of a spear, from an inoffensive to an offensive position, that the play, as it were, first speaks. Before one of its characters utters a word, that silent gesture reaches out into the auditorium, to coerce, marshal, and decisively direct the emotional traffic. Of course, all art engages in this sort of thing. All plays have designs on their audiences, which they promote through the wide variety of means the medium places at their disposal. But *Hamlet* seems remarkable for the degree to which it seeks to prescribe, moderate, or "police" responses to itself and, ultimately, for the self-consciousness with which it draws attention to its own activities in this sphere. "Look," it periodically seems almost to boast, "See how I can control you."

4. MAKING A STATEMENT

I refer deliberately to the *play*'s activity in this regard, not to those of any of its characters, although they too, as we have seen, will be individually involved. Indeed, it is almost a commonplace that most of them engage in some sort of policing or surveillance activity. The Ghost watches, and comments on Hamlet's remonstration with his mother; Polonius notoriously spies on Laertes, and on Hamlet and Ophelia, and in fact meets his death while spying. In truth, Hamlet himself seems to act very much as a kind of policeman in his own play. He constantly tries to tell us what to think, how to assess the events we encounter. His soliloquies are nothing if not a series of urgent recapitulations, siftings of evidence, and "briefing" interventions into the tumultuous action. Like other "great ones," rarely "unwatched" in Claudius's court, the Prince "polices" Ophelia's funeral, and, most famously, uses a performance of *The Mousetrap* to place Claudius under observation and secure evidence against him. It's hardly surprising that the cumulative effect of all these individual efforts at molding, shaping, or recording the behavior of others is to confirm *Hamlet* as a play of supervision, watching, eavesdropping, and trap-setting. That the Prince should finally picture his own condition as one of penal confinement, "Denmark's a prison" (2. 2. 243), and present his own demise in terms of resolute police action. ". . . as this fell sergeant Death/Is strict in his arrest" (5. 2. 341–42) comes as no surprise.

Less overt moments of policing are not hard to find. One of the most startling occurs in Polonius's interchange with his spy Reynaldo:

> *Polonius*:   Marry, sir, here's my drift . . .
> . . . .
> Your party in converse, him you would sound,
> Having ever seen in the prenominate crimes
> The youth you breathe of guilty, be assur'd
> He closes with you in this consequence:
> "Good sir," or so, or "friend," or "gentleman,"
> According to the phrase or the addition
> Of man and country.
> *Reynaldo*:   Very good, my lord.
> *Polonius*:   And then sir, does a this—a does—what was I about to
> say? By the mass, I was about to say something. Where
> did I leave?
> *Reynaldo*:   At "closes in the consequence."
> *Polonius*:   At "closes in the consequence," ay, marry.
> He closes thus: "I know the gentleman . . ."
>
> (2. 1. 38–55)

The introduction into any play of a moment when an actor appears to forget his or her lines, is a high-risk strategy. It risks unraveling the very fabric of the art. It courts that disaster in the hope of gaining advantage, using "error" to pursue a more subtle accuracy and, by its sly turning of the nuts and bolts of the play into a statement that the play itself suddenly makes, engages in "policing" of considerable subtlety.[6]

Polonius's concern here, after all, is with spying: with the ways in which concrete information yields itself to the resourceful probing of a secret agent who may "By indirections find directions out." When he seems to forget his lines, the serpentine plotter of the play's world turns abruptly into a mere performer caught short in ours. As Polonius collapses into the actor who is playing him, his tawdry guff about truth crumbles in the face of a contesting "reality," which bursts out from the stage to land explosively in the middle of the audience. The actor who momentarily and apparently disastrously peeps out from behind the figure of Polonius calls that figure's entire project into question by indicating to us that this is a play: that he who has been talking of investigative pretense, of carefully misleading suggestion, of acting a part, is himself, here and now, acting.

The impact on the audience must be considerable. It's as if, at a stroke, we found ourselves unceremoniously pitched backstage, into the play's material, quotidian innards. A dizzying epistemological gulf suddenly yawns. Who is speaking here, actor or "character"? Where is reality located, on or off the stage? In that sudden, explosive confusion, before its hasty resolution by Reynaldo, the audience feels itself firmly nudged in the direction of one of *Hamlet*'s central concerns. It's a calculated moment of jolting realignment. Those who entered the theater as spectators suddenly find themselves stumbling, as participants, in a no-man's land whose indistinct and tangled paths lead inexorably to *The Mousetrap*.

5. HOSTILE WITNESS

Of course, *Hamlet* is well-known for its exposition of the notion that plays are able to police their audiences rather more directly: that they have a forensic potential which can even provoke spontaneous confession. The Prince's claim that a powerfully delivered speech can "make mad the guilty and appal the free" (2.2.558) does not lack confidence and his assurance—

> I have heard
> That guilty creatures sitting at a play
> Have, by the very cunning of the scene,
> Been struck so to the soul that presently
> They have proclaim'd their malefactions.
> For murder, though it have no tongue, will speak
> With most miraculous organ. (2.2.584–90)

—reflects a playwright's self-interest in connecting the performance of *The Mousetrap* with a long and substantial anecdotal tradition confirming the link between "playing" and the actual social world. The understanding that the one carries imperatives for the other is reinforced by the suggestion that plays harbor a summary, prosecuting power enabling them somehow to reach out and make a kind of juridical contact with their audiences' private lives and individual consciences.[7]

But the flurry of play and stage-references preceding *The Mousetrap* scarcely prepares us for the breathtaking audacity of what happens during its performance, although it does serve, by its references to playing companies, the war of the theaters, and even by the player's graphic presentation of Pyrrhus as a Hamlet-like revenger, frozen on the brink of action, to construct an appropriate context. Thus Hamlet's account of a once-seen "excellent play, well digested in the scenes, set down with as much modesty as cunning" (2. 2. 435ff.), his comments on the "purpose of playing," his advice to the actors, and his remarks on dumb shows and on Polonius's acting can be seen as part of a deliberate strategy. When actors talk, in a play, about the mechanics of acting, the effect must be to intensify an audience's awareness of its own presence and function. Polonius's ready assumption of the applauding spectator's role in respect of Hamlet's rendition of lines from a play, "Fore God, my lord, well spoken, with good accent and good discretion" (2.2.462–3), offers a coercive model.

The climax then comes when the issue of audience-response moves to the center of the stage. Claudius's blankness in the face of the plain depiction of his crime in the dumb show has of course famously exercised critics over the years. How is it that he remains apparently unmoved? Does his silence indicate superb self-control, which breaks down only when the performance proper begins? Does it suggest that the murder of his brother did not in fact follow the sequence or use the method described by the Ghost? Does it therefore mean that the Ghost is unreliable? Does Claudius in fact fail to notice the dumb show? Does he watch it but, because of its formal elaboration, fail to notice that it applies to him? No doubt there are a number of other possible explanations.[8]

It's an interesting reflection of modern presuppositions concerning art, and especially drama, that this matter should be thought to constitute a "critical problem" or even a playwright's error. For it now seems reasonable to argue, to the contrary, that Claudius's null response represents another of those moments when the play, rather than one of its characters, speaks. Having primed its audience to raise its own awareness of itself, having led it to expect that audiences should and will respond in a specific mode, that guilty creatures sitting at a play will proclaim their malefactions, it suddenly and sensationally presents us with a very important member of an audience who does none of these things.

Claudius's failure to respond to the dumb show is not an "error" or a "mistake" made by Shakespeare. It's not something that goes "wrong." Or, rather, like Polonius's forgetting of his lines, it's the sort of "wrongness" which, once confronted, begins to reveal what our inherited notions of "rightness" conceal from us. In effect, directed as it is at the audience of *Hamlet* as much as at the "inner" audience of the Prince and Horatio, it represents—once more, as right at the play's beginning, by movements made in silence—a breathtaking defeat of expectations that have been carefully and stealthily aroused and unthinkingly embraced. Any confusion or dismay it generates—soon dispelled by subsequent events—not only mimics in us the roller coaster of emotions depicted on stage by the Prince. It also deepens and sophisticates our perception of both Hamlet and Claudius. In any event, *The Mousetrap* doesn't work very effectively and Hamlet's assertion to the contrary hints at both perversity and desperation. Indeed, the fact that Claudius remains largely impervious to the cardboard accusations of a Player King and Queen operates to his distinct advantage. Suddenly, Hamlet's opponent seems stronger, subtler, more sophisticated. He begins to intrigue, bewilder, and perhaps ever so slightly to charm us as much as he disturbs and repels.

In short, *The Mousetrap* sets in motion a new and intricate seesaw. For if *Hamlet* shows us anything at this point, it shows us a highly complex villain whose corruption demands to be viewed in the light of, if not to be mitigated by, the pitiable human situation it generates: that of a man torn by the conflicting demands of criminal passion and remorse, and held to the flames by an obduracy which is also self-control. In addition, and by the same token, it presents us with a no less complex and increasingly reckless protagonist who, in the name of "justice," will impulsively commit violent murder before our eyes: the same crime that he is dedicated to revenge. Hamlet's role as both killer and avenger, an identity clearly symbolized by the figure of Pyrrhus, cannot but complicate the play. In the view of Harold Jenkins, it ranks as a factor "of the most profound significance, without a grasp of which the play cannot be understood."[9] In the end, far from simply representing corruption on the one hand and justice on the other, Claudius and Hamlet seem, as "mighty opposites," to be not unequally matched. In the final moments of the action, with bodies strewn about the stage, Fortinbras orders:

> Let four captains
> Bear Hamlet like a soldier to the stage,
> For he was likely, had he been put on,
> To have prov'd most royal; and for his passage,
> The soldier's music and the rite of war
> Speak loudly for him.
> Take up the bodies . . .   (5.2.400–6)

It's tempting to propose that if "he" in line 402 refers to Hamlet, then "his" in line 403 refers to Claudius.

6. ROYCE'S CHOICES

If *Hamlet*'s "policing" interventions serve ultimately to cloud the differences between hero and villain, they do so as part of a broader function which not only muddies the distinction between play-world and real world, but disturbingly

reduces the distance between right and wrong. In the end, this hugely complicates the play, making its dilemmas to some extent unresolvable, and perhaps
constituting the basis of the enigma from which its capacity to arrest and disturb
derives.

If we now return to Berlin in 1945, it thus seems proper to ask on what basis
a play as fundamentally complex as this could have recommended itself to the
United States military authorities as an exemplary moral and political instrument,
especially in terms as apparently straightforward as its treatment of "corruption
and justice"? It's a particular and instructive instance, perhaps, of a larger, well-
attested tendency whereby a peculiar intimacy has often been felt to pertain
between Shakespeare's world and the oncoming modern one. It hints, seductive-
ly, that we constitute a uniquely sympathetic audience for his plays. Indeed, a
case can be made that the familiar—and evidently absurd—impression that
Shakespeare somehow wrote his plays specifically "for" us may rest on something more than fantasy. It doesn't imply—except metaphorically—that a post-
war society could reasonably claim to be the audience at which the plays were
actually aimed. But it does suggest that our sense of being present at the end of
processes whose beginnings the plays signal might generate a particularly
intense and hitherto unavailable feeling of recognition. For what confronts us in
the plays, such a view suggests, is not the set of permanent, history-transcending
truths of whose presence some critics have managed to convince themselves. It
is more the outline—dimly perceived, yet now increasingly discernible—of a
matching ideological relationship. A group of twenty-first-century theatre-goers
might, after all, legitimately claim to share something unique with the plays' first
audiences. That is, nothing less than a close encounter with "modernity"; they at
its beginning, we at its end; they from the point of view of the "early" modern,
we from that of the "post."[10]

If uncomplicated notions of universality and transcendence serve only to
mask the specificity of our present, a criticism more responsive to its opportuni-
ties (or demands) must be one whose roots in and connections with the here and
the now are fully and actively sought, deliberately foregrounded, exploited as a
first principle. It's a critical stance that has recently attracted a rather clumsy but
distinctive name: Presentism. A presentist criticism's engagement with the text
takes place precisely in terms of those dimensions of the modern world that most
ringingly chime—perhaps as ends to its beginnings—with the events of the past.
Its center of gravity is accordingly "now," rather than "then." Of course, a bland,
unthinking confidence that the contours of the past will neatly match those of our
own day—a view effectively skewered by those historian's gibes which employ
"Presentism" as a term of disapprobation—is not in question. A newly committed, self-consciously Presentist literary criticism stands as something of quite a
different order. It scrupulously seeks out salient aspects of the present as a crucial trigger for its investigations. Reversing, to some degree, the stratagems of
New Historicism, it deliberately begins with the material present and allows that

to set its interrogative agenda. Perhaps this simply makes overt what covertly happens anyway. Nevertheless, in practice, it calls for a heightened degree of self-awareness. In principle, it involves the fundamentally radical act of putting one's cards on the table.

The Shakespearean judgements made in Berlin in 1945 seemed to observers at the time to be quintessentially "American." They were also quintessentially "Presentist." There was good reason for both. Prior to the Hitler period, German culture had been the envy of the Western world and a very high proportion of that world's major philosophers, scientists, and theologians had worked and written in the German language. By contrast, the English-speaking culture of the United States was not particularly highly regarded—certainly not by Nazified Germans, who might prefer it to Russian culture, but undoubtedly considered it inferior to their own. Yet a major shift in cultural relationships was obviously now in the cards. The baton of leadership in the English-speaking world had passed from Britain to the United States. And if United States culture was to become a dominant world force in the years after 1945, one of its first acts in pursuit of that goal would have to be the imposition, in Berlin, of its lineaments, and the eradication of those that preceded them.

To exaggerate only slightly, the proposal that *Hamlet* was at this juncture preferable to *Coriolanus* heralds nothing less than a new world order. In it, the United States, not Britain, effectively speaks for a triumphant and belligerent Anglo-Saxon order, taking upon itself the responsibility of making a portentous assessment of the writings of its most prestigious author. Indeed, the portentousness is underlined by the fact that the judgment precisely reverses one made by an earlier, no less prestigious, but distinctly "Englished" American voice—that of T. S. Eliot, who had notoriously pronounced *Hamlet* an "artistic failure" and cited *Coriolanus* as "Shakespeare's most assured artistic success."[11] In other words, what confronts us here is a "Presentist" reading of *Hamlet*, made in and for the new "present" that began in 1945, and whose shape remains still just about discernible at the millennium's end. As the tip of a huge cultural and political iceberg, it offers a brief but revealing hint of some of the immense, if submerged, political, social and historical structures that sustain it. The sources of such a reading cannot fail to be of great interest. They lie in the career of Mauriz Leon Reiss.

He was a professional actor. Born on March 30, 1891, in Dolina, Galicia (latterly Poland), Reiss was employed in the German-speaking theater and, changing his name to Leo Reuss, enjoyed a successful career in Vienna, Hamburg, and Berlin, where he worked for a number of years with the likes of Erwin Piscator, Leopold Jessner, and Bertolt Brecht.[12] However, by 1935, the restrictive race-laws of the Nazi regime had virtually deprived Reuss of his livelihood. As a Jew, it became impossible for him to find work in Germany, and he retreated to Austria. There, *in extremis*, he hit upon an audacious strategy. Carefully acquiring a number of intently observed verbal and physical mannerisms, he manufactured and then took on a wholly new identity: that of a Tyrolean mountain peasant, rude, self-taught, but endowed with a range of "natural" acting talents, whose name was "Kaspar Brandhofer." Cloaked in this alter ego's rustic charm and protected by his Christianity, Reuss impressed men of the theater as influential as Max Reinhardt and Ernst Lothar, to the extent that "Kaspar Brandhofer" was given the important part of Herr von Dorsday in a dramatization of Arthur Schnitzler's story *Fräulein Else*.

The play's opening in Vienna proved memorable. "Kaspar Brandhofer" was hailed as a potential star and the *Reichspost* called him the "sensation of the evening." A glittering future seemed to beckon. Nonetheless, returning home after the first night, Reuss reported that he felt, not triumph, but emptiness and loneliness. Everyone was interested in "Kaspar Brandhofer," he claimed, but "niemand fragte nach mir, nach Leo Reuss." His creation threatened to become a monster (he uses the word Golem) which, colluding with the eradication of Leo Reuss, seemed to demonstrate that the Nazi race laws remained more powerful than the trick he had devised to defeat them. Shortly afterward, he and his wife emigrated to the United States, where he sought work as an actor in Hollywood. For this purpose he changed his name once more. As "Lionel Royce" he managed, before his death in April 1946, to secure a succession of small parts in a number of films ranging in quality from *Confessions of a Nazi Spy* (1939), to *Gilda* (1946). Inevitably, in most of these, he played the part of an unsavoury "German"; usually a Nazi.

No doubt the ironies of Royce's life story stir numerous echoes in the experience of many citizens of Europe and the United States during the 1930s and 1940s. His are remarkable only because the stratagem involved in the "Kaspar Brandhofer" episode brings to the fore particular aspects of an actor's situation. At its center lies the notion of some concrete, unified core, some indivisible, coherent "real self" from which acted parts are projected: the "me" that, in Royce's case, lies behind the "Brandhofer" he acts, as well as behind the part that "Brandhofer" acts. Obviously it would be of no help to him to point out that "Brandhofer's" success is itself a triumph of acting, or that the "real" Reuss is almost as much a confection as "Brandhofer" when set against an original "Reiss." The phonetic journey Reiss–Reuss–Royce marks an odyssey of part-playing, its cruelest irony unveiled in its final development, where "Royce's" acting turns him into the image of his own fundamental enemy, the villainous Nazi.

In Royce's particular case, however, the irony is peculiarly reinforced by the cunning of the Schnitzler story that fuels the success that finally undermines him, destroying his identity, necessitating the move to Hollywood and forcing the ultimate traumatic transformation from Reuss to Royce. *Fräulein Else* concerns a neurotic young woman who, while staying at a fashionable spa hotel, receives a letter from her mother to say that her father is disastrously in debt. The only way out of his situation is to procure an immediate loan, and her mother urgent-

ly requests that Else asks a friend of her father's, Herr von Dorsday, who is staying at the hotel, to come to the rescue. Von Dorsday agrees, but on one condition:
that Else permits him to view her naked for fifteen minutes. Considering the
proposition, the highly-strung Else becomes more and more hysterical, and finally adopts the sensational stratagem of appearing publicly naked in the hotel's
music room, in front of the hotel guests, including Dorsday. She then collapses,
feigns unconsciousness, and finally kills herself by taking an overdose of
veronal.

It's a disturbing, intensely erotic tale of the sensual and financial impulses
lying beneath the veneer of twentieth-century civilization, and it certainly casts
a number of brilliantly sardonic reflections on the theme of women's relationship
to men. Schnitzler's wry pre-Freudian insights abound. The notion that "everything in this world has its price" has broad implications, and leads ultimately to
Else's bitter comment on her parents, to the effect that "they've brought me up
to sell myself in one way or another" (Schnitzler 50, 64, 65). It's also evidently
a story of the primal challenge involved in human nakedness, of an animal and
fiscal final reality, initially cloaked by social convention, but then brutally
exposed by the same society's irresistible economic and sexual imperatives. The
manipulative character of von Dorsday contributes powerfully to this complexity and of course is of obvious interest to the story of Reuss/Royce.

Von Dorsday is an art dealer from Vienna, a "social climber" whose insistence on an unacceptable bargain involving money and human flesh might well
(to take up but one of its Shakespearean echoes) begin to imply, in Schnitzler's
world, the veiled possibility of his Jewishness. This irony clearly adds its own
dimension to Reuss's own assumption, as a Jew, of the Christian disguise of
"Brandhofer" in order to act the part. As a Jewish citizen of Vienna, Schnitzler's
sensitivities in the matter are often subtly in play throughout his work and Else's
Molly-Bloom-like and increasingly feverish musings make a point of the suggestion that, like "Brandhofer," von Dorsday may not be as Christian as he
appears: "What good does your first-class tailor do you, Herr von Dorsday?
Dorsday! I'm sure your name used to be something else . . ." and, later, "What's
the man's name? Herr von Dorsday. Funny name. . . ." [13] The reverberations of
that for his impersonator are evident. The story's prevailing sense of theatricality, its reiterated emphasis on role-playing, is further reinforced by Else's repeated references to the forthcoming unveiling of her own "real," finally naked self
as "the performance, the great performance." The connection with Reuss's own
"real" position gives this a disturbing dimension. Else's dismissal of Dorsday,
"He talks like a bad actor," perhaps adds its own ironic dimension to the "sensation of the evening" (Schnitzler 51).

Seen in the light of our subsequent experience, such ironies probe to a deeper, even more uncomfortable level. We know that in totalitarian societies, drama
often functions as a preferred vehicle for criticism, protest, or the assertion of an
alternative but officially impermissible worldview of how things really are.[14] A

play's nature as "public" art form, the fact that its art is made out of the virtual interaction of people with others, plus the actual interaction of the stage and the audience, make it an appropriate means of commentary upon the fabric of social intercourse from which "states" at large are made.

In such a setting, a play's power to disturb or involve rests on the notion that, beyond the *milieu* depicted on the stage, there exists a "real" material world to which it refers and on which it can impinge, somehow making a difference. Leo Reuss's sense—his outraged insistence—that, ultimately, he is not Brandhofer, even though both Reuss and Brandhofer are necessary to the realization of Dorsday, springs from this situation. Otherwise "Brandhofer" could simply stand as another milestone of nomenclature passed by the career of Reiss. Meanwhile, *Fräulein Else* operates—and disturbs—on a number of other levels. A paradoxical account of lust frustrated by the mode of its gratification, it casts its heroine as the central agent in a mini-drama, a play located within the main action, something that the stream-of-consciousness and feverish present-tense style of the narrative stresses. The climax of Else's "great performance" in this drama, in which the secret prize of her nakedness eludes Dorsday by being publicly manifested, manipulates a neat, even tricky irony, effectively neutralizing Dorsday's private fantasies by externalizing them. Convinced that she has nonetheless kept to the spirit of the appalling "bargain," thus forcing Dorsday to save her father, Else's stratagem bids to hoist the villain with his own petard even at the cost of her life. Her sudden disrobing is thus no mere act of hysterical abandon. A histrionic gesture at once vividly accusatory and conclusively damning, it ranks as an abrupt and carefully focused assertion of moral indignation: its aim, to "police" the presuppositions of its bourgeois audience through the sudden explosion in their midst of a contesting "reality."

A number of Shakespearean ghosts crowd on to the stage at such a moment. At the level of the plot, Shylock is of course readily discernible. But if we take into account Reuss's own situation, the figure of the Prince of Denmark is also hard to ignore. Like him, Reuss is using a play as a stratagem to pierce in the name of justice what he perceives as wholesale political and moral corruption: a move that aims to authenticate in the process his own "real" identity and being. However, such a project also contains the possibility that *Hamlet* considers: that the audience may respond with blankness, as Claudius does to *The Mousetrap*. In the performance of *Fräulein Else*, this happens on two levels; that of the play's world and, as we know, that of its spectators. Not only is the response of Else's "audience" to her nakedness in the hotel's music room one of blankness and bewilderment, but that of the Viennese audience present at the play's performance is evidently of a similar sort. Confronted by an almost naked revelation of the effect of the Nazi race laws, their response is—nothing. Nobody asks about Reuss.

Unlike Hamlet's, Reuss's victory seems thus only a pyrrhic one. His role as Dorsday, a man in pursuit of nakedness, is ironically only available to him when he's cloaked as another, "Brandhofer." The story of *Fräulein Else*, on this show-ing, is scarcely a vehicle for self-authentication. Rather, as the social product of a role-playing society, it seems to end by celebrating precisely that: role-playing itself. Perhaps the situation implies, at least in terms of a Jewish perception of the Viennese world at the time, that that is all there is. Role-playing is a common enough theme in the work of Schnitzler, to say nothing of Freud. The imminent rise of Hitler would crudely confirm its potency. The Holocaust would savagely lay bare its pretensions.

In *Hamlet,* on the other hand, the sudden defeat of audience expectation in fact turns out to be a powerful weapon. Its effect is to sharply increase awareness of the material presence of the play, the audience, and thus of the volatile rela-tionship between the two. Far from being simply negative, Claudius's blankness turns out, as we have seen, to offer nothing less than the most explosive and indeed subversive of reactions. Suddenly the whole forward motion of the action shudders to a halt, and we hear the play speak. What it seems to be saying is that drama doesn't always work: that the easy prognostications about guilt's self-rev-elation are unreliable, that with creatures as complex and as dangerously attrac-tive as Claudius, the aim of holding a mirror up to nature is not readily achieved, that the pathway from art to "real life" is by no means as direct and untrammelled as was sentimentally claimed, and that art's writ does not run easily in this cor-rupt and recognizably modern world of Elsinore. Here, as we its inheritors know all too well, one may still smile and smile and be a villain. Plays make nothing happen.

The bald, confirming truth is that the Prince succeeds in his aim despite the failure of *The Mousetrap.* Perhaps he does so even because of its failure. Certainly, as Polonius discovers, from that moment on Hamlet is prepared to use daggers as well as to speak them. For Reuss, as for any European Jew for whom Nazi persecution brought only the deadly response of nothingness, and finally its shocking material climax, *vernichtung, Hamlet* might well seem to be a play about the violent, murderous stratagems necessary to counter that peculiarly modern kind of corruption that takes the form of inertia, of willful blankness, of refusal to see. It might well seem to be about the need for a different kind of art: one that sets out to seize the initiative, to harry, cajole, persuade, and coerce its audience into some sort of redemptive action. And it might well be thought to speak of a Shakespeare who must, in the present and in the future, operate less as the passive Sweet William of romantic legend, and more as the intervening, directing, policing Old Bill appropriate to a harsher reality.

That surely is the Shakespeare invoked and given a clear political job to do in Berlin in 1945. As OMGUS began its mammoth, Fortinbras-like task amid the rubble, clearing the stage and taking up the bodies, its soldiers must have uncov-ered many ironies. Few could have matched those embodied in the fateful "black" and "white" lists administered by the Theater Officers. Their source was a letter, written from Hollywood, California, by a group of German–Jewish emigrés, in response to a request from the Office of War Information in Washington, D. C. Its controlling, marshaling purpose is baldly stated: to employ the German theater henceforth as "an instrument of reeducation." [15] Perhaps even the Prince of Denmark would have agreed that the letter's main signatory, and thus the instrument of *Hamlet*'s entry as policeman into a fresh world order, might now be hailed as one of the Bard's first Presentist critics. Playing what turned out, in the end, to be his most influential role, it was Lionel Royce.

NOTES

1. I am greatly indebted to Professor Balz Engler, who has kindly made his extensive knowledge of these matters available to me. Further details can be found in Lange, especially pp. 321–22; Stahl, and Hortmann. For an incisive and judicious analysis of this "massive theatre programme" in its larger political context as part of the "American response to the Soviet cultural offensive" see Saunders , pp. 20–21. Dr. Saunders's witty and provocative account of the cultural politics of the post-war world is illuminating on a large scale. I am extremely grateful to her for affording me access to copies of relevant documents.

2. Curiously, on May 3, 2000, the police eventually agreed to a declaration in the High Court that a number of their actions during the state visit of President Jiang Zemin had in fact been "unlawful."

3. The term "The Old Bill" or "The Bill" is nineteenth-century British thieves' slang for the police. It has now passed, through a television-driven process of gentrification, into polite parlance.

4. See Chambers, pp. 179–80. It is scarcely necessary to point out the *Hamlet* echoes of Agatha Christie's ingenious detective play *The Mousetrap*.

5. Greg, pp. 12–17. Greg's friend Frank Elliott was an "assistant commissioner" at the Yard. See F. P. Wilson, pp. 307–34, 320. See also John Dover Wilson, pp. 153–57.

6. We can discount immediately the less generous conclusion of some editors that such a case merely represents the vestigial, interpolated remains of an actor's actual difficulty, encountered in performance, and should thus rank as a theatrical "accretion" to the text, as Harold Jenkins terms it (p. 62). His rather odd judgement is that the Folio text is using "extra words" here, which "though they have usually been regarded as an omission in Q2, have the air of an actor's elaboration" (p. 232). In addition to driving a wholly illegitimate wedge between text and performance, the notion of "accretion" awards "the text" a pride of place that commits the play to the study rather than the theater. Worse, it risks missing a key moment where, once again, the play rather than one of its characters speaks.

7. See Jenkins, pp. 482–83.

8. Jenkins, gives a full account of these in his "long note," pp. 501–5.

9. Jenkins, p. 508. See also pp. 145, 156.

10. This point has most recently been made by Grady, pp. 4–25.

11. See Eliot, pp. 141–46, and Eliot (1964), p. 44. Of course, on one level, this is a mere debating point. Each set of judgments was made for quite different reasons and in completely different contexts. The symmetry is nevertheless startling.

12. For a full account of Royce's life, see Haider-Pregler. I am heavily indebted to Professor Haider-Pregler's work and she was also kind enough to make a good deal of

information available to me privately. A play about Reuss, *In der Löwengrube*, by Felix Mitterer, opened on January 14, 1999, in the Badisches Landestheater in Karlsruhe.

13. Schnitzler, pp. 14 and 92. On the subject of Schnitzler's situation as a Jew and the Jewish dimension of Vienna, see Raphael, pp. v–xvii.

14. See, for example, Hilsky and Gibinska.

15. OMGUS/RG260/Box 242/NARA, National Archives, Washington, DC. The letter is dated May 12th, 1945.

WORKS CITED

Chambers, Edmund. *A Short Life of Shakespeare* (abridged by Charles Williams), Oxford: The Clarendon Press, 1993.

Eliot, T.S. *Selected Essays*, 3rd edn., London: Faber and Faber, 1951.

———. *The Use of Poetry and the Use of Criticism*, London: Faber and Faber (first pub. 1933), 1964.

Gibinska, Marta. "Polish Hamlets: Shakespeare's *Hamlet* in Polish Theatres after 1945." *Shakespeare in the New Europe*, ed. Michael Hattaway, Boika Sokolova, and Derek Roper. Sheffield: Sheffield Academic Press, 1994. pp. 159–73.

Grady, Hugh. *Shakespeare's Universal Wolf: Studies in Early Modern Reification*, Oxford: Clarendon Press. 1996.

Greg, W. W. *Biographical Notes 1877–1947* Oxford: New Bodleian Library, 1960.

Haider-Pregler, Hilde. *Überlebens-Theater. Der Schauspieler Reuss*. Vienna: Holzhausen Verlag, 1998.

Hattaway, Michael, Boika Sokolova, and Derek Roper, eds. *Shakespeare in the New Europe* Sheffield: Sheffield Academic Press, 1994.

Hilsky, Martin (1994) "Shakespeare in Czech: an essay in cultural semantics." *Shakespeare in the New Europe*, ed. Michael Hattaway, Boika Sokolova, and Derek Roper. Sheffield: Sheffield Academic Press, 1994. pp. 150–58.

Hortmann, Wilhelm. *Shakespeare on the German Stage, Vol.2: the Twentieth Century,* Cambridge: Cambridge University Press, 1998.

Jenkins, Harold, ed. *Hamlet*, Arden Edition. London: Methuen, 1982.

Lange, Wigand. *Theater in Deutschland nach 1945: ZurTheaterpolitik der Amerikanischen Besatzungsbehörden* , Franfurt: Peter Lang, 1980.

Raphael, Fredric. Introduction to Arthur Schnitzler *Dream Story* (1926), London: Penguin Books, 1999.

Saunders, Frances Stonor . *Who Paid the Piper; The CIA and the Cultural Cold War*, London: Granta Books, 1999.

Schnitzler, Arthur. *Fräulein Else*, trans. F. H. Lyon (1925), London: Pushkin Press, 1998.

Stahl, Ernst Leopold. *Shakespeare und das deutsche Theater*. Stuttgart: Kohlhammer, 1947.

Wilson, John Dover. Contribution to a number of obituary notices of W.W. Greg in *The Library*, 5th series, Vol. XIV, No. 3, September 1959.

Wilson, F. P. "Sir Walter Wilson Greg 1875–1959," *Proceedings of the British Academy*, Vol. XLV, 1959.

Hamlet and the Canon

ANN THOMPSON

A TALE OF TWO CAN[N]ONS

In his essay, "Close Reading without Readings," Stephen Booth quotes a brief passage from the second scene of *Hamlet*, covering the end of the King's exit speech and the beginning of Hamlet's first soliloquy:

> No jocund health that Denmark drinks today
> But the great cannon to the clouds shall tell,
> And the King's rouse the heaven shall bruit again,
> Re-speaking earthly thunder. Come away.
> > *Flourish. Exeunt all but Hamlet.*
> O that this too too sullied flesh would melt,
> Or that the Everlasting had not fix'd
> His canon 'gainst self-slaughter. (1.2.125–32)1

He informs his readers: "As by now you will expect, my concern is for the twin cannons. The echo of artillery from line 126 in the word 'canon,' meaning 'law,' six lines later . . . ." (Booth 49). His readers will expect it because this is the kind of thing Booth does with Shakespeare's words, and he has set up expectations a few pages earlier when he writes that some "close readers" are "unlikely . . . to give serious attention to the pairing of the word 'nature' with the word 'art' when Edmund juxtaposes them in the first line of scene 2 of *King Lear* where he says 'Thou, Nature, art my goddess'" (44). His project is to pick up the echo of "cannon" as an example of what he calls the "casual, unobtrusive, substantively irrelevant relationships among *meanings*" (45), including "undelivered meanings" (43) which contribute to the richness of the effect of innumerable passages in Shakespeare.

When I first read Booth's piece—or rather heard it, because it was given as a conference paper at the 1989 meeting of the Shakespeare Association of

America in Austin, Texas—I assumed that this observation was original to him, but in fact it has rather a long history among editors and critics of *Hamlet*. (I'm not, of course, accusing Booth of plagiarism: I'm sure his rediscovery of the point was independent.) In his first edition of *The Works of Shakespear* in 1723, Alexander Pope spelled the word "cannon" in both instances (as indeed it is spelled in both the 1604/5 Second Quarto text and the 1623 First Folio), causing Lewis Theobald to remark in his critique of Pope's edition, *Shakespeare Restored*, that in the soliloquy the author "intended the Injunction, rather than the Artillery of Heaven" (Theobald 16–17). In the following century Joseph Hunter, in an extensive commentary on the play, said of the second "canon," "This is an unhappy word to use here. I fear the truth is that the noise of the cannon in the king's speech was still ringing in the Poet's ears" (Hunter ii, 218). Thomas Caldecott, who edited just two plays, *Hamlet* and *As You Like It*, contributed the curious point that "'Ordinance', which has the same sense as 'canon', differs also from 'ordnance' or artillery, in one letter only; and this difference in pronunciation is no way felt" (Caldecott 22).

In the theater, we actually hear the noise of the promised "cannon" celebrating the king's "rouse" two scenes later, when the Second Quarto gives the stage direction, "*A florish of trumpets and 2. peeces goes of*" (1.4.6), assuming the "pieces" (weapons, guns) are indeed cannons. Shortly afterwards, as Booth points out (Booth 50), Hamlet refers to his father's "canoniz'd bones" which have "burst their cerements" (1.4.47–48) as if they have themselves become projectiles. The cannon/canon pun has perhaps become more familiar to us than some of Booth's other "substantively irrelevant relationships" (45) because of the debates during the 1980s and 1990s about what should be taught in degree programs in English Studies when people published papers with titles like "Firing the Canon," arguing that canonical texts like *Hamlet* were being displaced (or perhaps ought to be displaced) by non-canonical texts written by women or people from ethnic minorities. My purpose in this essay is to consider some aspects of the recent trajectory (as it were) of the canonical *Hamlet*, and to speculate about its future.

THE PRE-EMINENCE OF *HAMLET*

"The collapse of Shakespeare is hard to imagine. But then, who could have imagined how easily the Berlin Wall would collapse?" writes Gary Taylor in his characteristically provocative essay on "The Incredible Shrinking Bard" (Taylor 205). Rejecting arguments that film, video, CD-ROM, and the Internet are expanding Shakespeare's influential domain, he asserts that his reputation "has passed its peak of expansion, and begun to decline" (Taylor 198): Shakespeare retains his dominant position in Western and indeed global culture only because of corporate capital and government subsidy, and Taylor views with equanimity a world in which "as Shakespeare gets smaller, the available cultural space for other writers—for Gloria Naylor, or Jane Smiley, or Thomas Middleton—gets

bigger" (Taylor 205). Harold Bloom, of course, sees the same world with considerable alarm, writing in *Shakespeare: The Invention of the Human* that
Shakespeare may be the only canonical writer "that can survive the debasement
of our teaching institutions, here and abroad. Every other writer may fall away,
to be replaced by the anti-elitist swamp of Cultural Studies. Shakespeare will
abide" (Bloom 17). Both writers turn quickly to *Hamlet* to sustain their arguments. Taylor admits:

> Most Americans know by heart a few tags from Shakespeare's plays even if
> they have not read them. A man on the street interviewed in New York by Al
> Pacino for his documentary *Looking for Richard*, or a Congressman in
> Washington, D.C. providing sound bites for the six o'clock news, can quote or
> parody the same rusty speech from *Hamlet* ("2B, or not 2B"). (Taylor 202)

Bloom announces rather startlingly that "After Jesus, Hamlet is the most cited
figure in Western consciousness" (Bloom xix), following this up with the claim
that "Perhaps indeed it is Falstaff and Hamlet, rather than Shakespeare, who are
mortal gods" (Bloom 4). In his chapter on *Hamlet*, he calls it "Shakespeare's
most famous play . . . . unsurpassed in the West's imaginative literature" and
asserts that "*Hamlet*'s eminence has never been disputed" (Bloom 383–84).

It is certainly true that *Hamlet* still has a high recognition factor: that same
"rusty speech," for example, has appeared in such a wide range of cinematic texts
as John Ford's Western *My Darling Clementine* (1946), Frank Launder's *The
Pure Hell of St Trinian's* (1960) where it accompanies a strip-tease, and Woody
Allen's *Everything You Always Wanted To Know About Sex, But Were Afraid To
Ask* (1972); not to mention the two films actually called *To Be Or Not To Be* (the
1942 original starring Jack Benny and directed by Ernst Lubitsch, and the 1983
remake, starring Mel Brooks and directed by Alan Johnson). Other specific
moments in the play appear over and over again as visual allusions in all kinds
of contexts, serious, burlesque, or banal. We can recognize at once the appearance of the Ghost on the battlements, the scene with Hamlet's attention fixed on
the guilty King, the drowning of Ophelia. The most familiar of all, of course, is
the man holding a skull: such an image immediately evokes Hamlet's stance in
the graveyard and his line "Alas, poor Yorick."

But, *pace* Bloom, *Hamlet*'s eminence has been disputed, most forcefully in
Hamlet versus Lear, published six years before *Shakespeare: The Invention of
the Human*, in which R. A. Foakes argues that, somewhere around 1960, *King
Lear* replaced *Hamlet* as "the best, the greatest, or the chief masterpiece of
Shakespeare," citing numerous distinguished critics who take this estimation for
granted (Foakes 1). Foakes demonstrates that this shift in critical esteem coincided with a radical change in the critical interpretation of *King Lear*: Formerly
viewed optimistically as Lear's journey toward redemption, it became a bleak
vision of suffering and despair appropriate to the period of the Cold War when

the ever-present threat of nuclear destruction made "the promised end" seem imminent. Tracing the traditional interpretations of both plays, and in particular their perceived relevance to political issues, Foakes draws a contrast between them:

> Although Hamlet was, as a character, abstracted from the play and privatised as a representative of everyman by Romantic and later critics, he also became in the nineteenth century an important symbolic political figure, usually typifying the liberal intellectual paralysed in will and incapable of action. By contrast, *King Lear* was depoliticized. . . . [U]ntil the 1950s the play was, in the main, seen as a tragedy of personal relations between father and daughter, or as a grand metaphysical play about Lear's pilgrimage to discover his soul. All this changed after 1960, since when *King Lear* has come to seem richly significant in political terms, in a world in which old men have held on to and abused power, often in corrupt or arbitrary ways; in the same period *Hamlet* has lost much of its political relevance, as liberal intellectuals have steadily been marginalised in Britain and in the United States. (Foakes 6)

He concludes that "for the immediate future *King Lear* will continue to be regarded as the central achievement of Shakespeare, if only because it speaks more largely than the other tragedies to the anxieties of the modern world" (Foakes 224). Foakes edited *King Lear* for the third series of the Arden Shakespeare (1997), and I am co-editing *Hamlet* for the same series with Neil Taylor (forthcoming, we hope, in 2002). While we agree with Foakes that the establishment of a "pecking order" of Shakespeare's plays is on one level merely an academic game, we nevertheless feel that as editors we must engage with the formidable status of our text and the historical and cultural contexts which have generated and continue to generate this status. Is it true that *Hamlet* has ceased to be regarded as "Shakespeare's greatest play," and if so, does it matter? Have modern ways of reading and writing about literary texts destabilized notions of "authorship" and "greatness" to such an extent that such questions have become meaningless or irrelevant?

Certainly, *Hamlet* is continuing to attract attention both inside and outside the scholarly community: since 1990, the average number of publications on the play listed in the *Shakespeare Quarterly Annual Bibliography* (which includes works in a wide range of categories: Editions and Texts; Translations and Adaptations; Sources and Influences; Textual and Bibliographical Studies; Criticism; Pedagogy; Productions and Staging; Ballet and Dance; Film; Cinema; Radio, and Television; Music; Readings and Audio Recordings; and Stage and Theater History) is 423, while the average for *King Lear* is 175[2]. *King Lear* has never had the high level of recognition enjoyed by *Hamlet*: it seems unlikely that the average "man on the street" in London or New York could quote or identify any lines from the play, and its most frequently illustrated moments—the opening scene with Lear dividing up a map of his kingdom, and the final scene with

Lear's entry carrying his dead daughter Cordelia—would probably not instantly signify *"Lear"* to most people in the same way that the man with the skull or the woman dead in the water signifies *"Hamlet."* For actors, of course, the title role of *Hamlet* remains one in which a young (or younger middle-aged) actor can make his mark as a potential "star" early on, while the title-role of *King Lear* is an older man's part, the confirmation or culmination of an already successful career. It is even arguable that the political topicality of *King Lear* perceived by Foakes is already dated, relating as it did to the period of the Cold War and the dominance of elderly politicians such as Leonid Brezhnev and Ronald Reagan. The Berlin Wall has indeed collapsed, but did it take *King Lear* rather than Shakespeare with it?

SHAKESPEARE EAST OF SUEZ

In one interesting review of *Hamlet versus Lear*, R. W. Desai upbraids Foakes for ignoring the international dimension of Shakespearean reception and study: "had the book's title been more limiting, say *Hamlet versus Lear in the Western Consciousness*, this umbrage would have been groundless, but to assume that east of Suez Shakespeare has not travelled is a notion that one would have thought had long ago been discarded." Desai accepts that Foakes's thesis may be true in Britain and North America, but argues that it is unproven in the rest of the world. He regrets Foakes's failure to mention *Hamlet Studies*, the journal in which he writes (and of which he is editor), which has been published in India for seventeen years—"and so far no *King Lear* studies has appeared" (Desai 153).

Books on Shakespeare outside the Anglo-American tradition have proliferated during the last decade: a brief list would have to include *Shakespeare on the German Stage* by Simon Williams (1990); *Foreign Shakespeare: Contemporary Performance* by Dennis Kennedy (1993); *Shakespeare in the New Europe*, edited by Michael Hattaway, Boika Sokolova, and Derek Roper (1994); *Hamlet and Japan*, edited by Yoshiko Ueno (1995); *Shakespeare and South Africa* by David Johnson (1996); *Shakespeare and Hungary*, edited by Holgar Klein and Peter Davidhazi (1996); *Post-Colonial Shakespeares*, edited by Ania Loomba and Martin Orkin (1998); and *Shakespeare and Eastern Europe* by Zednek Stríbrny (2000). Relevant studies have also appeared in collections such as *Shakespeare and National Culture*, edited by John J. Joughin (1997) and *Shakespeare and Appropriation*, edited by Christy Desmet and Robert Sawyer (1999).

Most of these books reflect the traditional dominance of *Hamlet* in both performance and criticism: a check of the index of *Shakespeare in the New Europe*, for example, reveals twenty-six references to *Hamlet*, plus references to forty-eight central and eastern European productions from one in 1922 at the Polski theatre in Warsaw to one in 1993 at the First Private Theatre in Sofia; there are three chapters entirely on *Hamlet*. By contrast, there are only eight references to *King Lear*, all passing references and four of them to Peter Brook's British touring production, which is indeed the only production of the play to be mentioned. *Shakespeare and South Africa* contains fifteen references to *Hamlet* and none to *King Lear*. The fact that the first production of *Hamlet* of which we have any record took place on board a ship bound for India but forced by storms to anchor off Sierra Leone for six weeks in 1607 attracts the attention of the post-colonial critics Ania Loomba (Loomba 111–13) and Michael Neill (Neill 171–72) who use it in their arguments about the global dominance and appropriation of Shakespeare. By contrast, perhaps, David Johnson quotes Chris Hani, "slain leader of the South African Communist Party and hero of the township youth," as saying, "I am fascinated by Shakespeare's plays, especially with *Hamlet*. . . . I want to believe I am decisive and it helps me to be decisive when I read *Hamlet*" (Johnson 201).

Two authors specifically address the "*Hamlet* versus *Lear*" issue. Tibor Fabiny contributes an essay on "*King Lear* in the new Hungary" to *Shakespeare and Hungary* in which he notes the relative absence of *Lear* from the Hungarian stage from the 1940s to the early 1980s, but

> around the political changes of 1989 *King Lear* became a very frequently per-
> formed play both in and out of Budapest. . . . *Hamlet*, of course, remained pop-
> ular on stage but usually it was not directly associated with the changing of the
> system. The paradigm shift Professor Foakes speaks about concerning the pri-
> macy of these two tragedies seems to have taken place also in Hungary but thir-
> ty years later than in Western Europe and North America. (Fabiny 195–96)

Fabiny sees *Lear* as appealing to his generation as a play inviting "compassion-ate love for tragically fallen parents" (Fabiny 205) who can only be forgiven because they "were different when they were young" (Fabiny 203).

Zednek Stríbrny's more wide-ranging study of *Shakespeare and Eastern Europe* records a large number of productions and adaptations of *Hamlet* that made extensive use of topical political allusions, from the overtly oppositional production by Roman Zawistowski in Cracow in 1956, "full of pain and hatred against Stalinist oppression and surveillance" (Stríbrny 100), to Alexandru Tocilescu's production in Bucharest in 1989, which played to packed houses for over 200 performances before and during the overthrow of Nicolae Ceausescu (Stríbrny 134). He notes that

> In the East, the position of *Hamlet* has been so strong that fully resonant pro-
> ductions of *King Lear* have been much slower in asserting themselves.
> Although Count Tolstoy's negative view of the tragedy was never fully accept-
> ed, it took such achievements as Kozintsev's film to draw the attention of large
> audiences [but]. . . . Irresistibly, *King Lear*, with its theme of the division of both
> kingdom and family . . . attracted Eastern Europe while the world of
> Communism was crumbling away. (Stríbrny 143)[3]

Two productions of *King Lear* played concurrently in Moscow for several years in the 1990s, the more "profound and rewarding" in Stríbrny's view being that directed by Sergei Zhenovach who had the small audience share the stage with the actors "while the auditorium was left empty, creating an impression of a vacuum characteristic of the Russian artistic and political situation of the period" (Stríbrny 144). Ironically, perhaps, in light of Foakes's view of the topicality of the bleakness of *King Lear* in the West,

> A crucial role in the spiritual revival and integration of both family and society was given to the younger generation, especially the self-sacrificing Cordelia and the surviving Edgar, as in Kozintsev's film. This time, however, the final lines of the play were spoken, in accordance with the Quarto version, by the Duke of Albany, who recognized "the weight of this sad time" but left some hope for young individuals such as Edgar, with his experience of living outside the acquisitive society, in close rapport with nature and the uncorrupted poor. Ecological reverberations were in the air. (Stríbrny 144)

THE FEMINIST RESISTANCE

Feminist critics have of course deplored the stereotypes of women in both plays. When Carolyn Heilbrun reprinted her essay on "Hamlet's Mother" and used it as the lead piece in her book on *Hamlet's Mother and Other Women* in 1990, she noted that when she first published it in 1957 she was "a feminist waiting for a cause to join." Her basic line of argument in the essay was that critics and readers of the play have been too ready to accept Hamlet's view of Gertrude without questioning whether the overall view taken by the play (or its author) might be different. Many have joined this cause since 1975, the date of Juliet Dusinberre's *Shakespeare and the Nature of Women*, the first full-length feminist study of Shakespeare, and the date selected by Philip C. Kolin as the starting point for his annotated bibliography of *Shakespeare and Feminist Criticism* (1991) which lists forty-four items published on *Hamlet* and thirty-eight on *King Lear* between 1975 and Kolin's cut-off point in 1988. Interestingly, these totals are lower than those for *The Merchant of Venice* (forty-eight), *As You Like It* (fifty) and *The Winter's Tale* (fifty-eight); *Hamlet* is only just ahead of *The Taming of the Shrew* (forty-three).

These statistics testify to the prominence of the comedies in this period of feminist criticism and to an understandable shift away from the overwhelmingly male-centered tragedies in which women tend to feature as victims or villains, angels or devils. *King Lear* has been a particularly difficult play for feminists. Joyce Carol Oates observes that "The disgust expressed in the play towards women is more strident and articulate, and far less reasonable, than the disgust expressed in *Othello* and *Hamlet* and certain of the Sonnets" (Oates, 65). King Lear, after all, has not suffered a specifically sexual betrayal, and at the points when he launches into his most sexually explicit attacks on his daughters and on women in general (his curse of Goneril at 1.4.267–81, for example, or his ravings about "the sulphurous pit" at 4.6.116–27), he is quite ignorant of his elder daughters' relations with Edmund and mistaken about the latter's "kindness" to his father. In an influential essay of the mid-1980s, Kathleen McLuskie writes:

> The misogyny of King Lear, both the play and its hero, is constructed out of an ascetic tradition which presents woman as the source of the primal sin of lust, combining with concerns about the family posed by female insubordination. (McLuskie 106)

She concedes that Lear's situation at the end of the play is so moving that "even the most stony-hearted feminist could not withold her pity even though it is called forth at the expense of her resistance to the patriarchal relations which it endorses" (McLuskie 102), making a point similar to Marianne Novy's. Novy noted that "there is so much sympathy with Lear at the end that it seems cold to turn from feeling with him to any further analysis of the play in terms of sex-role behaviour" (1984, 162). This record of resistance and even guilt about the greatness of *King Lear* is interestingly reflected in Jane Smiley's essay on the composition of her novel *A Thousand Acres* (1991) which has been one of the most widely read adaptations of *King Lear*, transferring the story to a farm in the American Midwest. She records her early dislike of the play:

> Beginning with my first readings of the play in high school and continuing through college and graduate school, I had been cool to both Lear and Cordelia. . . . These responses made me find the play less enjoyable than my favorite Shakespeare plays—*Hamlet, Measure for Measure, Much Ado About Nothing*. I felt an automatic resistance when people labeled *King Lear* Shakespeare's greatest tragedy, but I read my resistance as an idiosyncratic reaction, something not to mention in educated company—not exactly a failure in myself but more like a tiny tear in the social fabric that could be overlooked. (Smiley 1999, 160–61)

Bloom is dismissive of such objections—"Feminist critics will be unhappy with the mad old king for perhaps another decade" (Bloom 499)—but given that the majority of students of English Literature today are female, as well as an increasing proportion of their teachers, it is conceivable that *King Lear* may become demoted through neglect: women may prefer to read, teach and write about other plays.

It is possible to argue that *Hamlet* has fared somewhat better, perhaps because Hamlet's view of women, while deplorable, is, as Oates says, more "reasonable" than Lear's: he has specific grounds for feeling betrayed by both Gertrude and Ophelia. Many feminists have followed Heilbrun in reassessing Gertrude, often using material from the play's theatrical, textual and critical history. Ellen J. O'Brien, for example, examines the selective cutting of the Queen's role on stage from 1755 to 1900 and demonstrates that the result was to empha-size a negative view of the character and deprive her of any development after the closet scene (1992), while Dorothea Kehler argues that the representation of Gertred in the First Quarto was shaped in part by contemporary prejudices against "lusty widows" who remarried. The fiction writers such as Margaret Atwood in "Gertrude Talks Back" (1992) and John Updike in *Gertrude and Claudius* (2000) have used their greater freedom to give us more radically sympathetic readings of the Queen. Elaine Showalter's essay, "Representing Ophelia: Women, Madness and the Responsibilities of Feminist Criticism" (1985), has become something of a classic study, not only of the play, but of the subsequent use of Ophelia as an icon in painting, photography, literature, and psychiatry, tracing how treatments of the character reflect social attitudes toward women and madness. Jacqueline Rose's essay on "Sexuality in the Reading of Shakespeare" (1985) looks at the role of influential male readers of the play such as T. S. Eliot as well as Ernest Jones and the Freudians in defining "the problem of *Hamlet*" in terms of male anxiety about female sexuality. Curiously, as A. D. Nuttall points out, "Hamlet is much more 'Oedipal' than Oedipus" (Nuttall 129), giving the play an ongoing relevance to the nuclear family drama.

WHICH *HAMLET* IS THE CANONICAL ONE?

The performance history as well as the critical history of *Hamlet* has been affect-ed during the last twenty years by debates about the variant texts and particular-ly by the new wave of interest in the idea that Shakespeare revised his plays. If one is going to claim preeminent status for a play, one might ideally wish to establish what precisely one means by "the play": are we talking about the 1603 Quarto version of *Hamlet*, the 1604/5 Quarto version, the 1623 Folio version, or some (non-authorial) amalgam of two of these texts or even all three? Which words on which page of which text represent the true canonical *Hamlet*? Current orthodoxy is that the 1603 text is a "bad" one, reconstructed from memory by actors or reporters, and that the 1623 text is Shakespeare's revision of the play as represented by the 1604/5 text, but all of the evidence is internal and subject to challenge. Philip Edwards, who espouses the revision theory in his edition for the New Cambridge Shakespeare, printed the passages found only in the 1604/5 text in square brackets on the assumption that Shakespeare intended to delete them; the Oxford editors, Stanley Wells and Gary Taylor in *The Complete Works* (1986) and G. R. Hibbard in the Oxford Shakespeare volume (1987), go further by tak-ing them out of the main text and printing them as appendices. All of these edi-tors nevertheless adopt literally hundreds of individual readings from the 1604/5 text.

A comparable argument has been even more evident in the case of *King Lear*: Michael Warren's essay on "Quarto and Folio *King Lear* and the Interpretation of Albany and Edgar" (1978) was followed during the 1980s by no fewer than four books on the texts of *King Lear*: P. W. K. Stone's *The Textual*

History of "King Lear" (1980), Steven Urkowitz's *Shakespeare's Revision of "King Lear"* (1980), Peter W. M. Blayney's *The Texts of "King Lear" and Their Origins* (1982), and the collection of essays edited by Gary Taylor and Michael Warren on *The Division of the Kingdoms* (1983). Again, the consensus is that the Folio text is an authorial revision of the earlier Quarto, and in consequence the Oxford *Complete Works* contained two versions of *King Lear*, "The History of King Lear: The [1608] Quarto Text" and "The Tragedy of King Lear: The [1623] Folio Text", while the *Norton Shakespeare*, based on Oxford but with additional material by Stephen Greenblatt and others (1997), added a third version, a "traditional" conflated text.

Oxford and Norton contain only one version of *Hamlet*, although the Oxford editors are on record as saying that they regret this (Wells and Taylor 17). An interesting and relevant consequence of the textual debate is that scholars now argue over which text of *Hamlet* is better or more authoritative. The Cambridge and Oxford editors, believing the Folio to be an authorial revision, feel obliged to argue that it is superior as a play to the "good" Quarto: their commentary on the passages found only in the Quarto claim repeatedly that the supposed "cuts" improve the play. Philip Edwards, for example, says of Hamlet's last soliloquy, beginning "How all occasions do inform against me, / And spur my dull revenge" (4.4.32–66), the most extensively "cut," that "Although entire theories of the prince have been built on this speech, it is not one of the great soliloquies . . . . it is insufficient and inappropriate for Act 4 of *Hamlet*" (Edwards Introduction, 17). G. R. Hibbard scolds the author of the Quarto version for "self-indulgence" and an "inability to resist the temptation to quibble"; he finds that the passages omitted from the Folio "slow the action down" and merely repeat what has been said before (Hibbard Appendix A, 355–69). These apparent attacks on a canonical text by some of its most authoritative readers can be disconcerting for readers who are also rather dismayed to find that they need to study at least two versions of the play and attempt to grasp not only the differences between them but also the arguments about the reasons for those differences. All three of the editions of *Hamlet* published in the 1980s — Arden, Cambridge and Oxford — devote a large proportion of their introductions to textual matters, seeming to privilege them above everything else.

Neil Taylor and I are editing all three texts for Arden 3, but aiming to present them as independently meaningful. We shall not feel obliged to argue that the Folio is better (or more canonical) than the "good" Quarto. Even if we come to agree that it represents Shakespeare's second thoughts, we need not accept that every change must be one for the better; there are certainly enough examples extant of authors revising their work and making it worse. But in offering not one but three Arden *Hamlet*s are we contributing to a diminution of its status as preeminent within the canon?

On one level, it still seems difficult to think of a text written in English that is more canonical than *Hamlet*. In David Lodge's comic academic novel,

Changing Places: A Tale of Two Campuses, Howard Ringbaum fails to gain tenure at Euphoria State University after announcing publicly that he has never read *Hamlet* (Lodge 120). Yet the recent and rapid rise of *King Lear* to an eminence within the canon equal if not superior to that of *Hamlet* acts as a reminder that assumptions about such matters can change and that we are not dealing with issues of absolute inherent value, but with issues affected by cultural and sociological change. A brief look at productions of Shakespeare and work on Shakespeare outside the Anglo-American tradition reveals that we should be careful in claiming the total dominance of our own viewpoint. The potential collapse of *Hamlet*, or indeed the whole of Shakespeare, is envisaged by Gary Taylor, while the contributions of feminist critics again draw our attention to the fact that different critical approaches can privilege different texts in different ways. Textual problems further complicate the issue by challenging us to define what we mean by "*Hamlet*" speech by speech or word by word. In exploring what he calls "the twin cannons," Stephen Booth is deliberately turning away from serious "Readings"—what one might in this context call the heavy artillery of critical explications that strive to elucidate large patterns of overall significance. Perhaps we should be shrinking our expectations rather than shrinking Shakespeare, allowing the play of "undelivered meanings" in *Hamlet* as well as the claims of "immortality" made by Bloom.

NOTES

1. Quotations from *Hamlet* are from the Arden 2 text, ed. Harold Jenkins (London: Methuen, 1982).

2. The actual relative figures are as follows: 1990 *Hamlet* 400, *Lear* 197; 1991 *Hamlet* 365, *Lear* 184; 1992 *Hamlet* 479, *Lear* 212; 1993 *Hamlet* 459, *Lear* 204; 1994 *Hamlet* 456, *Lear* 188; 1995 *Hamlet* 418, *Lear* 168; 1996 *Hamlet* 400, *Lear* 165; 1997 *Hamlet* 451, *Lear* 202; 1998 (latest figures available) *Hamlet* 378, *Lear* 155.

3. See Tolstoy (1903). Grigori Kozintsev's film was released in 1964; see also his book about the making of the film (1977).

WORKS CITED

Atwood, Margaret. "Gertrude Talks Back," in *Good Bones*. London: Bloomsbury, 1992, pp. 15–18.

Blayney, Peter W. M. *The Texts of "King Lear" and Their Origins*. Cambridge: Cambridge University Press, 1982.

Bloom, Harold. *Shakespeare: The Invention of the Human*. London: Fourth Estate, 1999.

Booth, Stephen. "Close Reading without Readings." *Shakespeare Reread: The Texts in New Contexts*, ed. Russ McDonald. New York: Cornell University Press, 1994, pp. 42–55.

Caldecott, Thomas, ed. *"Hamlet," and "As You Like It": A Specimen of a New Edition of Shakespeare*. London: John Murray, 1832.

Desai, R. W. Review of Foakes, *Hamlet versus Lear, Hamlet Studies* 17 (1995), 152–55.

Dusinberre, Juliet. *Shakespeare and the Nature of Women.* London: Macmillan, 1975, 1996.

Edwards, Philip, ed. *William Shakespeare: Hamlet.* Cambridge: Cambridge University Press, 1985.

Fabiny, Tibor. "*King Lear* in the New Hungary." *Shakespeare and Hungary*, ed. Holgar Klein and Peter Davidhazi. New York: Garland, 1991, pp. 191–206.

Foakes, R. A. *Hamlet versus Lear.* Cambridge: Cambridge University Press, 1993.

Greenblatt, Stephen, Walter Cohen, Jean E. Howard, and Katherine Eisaman Maus , eds. *The Norton Shakespeare.* New York: Norton, 1997.

Hattaway, Michael, Boika Sokolova, and Derek Roper, eds. *Shakespeare in the New Europe.* Sheffield: Sheffield Acacdemic Press, 1994.

Heilbrun, Carolyn. *Hamlet's Mother and Other Women.* New York: Columbia University Press, 1990.

Hibbard, G. R., ed. *William Shakespeare: Hamlet.* Oxford: Clarendon Press, 1987.

Hunter, Joseph. *New Illustrations of the Life, Studies, and Writings of Shakespeare*, 2 vols. London: J. B. Nichols and Son, 1845.

Jenkins, Harold, ed. *William Shakespeare: Hamlet.* London: Methuen, 1982.

Johnson, David. *Shakespeare and South Africa.* Oxford: Clarendon Press, 1996.

Joughin, John J., ed. *Shakespeare and National Culture.* Manchester: Manchester University Press, 1997.

Kehler, Dorothea. "The First Quarto of *Hamlet*: Reforming Widow Gertred," *Shakespeare Quarterly* 46 (1995), 398–413.

Kennedy, Dennis. *Foreign Shakespeare: Contemporary Performance.* Cambridge: Cambridge University Press, 1993.

Klein, Holgar and Peter Davidhazi, eds. *Shakespeare and Hungary.* London: Edwin Mellen Press, 1996.

Kolin, Philip C., ed. *Shakespeare and Feminist Criticism.* New York: Garland, 1991.

Kozintsev, Grigori. *King Lear: The Space of Tragedy* trans. Mary Mackintosh. Berkeley: University of California Press, 1977.

Lodge, David. *Changing Places: A Tale of Two Campuses.* London: Secker and Warburg, 1975.

Loomba, Ania. (1997) "Shakespearian Transformations." *Shakespeare and National Culture,* ed. John J. Joughin. Manchester: Manchester University Press, 1997, pp. 109–41.

Loomba, Ania and Martin Orkin, eds. *Post-Colonial Shakespeares.* London: Routledge, 1998.

McLuskie, Kathleen. "The Patriarchal Bard: Feminist Criticism and Shakespeare: *King Lear* and *Measure for Measure*," *Political Shakespeare*, ed. Jonathan Dollimore and Alan Sinfield. Manchester: Manchester University Press, 1985, pp. 88–108.

Neill, Michael. "Post-Colonial Shakespeare? Writing Away from the Centre." *Post-Colonial Shakespeare.* ed. Ania Loomba and Martin Orkin, 1998, pp. 164–85.

Novy, Marianne. *Love's Argument: Gender Relations in Shakespeare.* Chapel Hill: University of North Carolina Press, 1984.

Nuttall, A. D. (1997) "Freud and Shakespeare: *Hamlet*," *Shakespearean Continuities*, ed. John Batchelor, Tom Cain and Claire Lamont. London: Macmillan, 1997, pp. 123–37.

Oates, Joyce Carol. "'Is This the Promised End?': The Tragedy of *King Lear*," in *Contraries*. London: Gollancz, (1981), pp. 51–81.

O'Brien, Ellen J. "Revision by Excision: Rewriting Gertrude," *Shakespeare Survey 45*, (1992), 27–35.

Rose, Jacqueline. "Sexuality in the Reading of Shakespeare," *Alternative Shakespeares*, ed. John Drakakis. London: Methuen, 1985, pp. 95–118.

Smiley, Jane. *A Thousand Acres*. New York: Knopf, 1991.

Smiley, Jane. "Shakespeare in Iceland." *Transforming Shakespeare: Women's Re-Visions in Literature and Performance*, ed. Marianne Novy. London: Macmillan, 1999, pp. 159–79.

Showalter, Elaine. "Representing Ophelia: Women, Madness, and the Responsibilities of Feminist Criticism." *Shakespeare and the Question of Theory*, ed. Patricia Parker and Geoffrey Hartman. London: Methuen, 1985, pp. 77–94.

Stone, P. W. K. *The Textual History of "King Lear."* London: Scolar Press, 1980.

Stríbrny, Zednek. *Shakespeare and Eastern Europe*. Oxford: Oxford University Press, 2000.

Taylor, Gary. "The Incredible Shrinking Bard." *Shakespeare and Appropriation*, ed. Christy Desmet and Robert Sawyer. London: Routledge, 1999, pp. 197–205.

Taylor, Gary and Michael Warren, eds. *The Division of the Kingdoms*. Oxford: Clarendon Press, 1983.

Theobald, Lewis. *Shakespeare Restored*. London: R. Francklin et al., 1726.

Tolstoy, Leo. "Shakespeare and the Drama." Preface to Ernest Crosby, *Shakespeare and the Working Classes*. London, 1903.

Ueno, Yoshiko, ed. *Hamlet and Japan*. New York: AMS Press, 1995.

Updike, John. *Gertrude and Claudius*. New York: Knopf, 2000.

Urkowitz, Steven. *Shakespeare's Revision of "King Lear"*. Princeton, NJ: Princeton University Press, 1980.

Warren, Michael. "Quarto and Folio *King Lear* and the Interpretation of Albany and Edgar." *Shakespeare, Pattern of Excelling Nature*, ed. David Bevington and Jay L. Halio. Newark, Delaware: University of Delaware Press, 1978, pp. 95–107.

Wells, Stanley and Gary Taylor, eds. *William Shakespeare: The Complete Works*. Oxford: Oxford University Press, 1986.

Wells, Stanley and Gary Taylor (1990) "The Oxford Shakespeare Re-Viewed by the General Editors," *Analytical and Enumerative Bibliography*, 1990, N.S. 4, 6–20.

Williams, Simon. *Shakespeare on the German Stage*. Cambridge: Cambridge University Press, 1990.

Can We Talk about Race in *Hamlet*?

PETER ERICKSON

My title question presupposes a prior question: How do we define race for the purposes of this inquiry? Is there a historically valid concept of race that can be applied to *Hamlet*? The essays by P. E. H. Hair and Robin Law and by David Richardson from the first two volumes of the *Oxford History of the British Empire* offer a useful starting point because together they provide a sufficiently long time span to document England's comparatively late entry into the Atlantic slave trade. Massive British involvement begins only in the 1640s (Hair and Law 247, 255; Richardson 454), a historical marker that any discussion of race in the early modern period must acknowledge.

In literary terms, this historical dividing line can be expressed as a contrast between the respective careers of the two major figures of Shakespeare (1564–1616) and Milton (1608–1674). As Maureen Quilligan's cogent analysis of Milton's engagement with the implications of slavery shows, Milton's work as a writer coincides with the rapid growth of the British slave trade, while Shakespeare's oeuvre entirely predates this phenomenon (Quilligan 220). However, this clear-cut historical difference does not permit us, in a triumphant spirit of case-closed Q.E.D., to announce the end of the story. Rather, it is only the beginning, because we are left with a further question: if the British contribution to the institution of plantation slavery in the new world is a historically later, post-Shakespearean development, what preceded it? Two answers are on offer. The first claims that no discussion of race before England's full-scale participation in the Atlantic slave trade is historically valid; in effect, the British Renaissance is a blank with regard to race. The second argues that there is a prior stage with its own distinct and historically appropriate conception of race.

The first approach is exemplified by P. E. H. Hair's adjunct essay "Attitudes to Africans" (cited in Hair and Law 249 n. 26). Hair's main point about the overall historical time frame is extremely valuable and cannot be denied. But his exclusive one-note emphasis on the Atlantic slave trade prevents him from recognizing any other definition of race and compels him categorically to dismiss any examination of historically earlier forms of race. This wholesale dismissal leads Hair to make rhetorical moves that are attitudinal rather than factual. For instance, Hair adopts a glib posture of chauvinist scapegoating to dismiss the authors of a body of interpretation counter to his own: "all are North American, their works are published in North America, and their arguments are addressed to North American readers concerned about North American social problems" (Hair, "Attitudes" 45). The suggestion that no British critic could pursue the issue of race or that England is without racial problems will not withstand even minimal scrutiny. At a more substantive level, Hair's recourse to the concept of xenophobia (Hair, "Attitudes" 47) as a catch-all term covering the English response to any outsider is unconvincing in the incuriosity with which it over-rides possible distinctions among foreign groups in favor of a vaguely excusatory yet apparently self-evident notion of "the time-honored and universal way of cultural self-protection" (Hair, "Attitudes" 44).

As an alternative to Hair, I argue that race-specific perceptions exist in England prior to the full-fledged commitment to the Atlantic slave trade. The material base for this previous phase is the traffic in black Africans as personal servants and as performers in court entertainments across Europe. The representational effects of the use of Africans as objects of display and as status symbols are varied, complex, and not always easily controllable (Erickson, "Representations of Blacks and Blackness" and "Representations of Race"). Material base and representational effects together comprise a significant symbolic field worthy of careful scholarly investigation. Further, not only is there a prior early modern phase that has its own relevant sense of race, but also this phase can itself be divided into precursor and emergent stages corresponding to the broad distinction between Elizabethan and Jacobean.

My specific interest is in the transition from *Hamlet* (1600) to *Othello* (1604), but this shift is situated in the larger context of the transition from the monarchy of Elizabeth I to that of James I. Steven Mullaney's insightful study usefully indicates that this transition should not be confined to one point in time—the exact moment of Elizabeth's death and James's accession—but should rather be thought of as an extended period of cultural adjustment and transformation. To Mullaney's focus on the "regendering of monarchy" (139) as the cultural work that occurs during this period, I would like to add a consideration of how monarchal power is raced.

Through the sixteenth century, the tradition of the cultural display of black Africans is far more prominent in Scotland than in England. James's move from the former to the latter brings an infusion of greater visibility to racial difference into English culture. The historical example of Scotland is instructive for two reasons. First, its Northern location serves to counteract the tendency to assume that the diffusion of Africans throughout Europe stems from a single point of origin in the Southern Renaissance countries adjacent to the Mediterranean. Paul

Edwards's accounts suggest that the patterns of circulation by which blacks arrived at various European sites involve more multiple networks and routes (Edwards; Edwards and Walvin). Second, while the study of the Atlantic slave trade is necessarily concerned with the huge numbers that measure and quantify its vast scale, the orchestrated displays in sixteenth-century Scotland show that deployment of a very small number of Africans can have a significant, even disproportionate, cultural impact (Fradenburg; Andrea).

Recent work has focused on the 1605 performance of *The Masque of Blackness* as a key landmark at the outset of the Jacobean era that demonstrates both Queen Anne's independent role (Barroll; Orgel) and the higher profile for race (MacDonald; Hall, "The *Masque of Blackness* and Jacobean Nationalism"; Floyd-Wilson; Andrea), a profile also on display in Paul van Somer's more conventional portrait of the Queen accompanied by a black attendant (c. 1616). In conjunction with *The Masque of Blackness*, *Othello* not only participates in the new attention to figurations of blackness but helps to create it.

The greater visibility accorded to race in Jacobean culture does not mean that race was completely absent under Elizabeth, as her proclamation of 1601 ordering the deportation of "Negroes and blackamoors" attests. The difference is rather that, compared to the new Jacobean ethos, attention to race during Elizabeth's reign was more muted, sporadic, and fragmentary, with the result that it did not register so strongly as a concerted, coordinated force. In *The Merry Wives of Windsor* (c. 1597), for example, Falstaff's early allusion to Guiana (1.3.63–66) just barely establishes an international framework that enables us to construe the later nationalist celebration of "our radiant Queen" (5.5.45) as projecting a radiance consistent with racial whiteness. Nevertheless, Elizabeth's whiteface is far slighter in its effect than Queen Anne's dramatic blackface. My thesis is that this relative Elizabethan–Jacobean contrast correlates with the transition from *Hamlet* to *Othello*. As *Othello*, consonant with its Jacobean context, is explicit in its turn to race (Erickson, "Images of White Identity"), so *Hamlet*, in keeping with its Elizabethan milieu, touches race only obliquely and its racial discourse thus remains latent, implicit.

In rethinking the sequence from *Hamlet* to *Othello*, I begin with two ethnic references in the former. The first is Hamlet's parenthetical phrase "if the rest of my fortunes turn Turk with me" (3.2.259–60) in the burst of glee after his success in catching Claudius with *The Mousetrap*. The second occurs when Hamlet, berating Gertrude, sharply contrasts his father with Claudius—"Could you on this fair mountain leave to feed, / And batten on this moor?" (3.4.67–68)—and the term "fair" activates a second, racial meaning implicit in the word "moor." Both instances are incidental, fleeting, and admittedly low-level. Yet they are noteworthy because both are uttered by the play's central character and both anticipate motifs that will become fully charged major themes in *Othello*: Othello is the Moor who ultimately turns on the Turk in himself. The potential resonance of Hamlet's evocations of Turk and Moor increases when we take into account the expanded geographical range implied by the play's performance history. For the play is not restricted to the Northern tier of its Scandinavian–English setting or to the site of its production in London theater. Michael Neill's observation that "Shakespeare had begun to move out along the arteries of Empire even in his own lifetime" is occasioned by an onboard staging of *Hamlet* off the coast of west Africa in 1607, a performance suggesting the play's capacity for "performing Englishness" in distant locations (Neill 171–72; also Hair, "Hamlet in an Afro-Portuguese Setting").

Beyond Hamlet's relatively minor allusion to Turk and Moor is a network of deep imagery regarding whiteness. Recent critical studies have brought into focus the construction of white identity as an emergent racial category in the early modern period (Hall, "Fair Texts/Dark Ladies" and "'These bastard signs of fair'"; Bowen; Callaghan; Erickson, "'God for Harry'"). My goal here is to extend this discussion to *Hamlet* by drawing in particular on Mary Floyd-Wilson's analysis of whiteness in the moment before it is securely established as a dominant political force. Her account shows that early modern white identity has to be seen as being in the process of formation and hence in flux and unstable. In addition, this fashioning of white identity does not unfold in a neutral context because whiteness carried negative connotations that had to be overcome. The perception of whiteness as flawed and on the defensive creates an active sense of insecurity and anxiety.

This association of whiteness and vulnerability is one of the underlying motifs *Hamlet* dramatizes. In approaching white imagery in the play, I examine two distinct strands, the first concerning male interaction and the second associated with the representation of women. However, in both cases whiteness is present as an ideal lost beyond recovery, and in this sense *Hamlet* participates in the interim crisis of whiteness described by Floyd-Wilson. As the play appeals to images of snow and of milk, it asks us to reimagine these familiar metaphors in the context of a newly emerging world picture keyed to racial difference and conflict.

One meaning of betrayal in *Hamlet* is the betrayal of whiteness. The white imagery connected with the ghost conveys not only violation but vulnerability and helplessness, and this link between whiteness and weakness is an element that no action in the play can remedy or reverse. The initial cues to the Ghost's white coloration are slight: there is the metamorphosis of the former "fair and warlike form" (1.1.47) into the "very pale" countenance of his current state (1.2.230–33). This paleness, however, is soon further transformed by the Ghost's graphic disclosure of the physical process of his death. The action of the "leprous distilment" results in a whitening that is both internal—"And with a sudden vigour it doth posset / And curd, like eager droppings into milk, / The thin and wholesome blood"—and external—"And a most instant tetter barked about, / Most lazar-like, with vile and loathsome crust, / All my smooth body" (1.5.64–73).

At the core of the first act's climax is a horrifying disfigurement of white identity that makes loss of stature a matter of skin condition.

This melodramatic deformation of white identity is further emphasized by young Hamlet's equally theatrical conception of his father's murderer as black:

> The rugged Pyrrhus, he whose sable arms,
> Black as his purpose, did the night resemble,
> When he lay couched in the ominous horse,
> Hath now this dread and black complexion smeared
> With heraldry more dismal.   (2.2.443–47)

As with Hamlet's father, the victim Priam is imagined in terms of innocent whiteness whose graphic physical violation is irreparable: "'the milky head / Of reverend Priam'" (469–70). The racialized implication of Claudius as a Moor is consistent with the overall white-black color scheme. This pairing tacitly gives expression to a fear that such a terrible demise of white identity could only be motivated and carried out by its racial opposite.

With regard to women, the ideal imaged in Hamlet's addressing himself to Ophelia's "'excellent white bosom'" (2.2.112) is dramatized from the beginning as irretrievably lost, already nullified by Hamlet's denial: "be thou chaste as ice, pure as snow, thou shalt not escape calumny" (3.1.137–38). The only value remaining in the language of whiteness is the use Ophelia makes of it in mourning her father—"White his shroud as the mountain snow" (4.5.35), "His beard as white as snow" (195)—where her very plaintiveness signifies the inefficacy of white imagery. Hamlet's brief recovery of a positive dimension after her death—"What, the fair Ophelia!" (5.1.233)—has been canceled in advance by his sarcastic verbal shakedown—"Are you fair?" (3.1.106) and "That's a fair thought to lie between maids' legs" (3.2.110). As Kim Hall's studies of the word "fair" demonstrate ("Fair Texts/Dark Ladies" and "'These Bastard Signs of Fair'"), this term increasingly bears racial as well as sexual connotations. *Othello* subsequently intensifies the rhetorical pressure on the meanings of "fair" not only in Iago's wordplay with Desdemona (2.1.132–62) but also in the Duke of Venice's ostensible praise of Othello as "far more fair than black" (1.3.288–89). Yet this interrogation of the word is a point of contact between the two plays.

Just as Hamlet finds in Claudius a blackened counterpoint to his father's violated whiteness, so he locates a blackened foil in his mother. Having just overseen Claudius's confession that his "bosom black as death" prevents "the sweet heavens" from "wash[ing]" his "cursed hand" "white as snow" (3.3.43–46), Hamlet proceeds to extract a parallel confession from his mother: "Thou turn'st mine eyes into my very soul, / And there I see such black and grained spots / As will not leave their tinct" (3.4.81–83). Both Gertrude's striking word "tinct" and Claudius's recognition of failed absolution convey an idea of indelibility that is uneasily reminiscent of the standard epigram about the impossibility of washing the Ethiop white. Though lacking racial specificity, the play's general preoccupation with a vocabulary of black and white imagery conveys a symbolic world characterized by the erasure of whiteness and the dominance of blackness. Without being explicitly formulated, racially toned anxieties appear just under the surface.

For interpretive convenience, I have traced figurations of whiteness in separate male and female contexts. In the end, the two fields operate together to suggest that a reliable source of whiteness is nowhere available in the play. This conclusion provides another way to understand the extraordinary torment and anguish the play so vividly communicates. This mode of interpretation by no means supplants all the others, but it should be added to the rest. The study of race in Shakespeare is unduly hampered if it is limited to a narrow focus on literal black characters. The scope of inquiry should rather be expanded to include the broader sphere of rhetoric and imagery that make it possible to answer yes to the question in my title.

WORKS CITED

Andrea, Bernadette. "Black Skin, The Queen's Masques: Africanist Ambivalence and Feminine Author(ity) in The Masques of *Blackness* and *Beauty*." *English Literary Renaissance* 29 (1999): 246–81.

Barroll, Leeds. "Inventing the Stuart Masque." *The Politics of the Stuart Court Masque*, ed. David Bevington and Peter Holbrook. Cambridge: Cambridge University Press, 1998, pp. 121–43.

Bowen, Barbara. "Aemilia Lanyer and the Invention of White Womanhood." *Maids and Mistresses, Cousins and Queens: Women's Alliances in Early Modern England*, ed. Susan Frye and Karen Robinson. New York: Oxford University Press, 1999, pp. 274–303.

Callaghan, Dympna. "'Othello was a white man': Properties of Race on Shakespeare's Stage." *Shakespeare without Women: Representing Gender and Race on the Renaissance Stage*. London: Routledge, 2000, pp. 75–96.

Edwards, Paul. "The Early African Presence in the British Isles." *Essays on the History of Blacks in Britain: From Roman Times to the Mid-twentieth Century*, ed. Jagdish S. Gundara and Ian Duffield. Aldershot, England: Avebury, 1992, pp. 9–29.

Edwards, Paul, and James Walvin. "Africans in Britain, 1500–1800." *The African Diaspora: Interpretive Essays*, ed. Martin L. Kilson and Robert I. Rotberg. Cambridge: Harvard University Press, 1976, pp. 172–204.

Erickson, Peter. "'God for Harry, England, and Saint George': British National Identity and the Emergence of White Self-Fashioning." *Early Modern Visual Culture: Representation, Race, and Empire in Renaissance England*, ed. Peter Erickson and Clark Hulse. Philadelphia: University of Pennsylvania Press, 2000, pp. 315–45.

———. "Images of White identity in *Othello*." *New Critical Essays on Othello*, ed. Philip Kolin. New York: Routledge, 2001.

———. "Representations of Blacks and Blackness in the Renaissance." *Criticism* 35 (1993): 499–527.

———. "Representations of Race in Renaissance Art." *The Upstart Crow: A Shakespeare Journal* 18 (1998): 2–9.

Floyd-Wilson, Mary. "Temperature, Temperance, and Racial Difference in Ben Jonson's *The Masque of Blackness*." *English Literary Renaissance* 28 (1998): 183–209.

Fradenburg, Louise Olga. "The Black Lady." *City, Marriage, Tournament: Arts of Rule in Late Medieval Scotland*. Madison: University of Wisconsin Press, 1991, pp. 244–64.

Hall, Kim F. "Fair Texts/Dark Ladies: Renaissance Lyric and the Poetics of Color." In *Things of Darkness: Economies of Race and Gender in Early Modern England*. Ithaca: Cornell University Press, 1995, pp. 62–122.

———. "The *Masque of Blackness* and Jacobean Nationalism." *Things of Darkness: Economies of Race and Gender in Early Modern England*. Ithaca: Cornell University Press, 1995, pp. 128–41.

———. "'These Bastard Signs of Fair': Literary Whiteness in Shakespeare's Sonnets." *Post-Colonial Shakespeares*, ed. Ania Loomba and Martin Orkin. London: Routledge, 1998, pp. 64–83.

Hair, P. E. H. "Attitudes to Africans in English Primary Sources on Guinea up to 1650." *History in Africa* 26 (1999): 43–68.

———. "Hamlet in an Afro-Portuguese Setting: New Perspectives on Sierra Leone in 1607." *Africa Encountered: European Contacts and Evidence, 1450–1700*. Aldershot, England: Variorum, 1997, pp. 21–42.

Hair, P. E. H., and Robin Law. "The English in Western Africa to 1700." *The Origins of Empire: British Overseas Enterprise to the Close of the Seventeenth Century*, ed. Nicholas Canny. The Oxford History of the British Empire 1. Oxford: Oxford University Press, 1998, pp. 241–63.

MacDonald, Joyce Green. "'The Force of Imagination': The Subject of Blackness in Shakespeare, Jonson, and Ravenscroft." *Renaissance Papers* (1991): 53–74.

Mullaney, Steven. "Mourning and Misogyny: *Hamlet, The Revenger's Tragedy*, and The Final Progress of Elizabeth I, 1600–1607." *Shakespeare Quarterly* 45 (1994): 139–62.

Neill, Michael. "Post-Colonial Shakespeare?: Writing away from the Centre." *Post-Colonial Shakespeares*, ed. Ania Loomba and Martin Orkin. London: Routledge, 1998, pp. 164–85.

Orgel, Stephen. "Marginal Jonson." *The Politics of the Stuart Court Masque*, ed. David Bevington and Peter Holbrook. Cambridge: Cambridge University Press, 1998, pp. 144–75.

Quilligan, Maureen. "Freedom, Service, and the Trade in Slaves: The Problem of Labor in *Paradise Lost*." *Subject and Object in Renaissance Culture*, ed. Margreta de Grazia, Maureen Quilligan, and Peter Stallybrass. Cambridge: Cambridge University Press, 1996, pp. 213–34.

Richardson, David. "The British Empire and the Atlantic Slave Trade, 1660–1807." *The Eighteenth Century*, ed. P. J. Marshall. The Oxford History of the British Empire 2. Oxford: Oxford University Press, 1998, pp. 440–64.

Shakespeare, William. *Hamlet*. Ed. G. R. Hibbard. Oxford: Clarendon, 1987.

Hamlet, Laertes, and the Dramatic Functions of Foils

RICHARD LEVIN

My only excuse for adding another item to the megagigantic body of commentary on *Hamlet* is that I can claim a certain uniqueness in the current critical scene—in fact, ten kinds of uniqueness:

1. I actually admire the play.
2. I think it is much more important and much more valuable than anything I could say about it.
3. I think it was consciously designed and written by an author, and I also admire him.
4. I think it presents Hamlet as an individual with a personality, and I admire him as well.
5. I do not think that it is really about the socio-economic conflicts of 1600 or 2000.
6. I do not think that it confirms my own views or "positionality."
7. I do not think that my remarks on it constitute a remarkable discovery that will invalidate all previous criticism of the play.
8. I do not think that these remarks constitute an "interrogation" of the play that will force it to yield up its concealed real meaning against its will.
9. I do not think that they constitute an "intervention" that will help to bring about a complete (but unspecified) "transformation of society" that will eliminate all oppression based on race, gender, class or anything else.
10. I do not think that critics who disagree with my interpretation of the play or adopt a different approach to it are "complicit," wittingly or unwittingly, with a reactionary, multinational conspiracy to perpetuate the aforementioned oppression, or that they feel "threatened" by me, or even that they are less intelligent, virtuous, or sincere than I am.

The fourth point would seem to be the most significant for my purpose here, because *Hamlet* is dominated by Hamlet, who has a more important role in "his" play than Shakespeare's other tragic protagonists. There are several reasons for this. One of them is simply the number of lines he speaks and the number of scenes where he appears. [1] Another is that no one else in the cast offers him any serious competition for our attention, whereas most of the other protagonists come in couples (Romeo and Juliet, Antony and Cleopatra) or with major antagonists (Aaron in *Titus Andronicus*, Mark Antony in *Julius Caesar*,[2] Iago in *Othello*, and Edmund in *King Lear*) who are fascinating in their own right. Hamlet is certainly surrounded by a number of interesting characters, but none of them captures our interest in the special way that he does, and we are interested in them primarily in terms of their effect upon him.

Our special interest in Hamlet, however, cannot just be the result of this absence of competition, since three other Shakespearean tragic protagonists— Macbeth, Timon, and Coriolanus—also have no serious competitors but are not as interesting as he is. Therefore it must have something to do with his character or personality, but this idea, as my fourth point indicates, brings me up against many of our recent critics, who tell us that any reference to the individual character of a Shakespearean character is anachronistic because there was no conception of individuals in early modern (formerly Renaissance) England and hence the drama of this period never portrayed them. Their claim is demonstrably wrong, but since I have presented the evidence to demonstrate this elsewhere, I will ignore it here.[3]

A number of these same critics also reject discussions of the character of a Shakespearean character because it is an "illusion" that we "construct" in our own minds. This claim, unlike the preceding one, is true, but it does not invalidate such discussions. While we certainly do construct the personality of a dramatic character by inferences from his words and deeds, that is exactly how we come to know the personality of all of the real individuals that we meet, which we do not think is an illusion. The obvious difference is that these real individuals are the source of their words and deeds and are not (usually) trying to create our conception of their personalities, whereas the source of a dramatic character's words and deeds is the playwright, who *is* trying to create such a conception in the audience.[4] The dramatic characters, however, are not aware of their effect on the audience because they do not know that they are in a play; they are acting (in both senses) as real people who generate their own words and deeds. It is crucial, therefore, to distinguish a character's problems and purposes from those of the playwright. I will return to this point later, but now I want to proceed to a consideration of Hamlet's personality and the reasons why it is so interesting to us.

Probably the most important of these reasons is the extraordinary complexity of this personality. Of course, complexity in a dramatic character (as in most other things) is a relative matter. In his mature work Shakespeare did not create any simple tragic protagonists. Fortunately the time has passed when some critics tried to reduce these protagonists to the level of Ben Jonson's single-trait "humor" characters by finding that each of them is completely dominated by one "tragic flaw" that explains his tragedy—that Othello's downfall is caused by his "jealousy," and Lear's by his "rage," and so on, and that *Hamlet*, according to a voice-over at the beginning of the Olivier film, is "the tragedy of a man who could not make up his mind."[5] Such simplifications are not true of any of these characters and surely not of Hamlet, who is much more complex than the others, including Macbeth, Timon, and Coriolanus, the protagonists of the other "one-man" tragedies. He is constantly surprising us by exhibiting new qualities and attitudes that do not cohere easily within a single personality and sometimes even seem to be contradictory, and it was largely because of this complexity that T. S. Eliot called the play "the 'Mona Lisa' of literature" (Eliot 124). Indeed so much has been written about this aspect of Hamlet that it is unnecessary to develop the point here. A good deal of this commentary comes from critics who are trying, like Rosencrantz and Guildenstern, to "pluck out the heart of [his] mystery" (3.2.365–66) by identifying a single master key that underlies and explains his complexity. I am not going to join this project, which I think is only a more sophisticated version of the attempt to reduce him to one dominant trait or "tragic flaw," but it seems clear that the search itself is testimony that the complexity of Hamlet's character is one of the major causes that makes him so interesting.

The second major cause of our special interest in Hamlet is his ability to evoke and maintain our intense sympathy and admiration, which further distinguishes him from the protagonists of the other "one-man" tragedies. The proof is that no critics, as far as I know, have likened themselves to Macbeth, Timon, or Coriolanus, whereas many have felt a close personal affinity to Hamlet. Some of them, in fact, have even rewritten the conclusion of the play in order to recreate Hamlet in their own image. Thus David Leverenz, who believes that the play (and presumably real life) is divided into an evil, unnatural "world of fathers," dominated by reason, public roles, ambition, power, and war, and a good, natural, feminine world of emotion, private selves, sensitivity, and harmony, claims that in the final scene Hamlet, in response to "the unspoken woman in him," has "inwardly . . . already left the world of fathers . . . to rejoin Ophelia and Gertrude" (Leverenz 123), which ignores the inconvenient fact that in his dying moments Hamlet is very busy with masculine business, such as killing Laertes and Claudius (twice) and settling the Danish succession; and Helen Vendler calls the play "a celebration of skepticism" (presumably her own position) because it shows Hamlet's "repudiation" of Christianity, which ignores the inconvenient fact that in the final scene he is much more explicitly Christian than before in affirming the role of "divinity" and "providence" and the "felicity" of heaven (5.2.9–11, 219–20, 347). This is another project that I have no intention of joining, since I do not want to make Hamlet resemble me or make the play conform to my own beliefs (as stated in my sixth point at the outset), but I would like to focus for the rest of this essay on the most important factors involved in Shakespeare's effort to maintain our sympathy and admiration for Hamlet.

Maintaining these positive feelings for Hamlet is no simple task. As we see him in this play, he is certainly not a nice young man. Indeed, it is easy to draw up a very severe indictment against him, which a few critics have done. He is responsible, directly or indirectly, for many deaths, and he does not show the least remorse for any of them—in fact he explictly rejects any feelings of guilt for stabbing Polonius (3.4.212–15) and for sending Rosencrantz and Guildenstern to be executed in England (5.2.57–62).[6] And his speeches, while not deadly, can be just as cruel. He launches savage (and sexist) attacks on Ophelia in 3.1 and on Gertrude in 3.4, and directs his bitter, parodic wit against Claudius, Polonius, Rosencrantz, Guildenstern, Osric, and just about everyone else whom he encounters except Horatio, the players, and the gravediggers. He certainly is not trying to evoke our sympathy and admiration.

Shakespeare, however, is trying to evoke and maintain a positive response to his protagonist. For one thing, he endows Hamlet with a number of traits that are very admirable in themselves. Like his complexity, this aspect of Hamlet has been discussed so extensively by the critics that it will be enough here to survey them very briefly. Probably the most striking of these traits is what Harold Bloom calls (four times, with variations) his "supreme intellect and capacious consciousness" (Bloom 388, 392, 394, 410),[7] which is exhibited in the astonishing number of subjects, ranging all the way from acting to the meaning of life and death, that he can comment on with considerable insight. Another impressive trait is his honesty, accompanied by a keen sensitivity to—and abhorrence of—deception and hypocrisy in others. He also is (or tries to be) completely honest about himself and frequently probes his own motives. He has a capacity for very strong emotional attachments, seen especially in his feelings for his father and Horatio, and an easy, unaffected manner in dealing with his social inferiors, and a brilliant sense of humor and of the ridiculous, and other less important but also admirable traits of character.

Our sympathy for Hamlet is maintained, not only by his possession of these positive traits, but also by several extenuating factors that serve to mitigate our negative judgment of some of his behavior. One of these is our realization that we do not see Hamlet before the events that initiate this tragedy have had a serious impact on him. In several of his other tragedies Shakespeare makes a special effort, early in the action, to show us the protagonist in what might be called his normal or optimal state, when he is functioning successfully at the height of his powers, which forms our crucial first impression of him and helps us to understand the extent and significance of his downfall. The first act of *Othello* is designed to give Othello an opportunity to display his best qualities (his self-confidence and self-control, his decisiveness and ability to command the situation), before Iago goes to work on him in 3.3. In *Coriolanus*, 1.4–9, we see Coriolanus in heroic action at Corioles, fighting fearlessly, rallying his troops, and winning

the battle (and his new surname), before the disastrous decision to seek the con-
sulship in 2.1. A similar function is served by the sergeant's report in *Macbeth*,
1.2, that describes Macbeth's feats as a loyal and brave general, before he meets
the witches in 1.3. And the opening scenes in *Timon of Athens* focus on Timon's
magnificent generosity in showering gifts upon all kinds of people, before he
runs out of money in act 2. But when we first see Hamlet (in 1.2), he is already
withdrawn, bitter, and deeply distressed because of his father's death and his
mother's hasty remarriage, and his encounter with the Ghost soon afterward
(1.5), with the revelations about the murder of his father and his mother's adultery and the injunction to take revenge, exerts much more pressure on him and
induces him to "put an antic disposition on" (172), so that during the entire play
he is never in his normal state.

    This does not mean, however, that we do not have a conception of Hamlet's
life before these events. Some recent critics insist that dramatic characters have
no existence until they first appear on the stage (or in the text), but if we believe
that this play is designed to represent the actions of life-like individuals (assumed
in my fourth point at the outset), we cannot believe that Hamlet is born, fully
grown, at the beginning of the second scene. We know that he is supposed to
have had a previous life, which we are supposed to construct, just as we construct
his personality, by inferences from the evidence in the play. Of course this kind
of interpretation can be abused, but that does not make it invalid. I am not going
to invent a childhood for Hamlet, like Ernest Jones (Jones 91–94), based on my
theory of human development.[8] (As indicated in my sixth point at the outset, I do
not think the play confirms any theory of mine.) But I believe that we can—and
are meant to—form an accurate picture of what Hamlet was like in the period
preceding his father's death, since we can be confident that we are dealing with
a gifted author (my third point at the outset) who gives us all the evidence that
we need in order to do this.

    Our most direct evidence of this earlier, normal Hamlet is Ophelia's solilo-
quy immediately following his attack on her in the "nunnery" scene:

> O, what a noble mind is here o'erthrown!
> The courtier's, soldier's, scholar's, eye, tongue, sword,
> Th' expectation and rose of the fair state,
> The glass of fashion and the mould of form,
> Th' observ'd of all observers . . .   (3.1.150–54)[9]

She is certainly not a disinterested witness, but she is an eyewitness, because she
is a member of the court where he was "Th' observ'd" and she was courted by
him (she "suck'd the honey of his music vows" [156]). We also have the testimony of Fortinbras, who says in the last speech of the play that Hamlet "was
likely, had he been put on,/ To have prov'd most royal" (5.2.397–98). Since
Fortinbras never saw him, as far as we know, this statement must reflect (and

confirm) the reputation of the earlier Hamlet as "Th' expectation and rose of the fair state" that Ophelia describes. And since it presents the play's final judgment of him, it is intended to weigh heavily in the impression that we carry away with us.

The testimonies of Ophelia and Fortinbras are corroborated, moreover, by several kinds of indirect evidence in the play. One of these is Hamlet's special relationship with Horatio, which extends back a number of years, as Hamlet tells us in his speech praising Horatio (3.2.63–74), and contributes significantly to our very favorable conception of the earlier Hamlet because he chose such a good man as his dearest friend (this being the main point of his speech of praise), and because he was able to earn the friendship and loyalty of such a good man, who feels so closely bound to Hamlet that he does not want to outlive him (5.2.340–42). A similar kind of evidence, on a much less serious level, is his warm camaraderie with the players, which also goes back several years ("O, old friend! why, thy face is valanc'd since I saw thee last" [2.2.422–23]) and shows us another, and very pleasant, side of the earlier Hamlet.

The most important kind of indirect evidence, however, is the Hamlet we see in the play, with all the positive traits—the wide-ranging intellect, the honesty, and the rest—that I just surveyed, since we can be sure that, like Hamlet himself, these traits could not suddenly come into existence in the second scene. His thoughts about human morality and mortality, for instance, were certainly colored by the events that precipitated this tragedy, but these events did not start him thinking about these things. He must have meditated long and deeply on them, and on many other subjects, for some time, because this is kind of mental activity is clearly habitual with him, and habits, we know, are developed very gradually and also change (if they do) very gradually. The same is true of his honesty and other traits, which are also habits and so must have belonged to the earlier, normal Hamlet. And it is our inferred picture of this earlier Hamlet that enables us to appreciate the impact of the recent events upon him and so helps to maintain our sympathy for him by extenuating some of his behavior in the play.

Another extentuating factor is the extremely difficult situation in which Hamlet finds himself, through no fault of his own. Except for his relationship with Horatio, he is completely isolated at the court. Indeed isolation is much too weak a term to describe his position there, since he is also constantly under attack. Not only must he face the more or less open (and expected) hostility of Claudius and Polonius, who acts throughout as Claudius's agent, but he also comes to learn that the very people that he should be able to trust—his mother, Ophelia, and his old schoolfellows Rosencrantz and Guildenstern—have betrayed him to Claudius and Polonius, so that he feels—correctly—that he is "benetted round with villainies" (5.2.29), surrounded by his enemies and the accomplices and spies of these enemies. When we add to this situation the terrible pressure placed upon him by the Ghost's injunction, we can undertand why he is not in his normal state, and sympathize with his predicament, and therefore judge some of his cruel behavior less harshly.

Another reason that we are less critical of Hamlet is our recognition that he is his own severest critic. That is clearly a direct consequence of several of his positive traits, including his honesty and his introspection, as well as the position in which he is placed, and it also contributes to our impression of his complexity. He can berate himself, especially in some of his soliloquies (in fact, in one of them, in 2.2.582–87, he even berates himself for berating himself), and at some other points in the play he shows a keen awareness of his failings—for example, in his confession to Ophelia of his many "offenses" (3.1.121–29) and in his regrets for his treatment of Laertes at the graveyard (5.2.75–76, 226–44). Thus this tendency also serves to extenuate his behavior, because it is hard for us to be very hard on him when he is so very hard on himself.

In addition to his positive characterization of Hamlet and his presentation of these extenuating factors, Shakespeare also maintains our admiration and sympathy for his protagonist by constructing Laertes as Hamlet's foil—a term adapted from the metal leaf that jewelers set behind a gem to bring out its luster. We do not hear much about dramatic foils today, but in the past we heard too much about them, since the concept was applied very loosely to almost any contrast between almost any two characters—even a relatively unimportant contrast between unimportant characters.[10] The fact that this concept was overused in the past, however, does not mean that it cannot still be helpful in interpreting a play, if our interpretation deals with the functions of the play's components. I do not want to legislate the difference between the correct and incorrect uses of this concept, because it seems more appropriate to place foils on a continuum ranging from these passing contrasts that we scarcely notice to striking and sustained contrasts between a minor character and the protagonist that significantly affect our response to that protagonist and to the play. Laertes clearly belongs at this second pole, because he functions as the most important and the most fully developed foil in all of Shakespeare's tragedies.

The conception and the function are stated explicitly by Hamlet himself in his pun on the foils that he and Laertes are selecting for their fencing contest:

> I'll be your foil, Laertes; in mine ignorance
> Your skill shall like a star i' th' darkest night
> Stick fiery off indeed.   (5.2.255–57) [11]

(In the play, of course, Laertes is the foil who makes Hamlet "stick fiery off," but Hamlet is being complimentary and, as I said, he does not know that he is in a play.) Earlier in this scene, he also states explicitly the basic similarity that underlies this foil relationship:

> But I am very sorry, good Horatio,
> That to Laertes I forgot myself,
> For by the image of my cause I see
> The portraiture of his.   (5.2.75–78)

Their obvious common "cause" is to revenge the murders of their fathers. In foil relationships, however, a basic similarity between the two characters invites a comparison of them that brings out their significant differences, which is how the foil can make the main character shine more brightly. In fact, we are asked to compare—and contrast—Hamlet and Laertes on their first appearance, in scene two, when Claudius warmly assents to Laertes's request to return to Paris ("Take thy fair hour, Laertes, time be thine" [62]), and, shortly after, emphatically rejects Hamlet's parallel request to return to Wittenberg ("It is most retrograde to our desire" [114]). [12] This contrast is heightened by the difference in their motives: Laertes sems to be bored at home (as we see in the next scene) and wants to pursue a life of pleasure in Paris, while Hamlet wants to escape from what he regards as an intolerable situation at home (which he emphasizes in his soliloquy in 129–59) and to go "back to school" (113).

Laertes's request not only sets up this contrast with Hamlet, but also leads directly into his departure from his family in the next scene. Although the main dramatic function of this scene (1.3) is to initiate Ophelia's rejection of Hamlet and the line of action resulting from this, it also serves to prepare us for Laertes's absence from the play (and thus for his return at the end) and to show us his feelings toward his sister and father. He seems to have an affectionate relationship with Ophelia (which is confirmed later by his reaction to her madness and her death), but with Polonius he is cold, formal, and even annoyed, as we infer from his remark to Ophelia, "A double blessing is a double grace" (53), which surely is sardonic. (Polonius shows a similar formal and impersonal attitude in this blessing, a collection of general platitudes that apply to any young man of their class,[13] and a much more unpleasant side in 2.1 when he orders Reynaldo to spy on Laertes in Paris.) This is very different from Hamlet's love and reverence for his father, which is expressed most forcefully in his comparison of the two portraits during the "closet" scene (3.4.55–63). And that difference is accentuated in their reactions to the deaths of these fathers: Hamlet is still grieving four months after his loss (for which Claudius reprimands him in 1.2.87–106), whereas Laertes does not mourn at all, as far as we can tell, but just wants revenge.

Hamlet also wants to revenge his father's death, but the parallel pursuit of this common "cause" by the two revengers establishes a number of other important differences between them. In contrast to Hamlet's hesitation and uncertainty about his course of action and his ability to undertake it (exhibited mainly in his soliloquies), Laertes, as soon as he arrives in Denmark, acts with "impiteous haste" to get instant satisfaction by stirring up a mob to storm the palace

(4.5.99–103). In contrast to Hamlet's fear, stated at the end of his soliloquy in 2.2.598–603, that in seeking revenge he may damn himself, Laertes exclaims:

> To hell, allegiance! vows, to the blackest devil!
> Conscience and grace, to the profoundest pit!
> I dare damnation. To this point I stand,
> That both the worlds I give to negligence,
> Let come what comes, only I'll be reveng'd
> Most throughly for my father.   (4.5.132–37)

In contrast to Hamlet's doubts about the Ghost's account of the murder and his decision to test it (explained in the same soliloquy), Laertes accepts without question Claudius's account of the murder of Polonius, even though Claudius is obviously an interested party seeking to exonerate himself.[14] In contrast to Hamlet's refusal to kill Claudius at prayer (3.3.73–96), Laertes later says that to take his revenge on the murderer of his father he would "cut his throat i' th' church" (4.7.126). Although he does not do that, he eagerly agrees to Claudius's scheme to use an unbated foil in the fencing contest, and even proposes to anoint the foil with poison (4.7.140–48), whereas it never occurs to Hamlet to descend to this kind of treachery for his revenge.

Most of these contrasts are quite obvious and have been pointed out by many critics, but very few, as far as I know, have noted an important difference in the motivation of the two revengers. Hamlet is impelled by his intense love for his father, by the commands of the Ghost (who explicitly invokes this love in 1.4.23), and by his outraged sense of justice. But Laertes has no such love for Polonius, as we saw, and no ghostly injunction, and he does not seem to be very interested in justice. His principal motive is expressed very clearly when he first confronts Claudius after his return from Paris:

> That drop of blood that's calm proclaims me bastard,
> Cries cuckold to my father, brands the harlot
> Even here between the chaste unsmirched brow
> Of my true mother.   (4.5.118–21)

He believes, in other words, that if he does not revenge his father's death he will bring dishonor to himself and his family—an idea that, again, never occurs to Hamlet.[15] It indicates not only that Laertes has no deep feelings for his father, who is seen here simply as the source of the sperm that produced him, but also that he is governed by an external and conventional conception of honor that seems to depend upon public opinion, and that emerges again in his protest that his father was buried with "No trophy, sword, nor hatchment o'er his bones, / No noble rite nor formal ostentation" (4.5.215–16). (This is quite different from his objection in 5.1.23 to the abridged "ceremony" of Ophelia's funeral, which reflects his real affection for her,[16] as well as his concern for her salvation, rather than for mere "formal ostentation.") And we see this conception once more in his reponse to Hamlet's plea for forgiveness for his behavior at Ophelia's grave:

> in my terms of honor
> I stand aloof, and will no reconcilement
> Till by some elder masters of known honor
> I have a voice and president of peace
> To keep my name ungor'd.   (5.2.246–50)

We would find it difficult to imagine Hamlet consulting such a panel of experts on a question about his honor.[17] He does not need anyone to tell him when his "honor's at the stake" (4.4.56).

It must be emphasized that, except for the unbated and poisoned foil, these contrasts do not make Laertes reprehensible. He is not presented as a bad person; he is a nice young man or "very noble youth," as Hamlet calls him (5.1.224), but a quite ordinary one, relatively shallow, thoughtless, and conventional, with no trace of the wit, the sensitivity, the broad intellectual interests, the probing insights, the tendency toward introspection and self-doubt, or the other special traits we noted earlier that serve to distinguish Hamlet. Shakespeare clearly intended this foil relationship to establish, not a simple moral opposition between vice and virtue, but a more shaded contrast between an ordinary and an extraordinary personality, in order to make these traits of his protagonist "stick fiery off indeed" and therefore elicit an even stronger positive response from the audience.[18]

Laertes's recourse to the poisoned foil, however, is essential for what is clearly his most important dramatic function in the play as a whole, which involves a very unusual transformation of his role. I cannot think of another foil who engages in direct and deadly conflict with the protagonist. That kind of action belongs to the antagonist, and in *Hamlet* the principal antagonist is Claudius, who enlists Laertes as his accomplice. Yet Laertes's transformation is a necessary consequence of his foil relationship to Hamlet, since this relationship is based on their common task as father-revengers, and to accomplish his task he must kill Hamlet.[19] While that is Laertes's (and Claudius's) purpose, Shakespeare has a quite different purpose—to create a satisfactory ending for the play, which means an ending where Hamlet gets his revenge and pays the price for it without losing our sympathy and admiration. The difficulty of this task can be seen very clearly when we consider what happens to the protagonists of the other major revenge tragedies of this same period—Hieronimo in Thomas Kyd's *The Spanish Tragedy* (*c.* 1587), Antonio in John Marston's *Antonio's Revenge* (*c.* 1600), and Vindice in the anonymous *The Revenger's Tragedy* (*c.* 1606), now often attributed to Thomas Middleton. Each of these three revengers devises an elaborate and deceptive scheme that enables him to trap and to kill the people who wronged him (and usually to kill several other people in the process), but, as a result, he incurs some guilt himself, so that at the conclusion Hieronimo commits suicide, Vindice is sentenced to be executed, and Antonio decides to enter a monastery.

Shakespeare avoids this kind of ending, which inevitably diminishes our sympathy for the protagonist–revenger, by the introduction of the poisoned foil in the fencing match, which means that Claudius, rather than Hamlet, devises the elaborate and deceptive scheme and that Hamlet can kill Claudius without any premeditation or trickery, as a direct and open response to Claudius's indirect, treacherous plot to kill him. Indeed his response seems more like an act of justified (although delayed) self-defense. And since he is already poisoned before he kills Claudius, there is no need for a separate action after it to penalize him. He has, in effect, paid the revenger's penalty in advance. It is a brilliant solution to the problem of bringing the tragedy to a successful conclusion—the most successful conclusion in all the revenge tragedies of this period—because it allows Hamlet to attain his goal, which we desire, without weakening our positive feelings for him, which we do not desire.

This ending also brings about a second transformation of Laertes's relationship to Hamlet, which is just as unusual as the first one. We are prepared for it by his only aside in the play, when he says, just before wounding Hamlet with the poisoned foil, that "it is almost against my conscience" (296). (We are not prepared for this aside, however, since he showed no signs of a conscience earlier and he himself suggested using the poison.) Then, after he is wounded with the same foil, he tells Osric that "I am justly kill'd with mine own treachery" (307), and acknowledges to Hamlet that "The foul practice / Hath turn'd itself on me," while insisting that "the King, the King's to blame" (317–20), and his dying words are both a plea and a verdict:

> Exchange forgiveness with me, noble Hamlet.
> Mine and my father's death come not upon thee,
> Nor thine on me! (329–31)

His verdict would hardly stand up in a court of law, since Hamlet did kill Polonius and Laertes and Laertes did kill Hamlet. But at this point we are not inclined to be legalistic, and we realize that Claudius was indirectly responsible for all three deaths (by agreeing to have Polonius hide behind the arras in Gertrude's closet, and by arranging the fatal fencing match), and ultimately for all of the other misfortunes in the play, which followed as consequences of his murder of his brother. Thus the effect of Laertes's death speech is to complete his transformation from Hamlet's foil to his deadly enemy and finally, with this reconciliation, to a fellow victim of Claudius, and thereby to focus all the guilt upon Claudius, which further justifies Hamlet's revenge and preserves our sympathy for him. It is because of these three phases in his relationship to Hamlet, each with its own distinctive dramatic functions, that I said earlier that Laertes is the most important and the most fully developed foil in Shakespearean tragedy.

A number of critics want to make Fortinbras a second foil to Hamlet as another father-revenger, but there are serious problems with this claim. For one thing, he has just two very brief appearances in the play (at the beginning of 4.4 and the end of 5.2), which are not enough to develop a significant foil relationship. Moreover, his father, unlike the fathers of Hamlet and Laertes, was not murdered but killed in a fair and open "combat," initiated by his own challenge under a "seal'd compact / Well ratified by law and heraldy" (1.1.84–87), and therefore is not subject to revenge. When we first hear of Fortinbras he is not trying to revenge this death (indeed the word "revenge" is never mentioned in connection with him); he only wants to recover the lands that his father lost to Denmark as a result of this combat (102–4), which is a very different thing. And a few scenes later, we learn that he has even abandoned this project and decided instead to attack Poland (2.2.60–80), after which we hear no more of the father whom, according to these critics, he is supposed to be revenging.

Actually, the claim that he is a foil to Hamlet rests not so much on his alleged attempt to get revenge as on the incident in 4.4 where the sight of him leading his army to Poland evokes Hamlet's soliloquy beginning "How all occasions do inform against me" (32–66, missing in F1). But Fortinbras's role in this soliloquy is parallel to the role of the First Player who evokes Hamlet's "O, what a rogue and peasant slave am I" soliloquy in 2.2.550–605. In both cases, Hamlet is responding to the action of someone (the actor weeping, the soldier going to war) who has a much weaker cause than he does, and as a result of this comparison he castigates himself for inaction and cowardice.[20] But no one seems to have suggested that the First Player is another foil to Hamlet; like Fortinbras, he simply provides Hamlet with an ad hoc contrast to his own situation that leads to a major soliloquy but then is not developed any further. And in Fortinbras's next and last appearance he has two other dramatic functions—to resolve the problem of the Danish succession and, as we saw, to pronounce the play's final judgment on Hamlet—neither of which has anything to do with his father or revenge or a role as foil.

I said earlier that I would not try to legislate the correct use of the concept of a foil. If some critics want to call Fortinbras (or the First Player, for that matter) a foil to Hamlet, that seems harmless enough, as long as they recognize the important differences between his role and Laertes's. The trouble is that once one joins the enterprise of foil-hunting, there is no place to stop. In the Watt-Holzknecht-Ross *Outlines*, Rosencrantz and Guildenstern are called "foils to Horatio" because they are "disloyal friends of Hamlet" while Horatio is a "faithful friend" (158), and by the same reasoning one could claim that Osric is a foil to the gravediggers, and even Marcellus to Barnardo, since contrasts can be found within each of these pairings.

Perhaps, then, it is time to drop the term foil from the critical vocabulary (where it is already languishing, as I said), and simply talk about the specific dramatic functions of each character. I do not think that would be much of a loss, but I think it would be a very great loss if we abandoned the concept of dramatic functions, which is the basis of this essay. And that concept is itself based on the concept of authorial intention, which determines and accounts for the dramatic functions of the components of a play, so it turns out that my third point at the outset, dealing with Shakespeare as the conscious designer of *Hamlet*, is really more important than the fourth, which deals with Hamlet as an admirable individual, since this is the result of Shakespeare's design or intention. Of course, invoking the author's intention places me again, for the last time, in opposition to many of our recent critics, who claim that this intention is unknowable or irrelevant or both, [21] which seems odd since they all must infer the author's (or speaker's) intention whenever they are on the receiving end of a communication, which is what makes successful communication possible. In the same way, I infer from the play that one of Shakespeare's intentions was to present Hamlet as an admirable individual, so it follows that some components of the play (including, as I have argued, the role of Laertes) will have dramatic functions designed to realize this intention and so can be explained in these terms. It does not follow, however, that this is the only correct way to interpret the play, because I am a pluralist and therefore believe that it is just one of several valid critical approaches, although I hope I have shown that it can illuminate aspects of the play that are neglected or obscured by many of the other approaches that now dominate academic criticism. I would maintain, then, that the most important of all the points that I listed in the beginning is the tenth, which affirms this fundamental pluralist position.

NOTES

1. He is present in all but seven scenes (1.1, 1.3, 2.1, 4.1, 4.5–7), and in all but two of these (1.1 and 4.5) he is a major presence in the dialogue. My reference text is *The Riverside Shakespeare*; unless I indicate otherwise, there are no significant differences between the second quarto (Q2) and first folio (F1) versions of the passages that I quote or cite.

2. I regard Brutus as the protagonist of this play.

3. I quote examples of this claim by Francis Barker, Catherine Belsey, Jonathan Dollimore, Malcolm Evans, Jonathan Goldberg, Stephen Greenblatt, Graham Holderness, Derek Longhurst, and Simon Shepherd, and assemble the evidence against it in "Unthinkable Thoughts," 434–44, 466–69; it is also refuted by David Aers. But this has not prevented Margreta de Grazia and Peter Stallybrass from announcing that Goldberg's discovery that in the early modern period there is no conception of individual character "has done nothing less than overthrow almost three centuries of 'character study'" of Shakespeare's plays (de Grazia and Stallybrass 273). Compare to my seventh point at the outset.

4. One of the more amusing results of the failure to make this distinction is Francis Barker's notorious assertion that Hamlet is trying to attain the "interior subjectivity" of the bourgeois "individual" but cannot succeed because of the "historical prematurity of this subjectivity," so that "at the centre of Hamlet, in the interior of his mystery, there is, in short, nothing," although this is "doubtless unknown to him" (Barker 163–64). (This is also an example of the claim, noted above, that there was no conception of an individual in this period, which explains its "historical prematurity.")

5. Shortly after writing these lines, I happened on a newspaper article by Matthew Gurewitsch that names the "tragic flaw" of each of Shakespeare's protagonists: "the ambition of Macbeth," "the jealousy of Othello," "Hamlet's indecision," "Mark Antony's self-indulgence," "King Lear's vanity," and so on (Gurewitsch 2.5). This reductionism is often based on what I think is a misreading of Aristotle's concept of *hamartia*, but I cannot argue the point here.

6. In the graveyard scene he does express his grief for the death of Ophelia (5.1.269–71), but gives no sign that he feels in any way responsible for it. And he seems to be motivated, at least in part, by a need to compete with Laertes, whom he thinks is trying to "outface" him (5.1.278).

7. For my criticism of his chapter on *Hamlet*, see "Bloom, Bardolatry, and Characterolatry."

8. Mary Cowden Clarke provides an earlier example.

9. Shakespeare uses the same triad, which apparently was conventional, in *Measure for Measure* 3.2.146 ("a scholar, a statesman, and a soldier") and *The Merry Wives of Windsor* 2.2.228 ("war-like, court-like, and learned"), and a shortened form in *The Merchant of Venice* 1.2.113 ("a scholar and a soldier") and earlier in *Hamlet* 1.5.141 ("scholars and soldiers").

10. Homer Watt, Karl Holzknecht, and Raymond Ross designate thirty-four of Shakespeare's characters as "foils" in their Dramatis Personae. At the opposite extreme, Jonathan Goldberg insists that the use of foils was "surely not part of Elizabethan dramaturgy" but was "timebound" to the nineteenth century (Goldberg 346, 348), which is another one of the new claims of anachronism that I refute in "Unthinkable Thoughts" (438, 466).

11. Shakespeare also applies this term to the relationship between two aspects of a single character when he has Hal predict that "like bright metal on a sullen ground, / My reformation, glitt'ring o'er my fault, / Shall show more goodly and attract more eyes / Than that which hath no foil to set it off" (*1 Henry IV*, 1.2.212–15).

12. Claudius first makes sure that Laertes has his "father's leave" (1.2.57), which may reflect Claudius's reliance on Polonius (47–49), but also assumes that the ruler of a state should uphold a father's rule over his family (compare to *A Midsumer Night's Dream*, 1.1.46–121, where Theseus reaffirms Egeus's power to dispose of his daughter Hermia). His opposite responses to the two requests are proleptic, since at the end he uses Laertes against Hamlet.

13. For a different view, see Harry Keyishian (p. 58).

14. Claudius offers to have his version of the death of Polonius judged by Laertes's "wisest friends" (4.5.204–6), but we hear no more of this; at their next meeting, Laertes has already accepted Claudius's account and only asks why he has not proceeded against Hamlet (4.7.5–9). (In 4.1.38–40 Claudius tells Gertrude that he will "call up our wisest friends" to hear his version, but not to judge it.)

15. He could not say this, of course, because he knows that his mother committed adultery; but my point is that he never thinks of his revenge in terms of such an external conception of family honor. (For another view, see June Schlueter and James Lusardi [53].) Apparently Polonius shares this conception of and concern for honor; he warns Reynaldo not to "dishonor" Laertes when inquiring about him in Paris, but explains that this does not exclude the accusation that he goes to brothels (2.1.21–31).

16. This difference is also evident when he states his losses in 4.7.25–29, devoting only one line to his "noble father" and four lines to the "perfections" of his sister.

17. Perhaps we are to relate this panel to Claudius's offer to be judged by a kind of jury of Laertes's "wisest friends" (see note 14), if we can assume that Claudius is astute enough to recognize Laertes's tendency to rely on external authority.

18. Several tragedies in the Beaumont–Fletcher–Massinger canon present a somewhat similar contrast between a man of extraordinarily refined sensitivity and scruples, who is usually the protagonist, and a more ordinary man of action, who is often a soldier and his friend— compare Amintor and Melantius in *The Maid's Tragedy* (*c.* 1610), Leucippus and Ismenus in *Cupid's Revenge* (*c.* 1612), Thierry and Martell in *Thierry and Theodoret* (*c.* 1617), and Virolet and the Duke of Sesse in *The Double Marriage* (*c.* 1620).

19. This point is developed by Harold Jenkins (pp. 98–99, 106–7).

20. It is significant, I think, that both soliloquies end on an upbeat note with Hamlet letting himself off the hook, as it were, by dedicating himself to action, although in neither case does this bring him any closer to his revenge.

21. See, for example, the attack on the concept of authorial intention in de Grazia and Stallybrass (273–79), which I refute in "Materialising" (97–98). Some of these critics claim that this concept is not only wrong but also reactionary (compare my tenth point at the outset).

WORKS CITED

Aers, David. "A Whisper in the Ear of Early Modernists; or, Reflections on Literary Critics Writing the 'History of the Subject.'" *Culture and History 1350–1600: Essays on English Communities, Identities and Writing,* ed. David Aers. Detroit: Wayne State University Press, 1992, pp. 177–202.

Barker, Francis. "Hamlet's Unfulfilled Interiority." 1984. *New Historicism and Renaissance Drama,* ed. Richard Wilson and Richard Dutton. London: Longman, 1992, pp. 157–66.

Bloom, Harold. *Shakespeare: The Invention of the Human.* New York: Riverhead, 1998.

De Grazia, Margreta, and Peter Stallybrass. "The Materiality of the Shakespearean Text." *Shakespeare Quarterly* 44 (1993): 255–83.

Clarke, Mary Cowden. *The Girlhood of Shakespeare's Heroines.* 3 vols. London: Smith, 1850–55.

Eliot, T. S. "Hamlet and His Problems." 1919. *Selected Essays 1917–1932.* New York: Harcourt, Brace, 1932, pp. 121–26.

Goldberg, Jonathan. Untitled review. *Shakespeare Studies* 16 (1983): 343–48.

Gurewitsch, Matthew. "A Warrior Whose Only Charm Is His Lack of It." *New York Times* September 3, 2000: 2.5, 7.

Jenkins, Harold. "Fortinbras and Laertes and the Composition of *Hamlet.*" *Renaissance Studies in Honor of Carroll Camden,* ed. J. A. Ward. Houston: Rice University Press, 1974, pp. 95–108.

Jones, Ernest. *Hamlet and Oedipus.* Garden City, NY: Doubleday, 1954.

Keyishian, Harry. *The Shapes of Revenge: Victimization, Vengeance, and Vindictiveness in Shakespeare.* Atlantic Highlands, NJ: Humanities Press, 1995.

Leverenz, David. "The Woman in Hamlet: An Interpersonal View." 1978. *Representing Shakespeare: New Psychoanalytic Essays,* ed. Murray M. Schwartz and Coppelia Kahn. Baltimore: Johns Hopkins University Press, 1980, pp. 110–28.

Levin, Richard. "Bloom, Bardolatry, and Characterolatry." *Harold Bloom and the Interpretation of Shakespeare: The Promises and Perils of Popular Criticism,* ed. Christy Desmet and Robert Sawyer. New York: St. Martin's, 2001. Forthcoming.

———. "The Old and the New Materialising of Shakespeare." *Shakespearean International Yearbook* 1 (1999): 87–107.

———. "Unthinkable Thoughts in the New Historicizing of English Renaissance Drama." *New Literary History* 21 (1990): 433–47, 463–70.

Schlueter, June, and James P. Lusardi. "Reading *Hamlet* in Performance: The Laertes/Hamlet Connection." *Shakespearean Illuminations: Essays in Honor of Marvin Rosenberg,* ed. Jay L. Halio and Hugh Richmond. Newark: University of Delaware Press, 1998, pp. 50–69.

Shakespeare, William. *The Riverside Shakespeare*, ed. G. Blakemore Evans et al. 2nd ed. Boston: Houghton Mifflin, 1997.

Vendler, Helen. "Hamlet Alone: A Celebration of Skepticism." *New York Times Magazine* April 18, 1999: 123.

Watt, Homer A., Karl J. Holzknecht, and Raymond Ross. *Outlines of Shakespeare's Plays.* Rev. ed. New York: Barnes and Noble, 1948.

Contributors

Catherine Belsey, Centre for Critical and Cultural Theory, Cardiff University.

Jerry Brotton, Royal Holloway University of London.

Philip Edwards, University of Liverpool.

Peter Erickson, Clark Art Institute, Williamstown, Massachusetts.

R. A. Foakes, University of California, Los Angeles.

Terence Hawkes, Cardiff University.

Arthur F. Kinney, University of Massachusetts, Amherst.

Richard Levin, State University of New York, Stony Brook.

E. Pearlman, University of Colorado, Denver.

Ann Thompson, King's College, London.

Paul Werstine, King's College, University of Western Ontario.

Index

233